Isabel Rosales Sandoval

STATES BEYOND BORDERS
A Comparative Study of Central American Sending States
and their Emigrant Policy (1998–2021)

CRITICAL STUDIES ON LATIN AMERICA
DEBATES AND ALTERNATIVES FOR SOCIAL CHANGE

Edited by Mariano Féliz

1   *Thiago Lima and Agostina Costantino (eds.)*
          Food Security and International Relations
          Critical Perspectives From the Global South
          ISBN 978-3-8382-1481-8

2   *Isabel Rosales Sandoval*
          States Beyond Borders
          A Comparative Study of Central American Sending States and their Emigrant Policy (1998–2021)
          ISBN 978-3-8382-1722-2

Isabel Rosales Sandoval

States Beyond Borders
A Comparative Study of Central American Sending States and their Emigrant Policy (1998–2021)

Bibliografische Information der Deutschen Nationalbibliothek

Die Deutsche Nationalbibliothek verzeichnet diese Publikation in der Deutschen Nationalbibliografie; detaillierte bibliografische Daten sind im Internet über http://dnb.d-nb.de abrufbar.

Bibliographic information published by the Deutsche Nationalbibliothek

Die Deutsche Nationalbibliothek lists this publication in the Deutsche Nationalbibliografie; detailed bibliographic data are available in the Internet at http://dnb.d-nb.de.

Cover image: © 2022 by: Simone Dalmasso/Plaza Pública

Dissertation at the Faculty of Business, Economics and Social Sciences, University of Hamburg, 2021.

ISBN-13: 978-3-8382-1722-2
© *ibidem*-Verlag, Stuttgart 2022
Alle Rechte vorbehalten

Das Werk einschließlich aller seiner Teile ist urheberrechtlich geschützt. Jede Verwertung außerhalb der engen Grenzen des Urheberrechtsgesetzes ist ohne Zustimmung des Verlages unzulässig und strafbar. Dies gilt insbesondere für Vervielfältigungen, Übersetzungen, Mikroverfilmungen und elektronische Speicherformen sowie die Einspeicherung und Verarbeitung in elektronischen Systemen.

All rights reserved. No part of this publication may be reproduced, stored in or introduced into a retrieval system, or transmitted, in any form, or by any means (electronic, mechanical, photocopying, recording or otherwise) without the prior written permission of the publisher. Any person who does any unauthorized act in relation to this publication may be liable to criminal prosecution and civil claims for damages.

Printed in the EU

About the Book series
'Critical Studies on Latin America.
Debates and Alternatives for Social Change'

This book series promotes the production and spread of original knowledge on Latin America from critical perspectives, mainly from the point of view of scholars working in Latin American setting. It includes analyses across all social science disciplines with an emphasis on the political economy, anthropology, and sociology.

While there is no shortage of critical research on Latin America, most studies tend to be produced by institutions and scholars from the Global North. Since the social context of production of knowledge is a key issue, we believe there is a need for Latin American scholars to be able to reach a wider audience. This will provide the global academic community of Latin American studies with a new, fresh perspective that is so far lacking, helping little known but highly relevant debates and researchers reach an international audience.

While books in the series may include contributions by non-Latin America based scholars, the series' main purpose is to provide rigorous research from scholars working in Latin American institutions.

Abstract

The study of migration in political science, and particularly in international relations, has tended to focus on the study of immigration. However, sending states are increasingly institutionalizing their policies and programs to include emigrants living outside the national territory. Empirical evidence shows that states are leading initiatives to develop transnational policies and, consequently, that state-led transnationalism is challenging traditional notions of sovereignty, nation-states, and citizenship. This research focuses on the factors that influence the implementation of the policies that sending states have adopted to reach out to their citizens abroad. Specifically, it investigates why and how sending states implement transnational emigrant policies. This comparative study of three Central American sending states— El Salvador, Guatemala, and Honduras—identifies four policy categories that these states have developed: 1) recognizing the emigrant community through the creation of institutions; 2) cultivating loyalties in the emigrant community through symbolic policies; 3) extending emigrant rights; and 4) extracting resources by incorporating migrants into the national economy. These policies are designed to reinforce the emigrants' sense of enduring membership with their country of origin. However, the motivation for the policies does not exactly correspond to the assumptions and typologies of existing theories on the subject, which tend to focus on international factors such as emergent norms, lobbying between sending and receiving states, and immigration reform. The argument presented in the study is that the characteristics of these three cases are better explained by domestic political factors. Correspondingly, it analyzes and explains three factors that account for the sending states' motivations to engage with their emigrant communities. These are: 1) the importance of the size and potential impact of the emigrant communities; 2) party system competitiveness; and 3) the sending states' institutional capacity to implement policies.

Zusammenfassung

Migration wurde in den Politikwissenschaften, insbesondere in den Internationalen Beziehungen, bislang meist aus dem Blickwinkel der Einwanderungspolitik erforscht. Allerdings institutionalisieren mehr und mehr Entsendestaaten ihre Richtlinien und Programme, um auch Auswanderer außerhalb ihres Staatsgebietes miteinzubeziehen. Empirische Evidenz zeigt, dass Staaten vermehrt Initiativen zur Entwicklung transnationaler Maßnahmen durchführen. Dieser Transnationalismus stellt eine Herausforderung für traditionelle Vorstellungen von Souveränität, Nationalstaatlichkeit und Staatsbürgerschaft dar. Die vorliegende Forschung fokussiert sich auf die Faktoren, welche die Implementierung von Maßnahmen der Entsendestaaten zur Erreichung ihrer Bürger im Ausland beeinflussen. Sie beschäftigt sich insbesondere damit, aus welchen Gründen und auf welche Weise Entsendestaaten transnationale Auswanderungspolitik umsetzen. Dazu wurde eine vergleichende Studie in drei Entsendestaaten durchgeführt: El Salvador, Guatemala und Honduras. Anhand dieser Forschung können vier politische Kategorien identifiziert werden, die von den untersuchten Staaten gewählt wurden: 1) Anerkennung der Auswanderergemeinschaft durch die Schaffung von Institutionen; 2) Kultivierung von Loyalität unter Auswanderern durch Symbolpolitik; 3) Ausweitung der Rechte von Auswanderern; und 4) Ressourcengewinnung durch Einbeziehung von Auswanderern in die nationale Wirtschaft. Diese Maßnahmen zielen darauf ab sicherzustellen, dass sich Auswanderer zu ihrem jeweiligen Herkunftsland dauerhaft zugehörig fühlen. Die Motivation für diese Maßnahmen deckt sich nur teilweise mit den bisherigen Annahmen und Typologien bestehender Theorien: Diese konzentrieren sich in der Regel auf internationale Faktoren, insbesondere auf entstehende Normen, Lobbyarbeit zwischen Entsende- und Empfängerstaaten, sowie Einwanderungsreformen. Diese Forschungsarbeit zeigt, dass die Charakteristika der hier untersuchten Fälle, besser verstanden werden können, wenn auch innenpolitische Faktoren miteinbezogen werden. Hierzu werden drei Faktoren analysiert und identifiziert, die den Motiven der Entsendestaaten, sich mit ihren Auswanderergemeinschaften zu beschäftigen zugrunde liegen: 1) Größe und potentieller Einfluss der Auswanderergemeinschaften, 2) Wettbewerbsfähigkeit des Parteiensystems, und 3) die institutionelle Fähigkeit zur Umsetzung von Politiken des Staates.

Our true nationality is mankind.

H. G. Wells

I am not an Athenian nor a Greek, but a citizen of the world.

Socrates

Acknowledgments

Transforming this book from a collection of loose ideas into a manuscript was truly a collective effort. Migrants, public officials, civil society members, invaluable interviewees, and the protagonists of this study in El Salvador, Guatemala, Honduras, Mexico, and the United States all participated in the endeavor. I am deeply indebted to the individuals and organizations that provided me with interviews and other material for this thesis.

I would also like to thank the individuals and institutions that in some way facilitated the research process. My research benefited greatly from extraordinary mentorship. I thank my first advisor, Detlef Nolte, for his unconditional support throughout the whole process, from my coming to Germany to starting and finishing my research; his guidance and constructive feedback were constant. I am also very grateful to my second advisor, Anita Engels, who encouraged me to submit the best work I could and inspired me by being an outstanding academic. I am thankful for her academic advice and willingness to share her knowledge.

I was fortunate to have a place to write and exchange thoughts in a helpful and cooperative environment: the GIGA German Institute of Global and Area Studies, in particular the Institute of Latin American Studies (ILAS). I thank Merike Blofield, Bert Hoffmann, Sabine Kurtenbach, and Mariana Llanos. I also thank the GIGA staff members, Doris Biesenbach, Julia Kramer, Peter Peetz, Steffi Stövesand, Maren Wagner, and Brigitte Waldeck, for all their support in helping me meet my needs and complete my research project. I am also grateful to Philip J. Williams and staff members from the University of Florida Center for Latin American Studies, where I wrote some of the resulting manuscript while I was a visiting research scholar. I thank Irene Palma and Jacobo Dardón from INCEDES, the institute that always welcomed me during my fieldwork and research visits in Guatemala.

I also gratefully acknowledge the Deutscher Akademischer Austauschdienst, the Übersee Club in Hamburg, the GIGA Doctoral Program,

Equal Opportunity Fund, the ILAS, and PIASTA at the University of Hamburg for providing financial support at different stages of my research.

I would also like to thank the colleagues who partially or completely read my work and provided me with invaluable feedback: Sofía Álvarez, Matthias Basedau, Jorge Gordin, Soledad Granada, Julio Hernández, Bert Hoffmann, Theresa Kernecker, Mariana Llanos, and Connie Thurston. I owe a debt of gratitude to the language and text editor of this work: Pamela Lalonde. Her comments and suggestions helped improve the manuscript in its final stages. I also thank Berta Ferrer for her support with the graphic design of this thesis.

I am thankful to friends and colleagues at the GIGA Doctoral Program with whom I have shared ideas and who supported me through the different stages of this process, making it a thoroughly enjoyable time, and leaving me with some unforgettable memories.

Finally, my deepest debt of gratitude is to my immediate and extended family, beginning with the Lemmermanns, who made me feel at home in Hamburg. I reserve my final thanks for my Guatemalan family. To my siblings: David and Ana, you were my main support system during the whole process and will continue to be forever. Thanks also to the little ones, Daniela and Juan. I thank my parents from the bottom of my heart: María and Julio for being my home and shelter. Thanks to Maynor and Leticia for their unconditional support for all my plans. I thank my Grandma Dina for reminding me of what is important in life. Lastly, I am grateful to my husband, César Díaz, who has encouraged and inspired me to accomplish my goals since I first met him and gives me all the support I need. I also thank my children, Elena and Camilo, for becoming the spark and joy of my world.

Contents

Abstract 7
Zusammenfassung 8
Acknowledgments 11
List of Figures 17
List of Tables 19
List of Abbreviations 21

Part I   **Introduction, State of the Art, Theoretical Framework, and Methodology** 25

1   Introduction 27
1.1   Overview 27
1.2   Questions and Aims 29
1.3   The Argument and Hypotheses 32
1.4   Reasons to Study the State-led Transnationalism of Sending States and their Emigrant Policies in Central America 35
1.5   Focus of the Study 36
1.6   Conceptual Clarifications 37
1.6.1 The Sending State and its Motivations to Engage 37
1.6.2 State-led Transnationalism 38
1.7   Organization of the Study 39

2   State of the Art 41
2.1   Introduction 41
2.2   Political Science Contributions to Migration Studies 43
2.3   The Links between the State and Migration 46
2.4   From a Migrant-Receiving to a Migrant-Sending State Approach 52
2.5   Migration Policy 56
2.6   The Literature on the Case Studies: Central America 60
2.7   Concluding Remarks 64

3	Theoretical Framework	67
3.1	Introduction	67
3.2	Sovereignty and the State	68
3.3	Migration Governance	70
3.4	Measuring the Dependent Variable: State-led Transnationalism	74
3.4.1	Emigrant Policy Mechanisms	76
3.4.2	State Involvement	78
3.5	Selection and Measurement of Three Explanatory Variables: Conditions for a Higher Degree of State-led Transnationalism in Emigrant Policy	81
3.5.1	The Size and Potential Impact of the Emigrant Community	83
3.5.2	Party System Competitiveness	84
3.5.3	The State's Institutional Capacity to Implement Policies	85
3.6	Concluding Remarks	86
4	Methodology	89
4.1	Introduction	89
4.2	Research Design: Case Study Methods	89
4.3	Case Selection: El Salvador, Guatemala, and Honduras; Similiar Features	90
4.3.1	Convergences	90
4.3.2	Divergences	91
4.4	Scope	91
4.5	Data Collection and Management	93
4.5.1	In-depth Interviews	93
4.5.2	Document Analysis	94
4.6	Concluding Remarks	94

Part II	Describing and Comparing State-Led Transnationalism in Central America	97
5	Policies to Build Relationships with the Emigrant Community	99
5.1	Introduction	99
5.2	Recognizing the Emigrant Community: Institutional Policies	99

5.2.1	Creating Institutions, Foreign Affairs Actions, the Expansion of Consular Services	100
5.2.1	Promoting Work Opportunities Abroad	107
5.3	Cultivating Loyalties in the Emigrant Community: Symbolic Policies	110
5.3.1	Days, Districts, and the Celebration of National Holidays	111
5.3.2	Declaring Responsibility for Migrants	113
5.4	Concluding Remarks	116
6	**Policies to Integrate the Emigrant Community**	**119**
6.1	Introduction	119
6.2	Extending Emigrant Rights	119
6.2.1	Out-of-Country Voting and Citizenship	119
6.2.2	Legislative Representation	125
6.2.3	Hometown Associations	128
6.2.4	Regional Institutions and Agreements	130
6.2.5	Providing Education, Health, and Labor Protection Services Abroad	139
6.2.6	Assisting the Arrested, Missing, and Emigrants in Transit; Receiving the Deported	143
6.3	Extracting Resources: Incorporating Migrants into the National Economy	150
6.3.1	Facilitating Investment Services, the Productive Use of Remittances, Matching Fund Programs	150
6.4	Concluding Remarks	153

Part III Explaining State-Led Transnationalism in Central America 157

7	**The Conditions for a Higher Degree of State-Led Transnationalism**	**159**
7.1	Introduction	159
7.2	Size and Potential Impact of the Emigrant Community in the Country of Origin	161
7.2.1	The Emigrant Community Size	161
7.2.2	The History of the Emigrant Community	163
7.2.3	The Emigrant Community's Degree of Organization	167

7.2.4	Current Remittances from the Emigrant Community	168
7.2.5	The Out-of-Country Voting Rights of Emigrants	171
7.3	Party System Competitiveness	173
7.3.1	Fragmentation	174
7.3.2	Polarization	182
7.4	The State's Institutional Capacity to Implement Policies	185
7.4.1	Adaptability	186
7.4.2	Stability	186
7.4.3	Coordination	187
7.4.4	Implementation and Enforcement	188
7.4.5	Efficiency	190
7.4.6	Public Regardedness	192
7.5	Different Degrees of State-led Transnationalism Regarding Emigrant Policy	193
7.5.1	State Emigrant Policy Mechanisms	193
7.5.2	State Involvement	195
7.6	Concluding Remarks	204
8	**Conclusion**	**209**
8.1	Key Question Answered	209
8.2	Key Findings	210
8.3	Theoretical Implications	212
8.4	Implications for Policy and Practice	213
8.5	Avenues for Future Research	214

Bibliography	215
Legal Sources	241

List of Figures

Figure 1	Measuring the Dependent Variable: State-led Transnationalism	75
Figure 2	Consular ID card Issued by a Guatemalan Consulate to an Undocumented Emigrant	105
Figure 3	A Canadian Job Opportunity Announcement, Published by the Ministry of Labor in the Main Newspapers in Honduras	109
Figure 4	Number of Registered Emigrants and their Votes in the 2014 and 2019 Elections in El Salvador	122
Figure 5	President of the Congressional Committee on Migration Recognizing the Emigrant Community in Los Angeles	126
Figure 6	"Don't Be One More Number, Don't Travel Illegally to the North!"	148
Figure 7	Emigrant Community Building Mechanisms in the NTCA	194
Figure 8	Emigrant Community Integration Mechanisms in the NTCA	195
Figure 9	Number of Emigrant Policies Proposed by each Actor in the NTCA	197
Figure 10	Recognizing the Emigrant Community by Actor in the NTCA	198
Figure 11	Cultivating Loyalties by Actor in the NTCA	199
Figure 12	Integration Mechanism by Actor in the NTCA	200
Figure 13	Degree of NTCA State Participation in Setting the Agenda for Emigrant Policy	201
Figure 14	State Influence on Emigrant Policy in the NTCA	203

List of Tables

Table 1	Possible Explanations for State-led Transnationalism in Central America	34
Table 2	State Emigrant Policy Mechanisms to Engage with the Emigrant Community	78
Table 3	Variation of State Involvement	80
Table 4	Conditions for a Higher Degree of State-led Transnationalism in Emigrant Policy	82
Table 5	State Policy Mechanisms to Engage with the Emigrant Community	160
Table 6	Explanations for State-led Transnationalism in the NTCA	161
Table 7	Number of Emigrants from Mexico and the NTCA Going to the US (2000–2019)	162
Table 8	NTCA Population by Country and Estimated Emigrant Population in the US in 2019	163
Table 9	US Apprehensions of Central American and Mexican Migrants, 2012–2019	164
Table 10	US Deportation of Central American Migrants by Country, 2012–2019	165
Table 11	Characteristics of those Considering Migration from the NTCA, 2019	169
Table 12	Emigrant Remittance Inflows (Million Dollars) from 2000 to 2019 and as a Share of Gross Domestic Product	170
Table 13	Out-of-Country Voting Average in each Election since it was Approved in the NTCA	172
Table 14	Size and Potential Impact of Emigrant Communities on a Sending State Proposing Emigrant Policy	173
Table 15	Effective Number of Electoral Parties in El Salvador, 2019	175
Table 16	Effective Number of Electoral Parties in Guatemala, 2019	177
Table 17	Effective Number of Electoral Parties in Honduras, 2017	179

Table 18	Effective Number of Parties in the NTCA, 2009–2019	180
Table 19	Evolution of Parties According to the Type of Party System	181
Table 20	Ideological Self-Positioning of Political Parties in the NTCA from 2004 to 2019	182
Table 21	State Institutional Capacity to Implement Policies since 1980 in the NTCA	185
Table 22	Global Freedom in the NTCA	196

List of Abbreviations

APH	Honduran Patriotic Alliance
ARENA	Nationalist Republican Alliance
BHW	Bi-National Health Weeks
CAMR	Center for Returned Migrants
CARECEN	Central American Resource Center
CARSI	Central America Regional Security Initiative
CEDOH	Honduran Documentation Center
CONAMIGUA	National Council for Guatemalans Abroad
CONAPROHM	National Council for the Protection of Honduran Migrants
CONMIGRANTES	Salvadoran National Council for the Protection and Development of the Emigrant and their Family
COPAREM	Regional Parliamentary Council on Migration
CREO	Commitment, Renewal, and Order
CRS	Catholic Relief Services
DC	Christian Democratic Party
DGM	Directorate for Migrant Services
EG	Together for Guatemala
ENEP	Effective Number of Electoral Parties
FA	Broad Political Front
FAFG	Forensic Anthropology Foundation of Guatemala
FCN	National Convergence Front
FMLN	Farabundo Martí National Liberation Front
FONAMIH	National Forum for Migration in Honduras
FRG	Institutional Republican Party
GANA	Grand Alliance for National Unity (El Salvador)
GANA	Grand National Alliance (Guatemala)
GDP	Gross Domestic Product
HTAs	Hometown Associations
IDHUCA	UCA Human Rights Institute

INCEDES	Central American Institute for Social Studies and Development
INSAMI	Salvadoran Migrant Institute
IOM	International Organization for Migration
IOs	International Organizations
LIBRE	Liberty and Refoundation Party
LIDER	Renewed Democratic Liberty
MLP	Movement for the Liberation of Peoples
MRE	Ministry of Foreign Affairs
MSSD	Most Similar Systems Design
NGOs	Non-Governmental Organizations
NTCA	Northern Triangle of Central America
OCAM	Central American Commission of Migration Directors
OPROMH	Office for the Protection of Honduran Migrants
PAC	Anti-Corruption Party
PAN	National Advancement Party
PAPTN	Alliance for Prosperity in the Northern Triangle
PARLACEN	Central American Parliament
PDI	Comprehensive Development Plan
PHG	Humanist Party of Guatemala
PINU	Party of Innovation and Unity
PLH	Honduran Liberal Party
PNH	Honduran National Party
PP	Patriotic Party
PUD	Democratic Unification Party
RCM	Regional Conference on Migration
RED COMIFAH	Network of Migrant Committees and Families
RROCM	Regional Network for Civil Organizations on Migration
SAWP	Seasonal Agricultural Worker Program
SICA	Central American Integration System

SLTN	State-led Transnationalism
STCA	Safe Third Country Agreements
TRICAMEX	Mexico-Northern Triangle Consular Consultation Program
TSE	Supreme Electoral Court
UCA El Salvador	José Simeón Cañas Central American University
UN	United Nations
UNDP	United Nations Development Program
UNE	National Unity of Hope
UNHCR	United Nations High Commissioner for Refugees
UNODC	United Nations Office on Drugs and Crime
URNG	Guatemalan National Revolutionary Unity
USAID	United States Agency for International Development
USC	Social Christian Union
VAMOS	Va Solidarity Movement (Honduras)
VAT	Value-Added Tax
VIVA	Vision with Values

Part I

Introduction, State of the Art, Theoretical Framework, and Methodology

Chapter 1
Introduction

> Without a doubt, the lack of policies designed specifically by Central American states contributes to the migration of Central Americans. If we do not become fully aware of this situation, if we do not eliminate the roots that cause social injustice, the great exodus of Central Americans will continue, with or without crisis.
>
> (Torres-Rivas & Jiménez, 1985)

1.1 Overview

After Hurricane Mitch in 1998, and especially after the events of September 11, 2001, a number of migrant-sending states[1] in Central America began to modify their emigrant policies. These changes were brought about by factors that included an increase in the monetary remittances sent to origin countries, tougher immigration policies in receiving countries, the disappearance of border crossers during transit, and stricter border enforcement and deportations, which have reached record highs in the Central America-Mexico-United States corridor. While emigration can be a perilous journey—increasingly so in recent years—the number of people leaving their countries of origin each year has risen from 173 million in 2000 to an estimated 281 million in 2020 (United Nations, 2020a). The factors that have caused migration to increase in many countries include agricultural export, forced migration during wars, the transnationalization of labor markets, increasing unemployment, natural disasters, and violence. In this context, it is perhaps not surprising that a migrant-sending state would be increasingly concerned about incorporating its citizens abroad into its domestic and foreign policy.

---

[1] This study bases its understanding of the "sending state" on the definition provided by (Gamlen, 2008), who argues that sending states can influence the ties between society and the country of origin beyond the reach of their territory (beyond borders), operating at a transnational scale. Sending states treat their citizens abroad as members of their home society with rights and obligations. The concept is discussed in more detail in the theoretical chapter.

Although Central American governments in the past scarcely engaged with their emigrant communities,[2] they are now actively appealing to the loyalty of their citizens abroad. These governments are creating and reinforcing transnational ties with their emigrant citizens by publicly taking responsibility for them. For instance, El Salvador's government has emphasized consular services and protection for its emigrants, with many of its efforts focusing on providing education and health, and facilitating investment services. Guatemala, in turn, has focused on creating institutions to support the emigrant community and their families left behind. For its part, Honduras has passed several laws and decrees that legally recognize the state's responsibility for its emigrant community. Honduras is the poorest of these three countries and, accordingly, has a strong focus on investment services and facilitating economic remittances sent back to the country. Central American presidents, members of congress, and general directors of migration have come together, while regional networks have emerged to tackle the lack of emigrant policies and make joint efforts as a region. In a press release regarding the situation of migrants in Central America, the Secretary General of the Central American Integration System (SICA), Vinicio Cerezo, urged Central American Foreign Affairs Ministries to:

> approve the Action Plan for Comprehensive Attention to Migration in the Region, which contains actions both at a national and regional level to respond to the needs of the migrant and refugee population, putting human rights at the center of the agenda. Migrants and refugees are not a threat to the national security of any state outside the region. They are people who have been forced to leave their countries, separated from their families because of violence or looking for access to better living conditions. We are not talking about numbers, but about the lives of human beings. Migration should be an option, not the only alternative. (SICA, 2021a)

---

2   "Diaspora" is the most commonly used term by scholars researching emigrant policies. The concept refers to an imagined dispersed community away from their homeland (Vertovec, 2009). This study uses the term "emigrant community" because "diaspora" has the connotation of being a very big and, over time, disperse community abroad. While the cases analyzed in this research have an important number of citizens living abroad in relation to their total population, their flows became steadier after the mid-1990s and are not disperse, in contrast to the Israeli, Mexican, and Philippine diasporas.

While the topic of emigrant policy as devised by sending states has been growing in academic importance, little research has been conducted to date on the criteria that determine how a sending state will reach out to its citizens abroad, and no comparative work has been done. Migration studies do not sufficiently explain the role of the state in shaping migration phenomena. Indeed, the excessive focus of migration studies on actors has relegated the role of the state and its policies to a secondary concern. Therefore, this study seeks to explain the motivations behind the engagement of sending states with their citizens abroad, arguing that migrants are not the only people initiating political transnationalism, as most of the literature claims, but that states are also promoting policies for their populations beyond borders. Therefore, it is normal for states to have a variety of strategies to influence extraterritorial groups. This comparative policy study analyzes over 20 years of migration policies, from 1998 to 2021, in Central America.

1.2 Questions and Aims

The study of migration in the social sciences has tended to focus on the economic, social, and cultural aspects of migration, shaping the life of communities and families as the main driving forces, and has paid less attention to the political aspects derived from migration. However, when those political aspects are considered, the approaches rarely include the emigrant policies of sending states. Therefore, this book addresses the question of how and why sending states adopt policies to engage with their emigrant communities abroad.

This study has two main aims. The first is to provide a systematic, detailed description of what sending states do (emigrant policy) and compare their overall levels. The second aim is to investigate why the levels of sending state engagement differ; in other words, to provide explanations for the determinants of sending states' emigrant policies.[3] The theoretical

---

[3] This study analyzes actions, press releases, programs, bills, laws, and decrees by sending states. The goal is to determine what subjects have been brought by states to the political agenda and are being publicly discussed in Congress, or what measures have already been passed. This study does not evaluate the outcome of all the policies.

objective of this study is to contribute to the general understanding of the determinants (motivation, intensity, time) that make some sending states more reluctant than others to reach out to their citizens abroad. The study uses as its starting point Goldring's concept of state-led transnationalism (SLTN), which includes "Institutionalized national policies and programs that attempt to expand the scope of a national state's political, economic, social, and moral regulation to include emigrants and their descendants outside the national territory" (2002, 64). To explain the empirical problem of why some states are more active than others with respect to emigrant policy, this investigation relies on existing theoretical approaches. At a broader level, the fact that sending states are increasingly addressing citizenries residing outside their national territory presents a paradox. States are implicitly undermining the basic principle of sovereignty, which has been defined by their political authority and has characterized the international system since the Peace of Westphalia in 1648. This has affected the nature of international relations and global policies of governance. For post-nationalists, the transnational movement of people opens a Pandora's box of nation-states and allows supranational legal and political orders to take over (Soysal, 1994). In contrast to post-nationalist approaches, sending states are observed to be "de-territorialized nation-states" (Basch et al., 1995). State boundaries are defined in social rather than geographical terms, and sending states engage in "re-territorializing" their citizens abroad by launching polices that re-include them not only in the nation, but also in the national economy and political life of their country of origin. The question of whether we are witnessing processes of de-territorialization or re-territorialization depends on how we assess the engagement efforts of sending states. In other words, sending states and emigrant policies challenge longstanding assumptions of nation-state sovereignty. Many scholars have argued that the rise in transnational actors and international institutions, the increase in people movement across borders, and new communication and transport technologies have reconfigured or even eroded the sovereign state (Soysal, 1994). Others argue that although boundaries are more porous and participatory patterns are changing, states are not fading but rather reinventing themselves (Levitt, 2001). In line with this argument, this study argues that the state matters and that, rather than disappearing or being subordinated to international regimes, sending states can potentially play a major role, along with other institutions such as civil, religious, political, and migrant associations.

The empirical objective of this study is to present a plausible explanation for the emigrant policy[4] choices made by sending states. The main interests of sending states are usually considered to be a) to secure the continuous inflow of economic resources; b) to mobilize political support and control subversive political dissidence; and c) to promote the upward social mobility of overseas nationals (Guarnizo, 1998; Itzigsohn & Villacrés, 2008; Østergaard-Nielsen, 2003a; Portes et al., 1999). This study seeks to answer how sending states engage with the emigrant community. In this regard, the research work done identified two emigrant policy mechanisms and four policy categories designed by sending states to reinforce emigrants' sense of enduring membership. The first mechanism that sending states use to build relationships with the emigrant community encompasses the following policy categories: 1) recognizing the emigrant community through the creation of institutions; and 2) cultivating loyalties in the emigrant community through symbolic policies. The second mechanism used by sending states to integrate the emigrant community includes the following policy categories: 3) extending emigrant rights; and 4) extracting resources by incorporating migrants into the national economy. To answer why sending states apply different levels of outreach towards the emigrant community, the study operationalizes the differences in state-led transnationalism and provides clarifications through three explanatory factors: 1) the importance of the size and potential impact of the emigrant community in the country of origin; 2) party system

---

4   Migration research to date has focused more on "immigration policies" made by migrant destination states than on emigrant policies made by migrant states of origin. In turn, this study adopts the term "emigrant policy" because it analyzes policies that are not immigration policies from destination countries. The term "emigration policy," on the other hand, can suggest that these policies are made by states so that migrants will leave their territory. "Emigrant policy" is a more accurate concept, since it implies that the policies are made for those citizens.

competitiveness; and 3) the sending state's institutional capacity to implement policies. These policy categories and the empirical findings are developed in Parts II and III of this work.

A comparative study of three sending states in Central America was conducted: El Salvador, Guatemala, and Honduras, referred to in the United States as the Northern Triangle of Central America (NTCA). Together, these countries comprise a region with high levels of human mobility, display similar migration dynamics, and have long been characterized by their rejection of the Mexican and United States governments and their immigration policies. Nevertheless, they have fundamental differences in terms of the degree to which their states engage with their citizens abroad. This investigation draws on data from a database created specifically for this study containing 400 official reports, laws, and bills from documents from civil society publications, government reports, pieces of legislation, and legislative and executive decrees from the three countries. I also conducted 70 in-depth interviews with former and current high-ranking public officials in the three NTCA states, Mexico (as a migrant-transit state), and the United States (as a migrant-receiving state).

1.3 The Argument and Hypotheses

The argument of this study is that sending state governments pay attention to emigrant policies depending on the political or economic gain that an emigrant community represents for the country of origin. However, those conditions alone are insufficient. Certain institutional capabilities must be present for sending states to be able to engage economically or politically with the emigrant community. Therefore, the study proposes a model to analyze the degree of a state's transnational emigrant community engagement (actions taking place simultaneously in both migrant-receiving and sending countries). This book operationalizes the degree of state-led transnationalism, the dependent variable of this study as: policy mechanisms to build relationships or to integrate the emigrant community and the states' involvement.

Emigrant policy mechanisms are the policies that states use either to build relationships or to integrate the emigrant community. To observe the variation in the states' involvement, this study takes the following as indicators:

a) the key actors involved in each policy;
b) the degree of state participation in setting the agenda for each policy; and
c) how state influence is exercised.

The analysis highlights the importance of some relatively unexplored factors for understanding the determinants of SLTN in emigrant policy, such as the states' political and economic motivations in their attempts to reach out to their expatriates, or how they integrate and recognize their emigrant community. Focusing on the state and paying attention to context-specific variables, this chapter proposes three main hypotheses.[5]

Hypothesis 1:
the importance of the size and potential impact of the emigrant community in the country of origin

H1: If the importance of the size and potential impact of the emigrant community in the origin country is high, sending states will reach out to it because of the possible economic or political benefits it may represent.

Hypothesis 2:
party system competitiveness

H2: The degree of engagement of political parties is important for creating debates over emigrant policies.

---

5   These hypotheses are derived from the works and theories of other scholars and are presented in depth in the theoretical chapter (Chapter 3), which also explains how they are supplemented by the research done for this study, as well as the operationalization of these hypotheses into explanatory factors.

Hypothesis 3:
the state's institutional capacity to implement policies

H3: If a state has strong institutional capacities, it will be more active in the implementation of emigrant policy to engage with its emigrant community. A state with low institutional capacities will delegate its functions to other actors such as civil society or international actors.

Table 1   Possible Explanations for State-led Transnationalism in Central America

State-led transnationalism (Y)	Importance of the size and potential impact of the emigrant community (X1)	Party system competitiveness (X2)	State's institutional capacity to implement policies (X3)

Note. Prepared by the author.

The starting point for selecting the above hypotheses is not a theoretical problem, but an observation that some migrant-sending states do more than others to reach out to their citizens abroad. The aim is to apply and test the theory of transnationalism. Transnationalism as a concept, theory, and experience has nourished an important body of literature in the social sciences. In practice, transnationalism refers to the increasingly functional combination of processes that cross borders (relations of individuals, groups, companies, and state actions) beyond the nation-state boundaries. Thus, individuals, groups, institutions, and states interact with each other in a new global space in which the cultural and political characteristics of national societies are combined with emerging multilevel and multinational activities (Basch et al., 1995). The main goal of this study is to explain this problem empirically, in order to see how states tackle the problem of managing and governing emigrants through emigrant policies. To that end, the study relies on theoretical literature based on the concept of state-led transnationalism. The idea behind this study is that these sending states engage in a variety of activities that must be systematically described and assessed, and that they appear to differ in their levels of engagement, a phenomenon that requires an explanation.

1.4 Reasons to Study the State-led Transnationalism of Sending States and their Emigrant Policies in Central America

This study offers a comparative analysis of the policies of sending states towards their nationals abroad. In doing so, it fills some holes in current comparative research on migration studies and on the political dimensions of migration. Specifically, the study helps to fill five gaps found in the literature on sending states and emigrant policies.

The first gap is disciplinary. Research on migration in political science has traditionally favored the policy choices of receiving states and immigration programs. Sending-state governments are frequently presented as pawns rather than players when it comes to migration management, because the receiving states are decisive in formulating the rules for immigrant visas related to work, asylum, return, or undocumented migrants. The political aspects of migration are usually considered in the field of political science from an international relations approach, leaving government institutions, interest groups, advocacy, and the policymaking process under-researched (Cornelius, Martin, and Hollifield 2004; Freeman 2004; Geiger and Pécoud 2010). This can be explained by the security paradigm that governs the international system, in which immigration is a threat and a violation of the receiving states' sovereignty (Waever et al., 1993).

Second, in terms of methodology, few comparative studies explain the similarities and differences in the motivations of sending states with regard to developing policies to engage their citizens beyond borders (Hollifield, 2004). Nevertheless, sending states (many of which are also receiving states) are increasingly emerging as significant actors in migration politics. Third, regarding the level of analysis, the impact of migration has been primarily examined from an individual, family, local, and community approach (Østergaard-Nielsen, 2003b; Vertovec, 2004; Williams, 2009). Thus, the analysis of transnationalism from below (migrant-led transnationalism) has overshadowed the study of transnationalism from above (state-led transnationalism). Fourth, the increasing amount of literature on non-state actors, including non-governmental organizations (NGOs), international organizations (IOs), and transnational processes in international relations makes an examination of the interests, motivations, aims, and policies of sending states a timely one (Hollifield, 2000).

Finally, there is a regional research gap. Some scholars have focused on regional migrations, the cultural and social impacts of migration, and migration during internal conflicts. However, only a few studies have looked at the emigrant policies and politics of Central American states (Castillo and Palma 2003; Palma 2004). Moreover, the researchers who have looked at these policies have done so mostly using a single case study, which makes it difficult to make broader or more comprehensive inferences about the topic.

1.5 Focus of the Study

This is a study of state motivations to engage and their degree of action regarding the emigrant policies affecting contemporary migration movements. Therefore, the analysis is limited to migrant-sending states and will not include migrant-receiving or transit states. The study also reconstructs the emigrant policies of sending states. The policies analyzed include emigrant communities abroad, in transit, and back in their countries of origin, either due to deportation or voluntary return. Thus, it does not research immigration policies in sending or receiving states. Third, the work deals with the political aspects of migration and its policies, without going into detail about the cultural and social aspects of these policies or considering the migrant perspective of the state. The actors considered in the work are largely limited to public officials, political parties, civil society organizations, and international organizations. Fourth, the focus is on contemporary policies in the post-Cold War period, specifically the last 20 years, from 1998 to 2021. This is because migration policies had other aims during the Cold War period and were largely oriented towards the "reintegration" of refugees. Between 1998 and 2021, the changes observed in the state system and institutions are related to the positions of civil society, political parties, and the world's security framework towards immigration. Thus, the focus of the work is on state actions regarding emigrant policies related to contemporary migration movements. The end of internal armed conflicts in the region, the impact of some natural disasters, and more stringent American immigration policies after September 11, 2001 all contributed to these changes. Accordingly, it is no surprise that political parties, civil society, and governments started to realize the political and economic benefits that their emigrant community could offer their countries of origin, and therefore modified their emigrant policies.

1.6 Conceptual Clarifications[6]

1.6.1 The Sending State and its Motivations to Engage

Scholars like Gamlen (2008), (Levitt & de la Dehesa, 2003), and Smith (2003) have explained the factors that lead states to engage with their citizens abroad, the forms that this engagement takes, and how states choose a particular type of engagement. The study of migration in general, and international relations specifically, has usually meant the study of (im-)migration. In the context of increasing international migration, sending states are actively implementing a variety of new policies with their emigrant communities. Nevertheless, in comparison to other dimensions of international migration phenomena, sending states have received less attention than receiving states. However, Gamlen, a geographer, responded to this issue with a quantitative study. His (2008) study of over 70 states and their citizens abroad shows that institutionalized state-emigrant community relations are actually more normal than what supporters of the modern geopolitical view of the world would have us believe. Traditionally, the view of state-emigrant community relations as backward or somehow abnormal has been commonly accepted, because most studies on states have been conducted from the point of view of the receiving state. This is also because studies of emigrant community initiatives have

---

6   This section on conceptual clarifications introduces the concepts used in the study. The explanatory factors will be outlined in detail in the theoretical chapter (Chapter 3).

involved cases of strong states or larger emigrant communities, such as the Irish or Italians in the United States, disregarding the valuable cases of less developed regions like Latin America and Asia. However, Gamlen found that many states devote a portion of the state apparatus to transnational activities and have policies to engage migrants that extend beyond their borders.

1.6.2 State-led Transnationalism

This shift in attitudes towards the state was also accompanied by increasing academic interest in the role of the state in transnationalism. Earlier literature tended to focus on how migrants engaged in transnational practices and created transnational space. In the last decade, however, researchers have studied the role of the state in facilitating or hindering transnational practices and creating transnational space to the point that there is now a division in the literature between migrant-led and state-led transnationalism.[7] Migrant-led transnationalism refers to "a range of practices and institutions linking migrants, people and organizations in their homelands or elsewhere in a diaspora" (Vertovec, 2009, p. 13). Examples include having immediate family members who live on either side of a border, maintaining kinship and social networks across borders, and sending or depending on remittances (Goldring 2002). State-led transnationalism is defined as "institutionalized national policies and programs that attempt to expand the scope of a national state's political, economic, social, and moral regulation to include emigrants and their descendants outside the national territory" (Goldring, 2002, p. 64). Emigration polices are a good example of how SLTN works. Examples of these policies include the creation of institutions to address the needs and demands of emigrants, efforts to control and channel remittances, incentives to invest, support for migrant cultural activities and organizations, enacting legislation regarding dual citizenship, political representation, and voting rights (Margheritis,

---

[7] While scholars tend to separate state-led and migrant-led transnationalism for analytical purposes, the boundaries between the two are not always clear. Migrants and the state often interact to create transnational space or practices, as discussed in Goldring (2002).

2011). These measures usually include a political discourse that aims to recognize emigrants as part of the nation (Gamlen 2008), seeking to enhance pride in nationhood.

1.7 Organization of the Study

This thesis is divided into three parts. Part I consists of the introduction (Chapter 1) and three further chapters. Chapter 2 provides a review of the literature relevant to sending states, immigration, and emigrant policy, as well as the approaches taken in international relations and political science. Chapter 3 provides the theoretical framework. It begins with an overview of sovereignty and the state and sending state actions, and then goes into more detail about state-led transnationalism and its types. It then discusses how sending states and emigrant policy call into question longstanding assumptions about nation-state sovereignty. Chapter 4, on methodology, explains the case selection, why a comparative case studies method was chosen, and how the data was collected and organized.

Part II has two chapters that examine the empirical findings. Chapter 5 analyzes the recognition of the emigrant community through the creation of institutions and describes how sending states aim to cultivate loyalties in the emigrant community through symbolic policies. Chapter 6 looks at the process of extending emigrants' rights, in addition to programs designed to protect vulnerable emigrants. This chapter also explains the process of how states work to integrate migrants by extracting economic and political resources from them by promoting programs to attract money for the national economy or to win votes.

In Part III, Chapter 7 discusses the findings related to the three explanatory variables and the differences in the degree of state-led transnationalism, namely 1) the importance of the size and potential impact of emigrant communities; 2) party system competitiveness; and 3) the sending state's institutional capacity to implement policies. These explanatory factors account for the differences in the sending states' motivations to engage with their emigrant communities. The chapter also analyzes how low institutional capacity leads to the delegation of state functions to civil society organizations or international organizations. Finally, the chapter examines the degrees of state-led transnationalism in the three case studies. Chapter 8, the final chapter, presents the main conclusions, beginning with a discussion of the key questions answered, followed by the key findings. It also reviews the theory and discusses implications for policy and practice. It concludes with avenues for future research related to emigrant policies in Central America and the overall contribution of this book to the field.

Chapter 2
State of the Art

2.1 Introduction

This chapter, which provides a review of the literature on the role of states in emigrant policy, mainly focuses on the case of Central America, a migrant-sending region. The chapter is divided into five parts. The first section presents an overview of the different disciplinary approaches in migration research, including contributions from political science to migration. The second section shows the links between the state and migration. The third section highlights the research gap between migrant-receiving and migrant-sending states (the great majority of emigrant policy research has focused more on policies from receiving states, neglecting the role of sending states in policymaking).[8] The fourth section examines the topics addressed by emigrant policy, both in the political realm, as well as in academic research. The final section provides an overview of the developments in migration studies in Central America following the events of September 11, 2001, showing how the Northern Triangle of Central America (NTCA) has been an under-researched region compared to the rest of Latin America.

The literature review also observes the pronounced research gaps in the study of the political aspects of migration. Thus, three gaps (receiving vs. sending states; focus on the micro level of migration; studies on Central America vs. other regions in Latin America) can be identified in current migration research. The first gap is reflected in the estimates that suggest that almost half of all international migration comes from the Global South; yet most studies focus their analyses on the policies in the North, thereby excluding analyses of sending states (United Nations, 2020a). A considerable preponderance of literature has looked at immigration policy, mostly in the United States, Canada, and some European countries,

---

8 This concept is discussed in greater detail in the theoretical chapter.

the most common receiving states. Some exceptions to research on sending states include China, the Philippines, South Korea (Hugo, 2010), and Mexico.

The second gap shows that research on migration has tended to emphasize the economic, social, and cultural aspects of migration. For instance, many researchers have looked at the social impact of migration shaping the life of communities and families, while only a few have paid attention to the political results of migration.[9] Hence, research on the connection between migration and the state, its policies, institutions, and interest groups is still underdeveloped.

Third, there is a hole in the regional research vis-à-vis the impact of migration in Central America. Leading works of migration research carried out in Latin America can be found that concern Argentina, Ecuador, and Mexico.[10] However, even though this region shares similar historical and contemporary socioeconomic challenges, there is still little research on the explanatory factors that account for the impact of migration in Central America. Due to its geographic position, Central America offers a bridge that allows migration from South to North America. There is an increasing body of research on intraregional mobility, especially from Nicaragua and Costa Rica, and single case studies of El Salvador, Guatemala, and Nicaragua. Still, comparative approaches that address Central America as a region or subregion remain scarce. The main argument in this chapter is that research on the political aspects of migration is necessary to understand future trends in emigrant policy, which is relevant both academically and in terms of policy.

---

9   Some exceptions are: (Baringhorst et al. 2006; Bauböck 2003; Faist 2004; Hollifield 2004; 2000; Levitt & de la Dehesa 2003; Zolberg 1999).
10 For some of the early research done from Argentina, see (Novick 2008 and Oteiza 2010). For studies from Ecuador, see Herrera et al. 2005. Some of the most relevant work done on Mexico (a vast amount) includes (Anguiano & López, 2010; Calderón, 2010; Castillo, 1994).

2.2 Political Science Contributions to Migration Studies

Many debates surround similar migration questions within the academic disciplines. At times, there is agreement across the disciplines about the nature of the issue and even the methodology. However, concurrence about a single explanation or model is unlikely. Within the social sciences, research that draws upon concepts in an interdisciplinary manner is very rare for migration studies. This section briefly looks at the contributions that the social science disciplines have made to migration studies. It begins with the analytical levels associated with historians, anthropologists, sociologists, demographers, and economists and ends by pinpointing the contribution from political science to migration studies, in order to shed light on the approaches missing in that discipline, which has focused more on "securitization" from an international relations perspective.

Within the social sciences, some scholars have engaged in micro-level research, examining the decisions and actions of individuals, families, and communities related to migration. Others approach the problem at a macro-level, analyzing structural conditions (political, legal, and economic). Meso-level theories focusing on social ties and networks are associated with the work of sociologists and anthropologists. In contrast, political science is principally concerned with the role of the state, and how it operates at a macro-level (Brettell & Hollifield 2000).

The main research questions for historians are related to place or time: what are the determinants and consequences of population movement? Who moves, when do they move, why do they move, and what is their experience during departure, migration, and settlement? These questions are generally applied to single groups or focus on individual migrants as agents. Researchers in this field appear to be less concerned with the influence of social structures on migrants' behavior (Brettell, 2000). Conversely, anthropologists tend to be as context specific as possible using ethnographic methods. Their goal is to explore the impacts of immigration and emigration[11] on social relations, for instance between men and women and among kin. Rather than focusing on the why, who, and when, these scholars concentrate on the experience of being an immigrant and the meaning of the social and cultural changes that result from leaving one context and entering another (Basch et al., 1995; Diner, 2000; Khagram & Levitt, 2008). Offering a different perspective, sociologists have argued that social relations are central to understanding the processes of emigration and immigration. These researchers work almost exclusively with destination societies, while anthropologists examine both the destination and origin societies (Brettell, 2000).

A growing body of literature has been developed by demographers, who have focused mainly on births, deaths, directions of migration flows, and population change. In contrast to anthropologists and sociologists, whose main concern is present behavior, demographers often make assumptions about future migration trends. Economists have largely researched migration from a supply-side theory, rather than looking at outcomes. They tend to use a microeconomic framework of individual choice and the minimization of risks as a motivating factor for migration (D. Massey & Taylor, 2004a). From an economic framework, some scholars have shown predictive models of employment patterns for immigrants in the American economy and general patterns of labor market insertion for the major foreign-born nationality groups (Zhou, 2004). In short, economists highlight labor markets in destination countries or the economy in sending states.

In contrast to the aforementioned disciplines, political scientists tend to study migration using the state as their primary unit of analysis, with contemporary literature on the politics and policy of migration being scarcely 30 years old (Freeman & Kessler 2008). The migration research done by political scientists emphasizes three main topics: the role of the nation-state in controlling migration flows and its borders; the impact of migration on institutions, sovereignty, and citizenship, as well as the link

---

11   Immigration refers to the movement of people into a country. Emigration is the act of leaving one's country.

between migration and foreign policy or national security; and the question of the integration of migrants in destination countries (Hollifield 2004; 2000). The role of political science in international migration research, especially in policymaking, has been reflected in a growing body of literature on migration in comparative politics (Castles 2004a; 2002; Cornelius et al. 2004; Hollifield 2004).

Many political scientists have drawn attention to the challenges regarding citizenship for immigrants, with some authors approaching citizenship from the point of view of integration policies in receiving states and others viewing it as a challenge for democracies. Although most of these studies emphasize citizenship in a context in which political identity and membership must be congruent with state territory, other researchers write about a deterritorialized citizenship, focusing on the rights of minorities in more than one country (Aleinikoff & Klusmeyer, 2001; Castles & Alastair, 2000; Fitzgerald, 2000).

Nevertheless, prior to the terrorist attacks of September 11, 2001, the traditional political science approach came from an international relations perspective that looked at questions like refugee crises (Castles & Miller 2009; Waever et al. 1993; Weiner 1993b; 1995). After 9/11, research began to focus more on human trafficking and smuggling, and types of border and visa controls (Koslowski, 2005). These studies were carried out by international relations scholars who linked neorealist and neoliberal approaches with the "securitization" of migration (Waever et al., 1993; Weiner, 1993a). Many researchers published studies on migration policy directed towards security and control (Cornelius et al. 2004; Freeman 1994; Geiger & Pécoud 2010; Weiner 1993a), some with a focus on development (i.e. Chappell 2009; de Haas 2008b). Other approaches of that type attempted to explain world politics from two perspectives, state-centric theories (mostly from realism and neoliberalism) and non-state-centric theories (linked to constructivism), which developed as alternatives to realism by focusing on transnational studies (Koslowski, 2005).

Further analysis will show that migration is rarely considered in political science research today. The following sections draw attention to the fact that most scholars from the political sciences concentrate on international relations and emphasize questions relating to world politics, such as the role of diasporas. One of the limitations with this approach is that it does not consider migrants in receiving states and the countries they left behind. Nor do these accounts sufficiently examine the implications of citizenship beyond the right to vote or acquiring rights and duties in the host society. Research in political science tends to focus on migration as a security issue for receiving states, disregarding many important aspects of emigrant policy relevant to sending states. Current international relations approaches (vs. a meso-level of analysis) examine migration using a transnational lens. A comprehensive review of emigrant policy between sending and receiving states is clearly needed.

2.3 The Links between the State and Migration

The following section spotlights the tendency to link migration and the state, mainly through control and management functions. There have been some efforts to quantify the role of the political processes of migration from political science (see: Bauböck 2003; 2006; Castles 2004b; Smith 2003) that pay special attention to institutions and interest groups. To examine the predominant approaches linking the state and migration, this chapter discusses the initial sources that trace migration to state activities, discussing three hypotheses using an international relations approach. These hypotheses underpin the contradiction of closed and open borders, confronting receiving and sending states dealing with migration. The chapter also shows how perspectives that link the state and migration through a security paradigm have been predominant in the literature (specifically, regional and human security), creating a migration-security nexus approach. Finally, it presents the research gaps related to the links between states and migration, highlighting the few studies that connect states with migration using institutional and interest group approaches.

Many scholars have acknowledged that migration is as much about state sovereignty and policy as it is about the people who migrate. Since the end of World War II, international economic forces (trade, investment, and migration) have pushed states towards greater openness, while the international state system and domestic political forces have pushed states towards greater closure. The problem is that transnational movements (such as cross-border investment, trade, and migration), challenge the sovereignty and authority of the nation-state. It has been conclusively shown that migration is a particular challenge to the nation-state because unauthorized migrants crossing borders violate principles of sovereignty (Hollifield 2004).

Political scientist Aristide Zolberg was one of the first to trace the sources of migration to the activities of the state. He argued that the formation of new states was one of the root causes of refugee migrations (Zolberg et al. 1989; 1999). In his book, *A Nation by Design*, the author explores American immigration policy from the colonial period to the present, discussing how it has been used as a nation-building tool (Zolberg, 2006). Hollifield, on the other hand, conducted a number of investigations connecting the liberal state and migration. He discusses migration with regard to three hypotheses from international relations theory: neorealist, globalization, and neoliberalism (1986; 1998; 2000; 2004).

The neorealist hypothesis posits that states open and close their borders in response to changes in the structure of the international system. Hollifield notes that the problem with this argument is that shifts in the distribution of power are very rare. The author then offers an alternative to the previous neorealist hypothesis: globalization theory. This theory is based on world systems arguments, where the international division of labor and restructuring of the global economy entails population movements that even the most powerful states are incapable of regulating. This is often referred to as the "global city," which is beyond the regulatory reach of the state (2000). Globalization theory proposes that it makes no sense to use a domestic or international politics approach to understand increases in international exchange (whether in the areas of finance, trade, or migration). Hollifield argues that sovereignty is an antiquated concept and that migration and the state must be thought of in terms of postnationalism.

Hollifield then proposed a third hypothesis, neoliberalism. Based on the continuing importance of the nation-state in international relations, Hollifield argues that increasing economic interdependence has altered the way that states use their power. Now, rather than using traditional military means to pursue their national interest as in neorealist theory, liberal states pursue collaboration in order to influence the international economy, reduce risks, and lower transaction costs. This argument shows that unlike neo-realists, liberal states are willing to look at domestic politics, especially those that relate to coalitions and institutions, suggesting that openness increases international cooperation (1998). In sum, Hollifield follows the neoliberal and neorealist arguments, suggesting that the rise in immigration in the postwar period is closely linked to three factors: a) the structure of the international system; b) domestic political coalitions (based on economic interests); and c) rights, from liberal constitutions to laws.

The security focus of international migration research emphasizes three main concepts in the classification of security: a) state security; b) regional security; and c) human security. A state-centric approach is the traditional security concept, focusing on territory, political independence, and the survival of the state. During the 1970s, this concept was challenged by theories that focused on regional security, which broadened the security agenda to include different kinds of possible threats and acknowledged the interdependence of states.

The most classic approach linking security with migration by Weiner (1993a; 1993b and 1995) stresses the rise of uncontrolled mass migration, resulting in the violation of national territory and border controls within the sovereign nation-state. Furthermore, Weiner argues that migrants can cause diplomatic conflict. For instance, when asylum is granted to a certain population, the sending state is then classified as one where people are persecuted. The hopes of migrants and refugees for a better life matches the fears of many citizens in receiving states that a massive influx of migrants could impose strains on the economy, upset the ethnic balance, and weaken national identity (Weiner, 1993a).[12]

---

12 One example of migrants perceived as a threat are the Syrian refugees from that country's civil war, who are being housed in camps in Turkey, Lebanon, and Jordan. They are considered a threat to the security of Italy, specifically, and Europe in general. The media has contributed significantly to this perception, frequently portraying overwhelming numbers of people crossing borders every day.

A focus on the tension over migrants, identity, and territory that builds up between societies gives rise to a security-migration approach, which according to Waever et al. (1993), is a "societal security dilemma." In their book on European receiving states, the authors explain that societies can experience processes in which perceptions of "the other" develop into mutually reinforcing "enemy-pictures" leading to the same kind of security dilemma that occurs between states. Another component of this dilemma is the argument that migrants may serve as a source of competing identity, because they pose a threat to societal security when identities are mutually exclusive, i.e. Christian versus Muslim.

The last approach—human security—emphasizes the view of individuals as a threat to security. The main risks considered here are civil wars within "security complexes," in which established neighboring regions affect another region (Angenendt, 2007). In this respect, daily newspapers in the Western world often carry articles about undocumented immigrants, asylum seekers, and other migrants. The focus of these articles varies greatly, from viewing migrants as a threat to one or another important societal interest, to presenting migrants as an important asset to those very societal interests. The overall impact is confusing: is migration an asset or a threat?[13]

The specific concept of a security-migration nexus has been discussed in recent political and, to a lesser extent, academic debates. Discourses on this nexus have usually revolved around four threatening scenarios. First, there is a fear of an uncontrollable rise in irregular migration (this matches the classic view put forth by Weaver and Weiner). This argument is often linked with fears of organized crime, trafficking in persons, migrant smuggling, and drug trafficking. Second, there is a fear of a "demographic imbalance." Fueled by current concerns regarding declining birth rates in many industrialized countries, this debate tends to overemphasize perceptions in the resident society that they will be outnumbered by large groups of unauthorized immigrants who will compete for

---

13 For example, in their book (Guild & van Selm, 2005) investigate these value assessments regarding migrants in Australia, Canada, Europe, and the United States.

jobs or housing (Marquardt et al., 2011). Third, this discourse is often connected to issues related to the lack of integration policies of both migrants and the resident society, such as fears of youth gangs, of "ghettoization," and of the development of "parallel societies" (Warnecke, 2007). In part this debate is fed by the thesis linking ethnic diversity and conflict in Huntington's *Clash of Civilizations*, where he postulates that post-Cold War conflict would most likely occur because of cultural rather than ideological differences (Huntington, 1998). Finally, intensified by the events of September 11, migration and terrorism have become linked in political debates. The public and the media call for stricter border controls to stop potentially dangerous "aliens" from entering.

The domestic comparative politics approach has been the least explored by political scientists. This is the gap that this work helps to fill, because it explains more about the links between state and migration from perspectives other than international relations, for two main reasons. First, those theories tend to lean towards explaining interactions between states, rather than policies focusing on the interaction between state and society. While international relations approaches are useful for the study of emigrant policies, they focus primarily on trade and the monetary and security policies of receiving states. Second, domestic politics theories reveal the impact of migration on state sovereignty, culture, and politics.

One middle-ground approach to states and migration combines realism, Marxism, liberalism, national identity, and institutionalism. For instance, in his comparison of theories of international immigration policy, Meyers (2000) analyzes the influence of theories from comparative politics, international relations, and sociology on immigration policy theories. His findings show that, whereas realism sheds light on refugee policy, Marxism and neo-Marxism highlight the role of migrant workers and undocumented immigration in the policies. Neoliberalism, conversely, may emphasize the importance of immigration policy in the European Union. In short, Meyers's interdisciplinary approach manages to disaggregate the state, beginning with the distinct roles played by bureaucracies, political parties, electoral arrangements, and executive-legislative relations in the policymaking process.

With regard to institutions, studies have attempted to explain the variation between states in shaping migration politics. These works have often focused on political opportunity structures that affect the capacities and incentives of interest and advocacy groups to organize and give voice to their preferences (Ögelman, 2003). Other studies have focused on interests groups, rights, and states (Freeman & Birrell 2001), linking policy demands to the concrete gains and losses of identifiable groups in the electorate and to the compromises they produce in pluralistic political systems. Scholars researching migration interest groups have focused on associations that are for or against immigration (Freeman, 1994; Joppke, 1998). Finally, other theories postulate that policies are designed to achieve national interests, but provide few guidelines to explain what that interest is in the case of immigration policy (Freeman & Kessler 2008). The model in this study, on the other hand, confronts the problem of explaining why liberal receiving states adopt widely different immigration and citizenship policies. To summarize, one of the many problems related to institutionalism is that there is little empirical evidence to support generalizations about the motivations driving different bureaucratic bodies and no consensus as to whether diverse institutional configurations yield diverse policy outcomes (Guild & van Selm, 2005). Although interest groups fill some gaps in the study of institutionalism, they fail to produce complete theoretical explanations for what moves groups to organize.

Research about institutionalism and migration policy is scarce, with the few exceptions related to domestic policies. Here, scholars have investigated the immigration preferences of mainstream parties (Money, 1999) and the effects of electoral arrangements on the success of anti-immigration parties (Art, 2011). Nevertheless, these accounts tend to overlook the importance of international factors on certain domestic policies. By applying a transnational lens to the study of sending state emigrant policy that combines different levels of analysis, including domestic interest groups, political institutions, and international actors, this text addresses some of these shortcomings.

2.4 From a Migrant-Receiving to a Migrant-Sending State Approach

As noted above, scholarly attention has usually prioritized receiving states over sending states, although some works have highlighted the need to go beyond nation-states and employ a transnational perspective. The focus of this section is the sending state. To better understand why sending states employ certain policies and programs, the factors that account for their different actions, such as the types of pressures they face and the direction their policies follow, both planned and unexpected, must be considered. A variety of researchers have attempted to explain the role of receiving states through immigration (rules of entry) (Hollifield 2004; 1986; Freeman & Kessler 2008; Weiner 1995), while less attention has been paid to emigration (rules of exit) (Castles & Delgado Wise 2008; Massey & Taylor 2004b; Schmitter Heisler 1985).

During the half century characterized by the rise and consolidation of the European empires, a significant amount of movement between continents took place. These were mostly Europeans migrating to the colonies to improve their economic situations and that of the home country (Juss, 2004). During this time, many Asians and Africans were also moved by the colonizers between continents to meet labor needs. The current system, where states have the sovereign right to exclude non-citizens from their territory, originated during the late 19th century and focuses on the receiving states. Ironically, its strongest supporters are the very Western states that benefited greatly from the free movement of earlier times (Juss, 2004). Most international migration now occurs from the rest of the world to Western receiving states. However, the opportunities these states can offer migrants at present are far exceeded by the demand. Given the increasing number of security measures and migration management policies, many individuals look for other alternatives to migrate.

One critical question that has been analyzed from the view of receiving states is asylum. Receiving states generally withdrew their commitment to asylum with the end of the Cold War, when it was expected that immigration levels would decline. At the end of the 1980s, the commitment of receiving states to an international refugee regime weakened. The Schengen Agreement in Europe, which suspended the right of asylum for some people, is one such example. Additionally, some countries like Germany eliminated the blanket right to asylum. This happened in the United States, as well, when the protection of asylum seekers was revoked in 1996 and the special status of Cuban refugees was restricted, even though they had enjoyed automatic access to asylum. According to Hollifield (1998), these changes indicate that receiving states were adjusting to new geo-political realities and thus attempting to restrict migration. Even so, international migration did not decrease after the Cold War. Another crucial topic involving receiving states is that of integration as a way to obtain rights, such as the right to vote, to work, and to settle in general (Escrivá et al., 2009; Lafleur & Martiniello, 2009; Landolt, 2001). Some researchers have focused more on the social and cultural consequences for migrants coping with host societies, or the ways in which migrants maintain their own customs in the receiving state (Brubaker, 1998; Hollifield, 1986; Joppke, 1998; Ögelman, 2003).

Other scholars have adopted a transnational lens to examine both receiving and sending countries together, demonstrating that the increased migration from some countries has an impact on the sending communities, too. These changes are associated with a number of circumstances from economic conditions to quality of life, family disintegration, changing gender roles, kinship, political engagement, and the like (Fitzgerald, 2000; Herrera et al., 2005; Levitt & Sørensen, 2004). They also influence the mechanisms through which the two communities remain connected, for instance through social, political, and economic remittances (Khagram & Levitt, 2008). Although this viewpoint takes the impact of migration in sending states into account, it looks at it from the perspective of the receiving state and what comes from there; in other words, what migrants send to their families in their country of origin. A few transnational studies have looked at the role of gender with regard to citizenship involving Mexican and Dominican women who went to the United States (Goldring 2001; Guarnizo 1998), while others have examined care chains related to the migration of Ecuadorian or Dominican women (Herrera et al. 2005; Guarnizo 1998; Piper 2006) to Europe (Piper 2006). Transnational migration studies, in short, highlight the importance of looking beyond the nation-state and its sovereignty, an approach that is highly useful when analyzing the dynamics of two or more places, even when the state continues to play an important role regarding migration (Pries 2007; 2008; Sassen 2000).

Recently, an increasing amount of literature has focused on the sending state. The earliest discussions of the political impact of migration from the sending states emerged in two texts, one by (Levitt & de la Dehesa, 2003) and the other by (Østergaard-Nielsen, 2003a). Looking at Brazil, the Dominican Republic, Haiti, and Mexico, Levitt & De la Dehesa (2003) analyzed how sending states play an important role in shifting policies toward their communities abroad, reconfiguring conventional understandings of sovereignty, citizenship, and membership. In her book on the sending state, Øestergaard-Nielsen (2003) offers a comparative study of the policies of sending countries towards their nationals abroad. Both pioneering texts concentrate on classifying the actions and policies of sending states. Later, (Gamlen, 2008) used quantitative methods to analyze 70 sending states around the world, and categorize the state mechanisms to reach out to its citizens. Other studies have also provided important insights regarding the operation of sending states, with some groundbreaking works on Central America (Aguayo, 1985; Castillo & Palma, 1996; Kron, 2011; Sørensen, 2019); Mexico (Cornelius & Lewis 2007; Choate 2007; Fitzgerald 2008; Taylor 2004); and South and Latin America in general (Domenech, 2009; Mármora, 1994; Oteiza, 2010; Pellegrino, 2010; Wehr, 2006). Wayne Cornelius (2004) examined the impact of migration on Mexico as a sending state, observing how sending states have a say on how to manage migration flows through temporary foreign worker programs, for instance the Bracero Program.[14] Other studies can be found on Filipino temporary foreign workers in the United States (Asis, 2008;

---

14 The Bracero program was a temporary foreign worker program during the mid-20th century between the governments of Mexico and the United States. There were also temporary foreign worker programs between Guatemala and Mexico in the Soconusco region in Chiapas.

Battistella, 2004). Some researchers have focused on the causes and consequences of migration on economic phenomena like poverty, job shortages, and the intraregional markets of sending states (Abella, 2004; Hujo & Piper, 2010; Taylor, 2004). The political impact of migration, on the other hand, has received little academic attention, although some work has been done on the policies implemented by sending states, such as voting rights and migrants' access to political rights abroad (Castillo et al., 2011; Lafleur & Chelius, 2011; A. I. López, 2018). The role of sending states has always been seen as submissive to the actions of the receiving states. In this regard, Rosenblum (2002) argues that Mexico has had "a policy of having no policy," although the Mexican state has designed a number of programs for its citizens.

One innovative concept in political science is "state-led transnationalism," first defined by (Goldring, 2002) as institutionalized national policies and programs that attempt to expand the scope of a national state's regulations to include emigrants and their relatives beyond the country's borders. This concept has been used to study domestic political factors such as the nature and internal dynamics of governments, political discourses, and projects, as well as other institutional factors in Ecuador and Argentina (Margheritis, 2007, 2011).

Massey et al. (1994) demonstrated that when sending states become involved in emigrant policymaking and agree to negotiate migration quotas with receiving states, better results can be achieved, thus benefiting migrants. For sending states, the effects of international migration have been a source of controversy among researchers and policymakers. Massey & Taylor (2004a) argue that this controversy is mainly about the unequal distributions of these effects, raising questions such as: why does international migration appear to promote development in some migrant-sending states and not in others? And, which social groups benefit from migration, which ones lose, and why?

There is a need for structured comparisons to explain the differences and similarities in the types of sending states, to add detail to the existing theories and generalizations. Theories on emigrant policy need to be contrasted and debated based on empirical data. Moreover, many migration studies focus on Western liberal democracies, downplaying the importance of sending states in, for example, Latin America, East Asia, and the Middle East. Finally, there is a gap in the research about the interests of sending states when formulating emigrant policy. This study helps to fill these gaps, contributing not only to contemporary research trends on migration, but also to the discipline of political science, since it analyzes states, their interests, and the way they handle certain policies, such as migration.

2.5 Migration Policy

Migration policymaking is not only about institutional and historical legacies, but also about the deliberate strategies employed by political actors involved in shaping policy alternatives. Public policy and policymaking can be linked with the concept of governance; this has its roots in sociological systems theory and empirical policy studies. For instance, Piper (2010) argues that migrant organizations are an important factor of influence on policymaking and concrete networking initiatives with government agencies at regional, national, and municipal levels, which connects with the concept of governance. Boswell (2007), on the other hand, argues that new institutional theories offer a sophisticated approach, but fall short on methodological and explanatory factors. Political economy explanations are theoretically strong, but at the price of over-simplification. As a third way to explain and theorize migration policy, the author suggests a theory that emphasizes the functional imperatives of the state in the area of migration, as they shape states' responses to societal interests and institutional structures.

The increasing number of temporary foreign worker programs in the world prompt questions about whether liberal states can control unwanted migration (Freeman 1994). Temporary migration programs are seen as a policy instrument for managing labor immigration. However, these programs have been the subject of criticism, because many past guest worker programs, most notably the Bracero program in the United States (1942–64) and the temporary foreign worker programs in Germany (1955–73), supposedly failed to meet their stated policy objectives, while generating several unanticipated consequences, including the non-return and eventual settlement of many guest workers and their families.

Some authors refer to this phenomenon as the unintended consequences of public policy. Castles (2004b) claims that to be effective, policies need to be fair and be perceived as fair by all the groups involved. This requires changes in legal frameworks and institutional structures. Some arguments in favor of migration emphasize the benefits for receiving countries in terms of meeting labor market shortages, for sending countries with regard to guaranteeing remittances for development, and for migrants through employment and control over the use of their wages (Ruhs 2008; Vertovec 2007).

Citizenship policies play an important role in this discussion as well. These often focus on the capacities and incentives of various groups to organize and give voice to their preferences (Faist et al. 2004; Hoffmann 2008; Piper 2010). Many authors have analyzed the challenges for citizens in the receiving states. For example, in their book, Baringhorst et al. (2006) analyze European and North American immigration societies, scrutinizing the specific value of citizenship for immigrants. The work done by Soysal (1994) contains perhaps the best known approach to the impact of values and norms that transcend traditional notions of national citizenship.

Some researchers have highlighted the political rights of migrants, specifically from a migrant-receiving state perspective, looking at, for example, Turks in Germany (Avci & Kirişci, 2008; Brubaker, 1998); Africans in Europe (Angenendt & Parkes, 2008; de Haas, 2008c, 2008a; Marfaing & Hein, 2008); Latin Americans in Europe (Martínez & Reboiras 2012), with a focus on Spain (Escrivá et al. 2009; Herrera et al. 2005; López 2005); and Latin Americans in the United States, especially Dominicans and Jamaicans (Sørensen 2007 and Levitt 2001) respectively; Cubans (Hoffmann 2006); and Central Americans (Maguid, 2010; Mahler, 2000a; Popkin, 2003). In this respect, scholars have concentrated on questions like multiple citizenships and the absentee rights of citizens as a matter of franchise, and how external citizenship is becoming much more important in structuring opportunities for migrants: Aleinikoff & Klusmeyer 2001; Bauböck 2003; 2006; Castles & Alastair 2000; Faist et al. 2004; Fitzgerald 2000; Fox 2006; Joppke 1999; Lafleur & Martiniello 2009; Smith 2003. The little research done on political rights from a migrant-sending state perspective has focused on Mexican immigrants in the United States keeping or acquiring political rights in their homeland, and not only in the receiving country: (Castillo 1994; Calderón 2010; Cornelius & Lewis 2007; Taylor 2004).

Other types of policies—again from the perspective of receiving states—are concerned with integration. Few topics generate as much heated public debate in the United States and Europe today as integration and assimilation policies. Integration policies, which aim to reduce the risks of conflict between citizens, generally involve language, education, taxes, and health systems, as well as the labor market. Assimilation policies, conversely, pursue adaptation and coercive norms for migrants in the host societies. Although various authors rely on a model of assimilation based on the Chicago School studies of the early 20th century, assimilation today no longer involves a core set of values by which to measure immigrant integration (largely based on concerns about racial and cultural purity (Arnold, 2011)). The works done on migration and human rights policies, in turn, are usually linked to undocumented migration and immigration for asylum (Bogusz et al., 2004) and are generally written under the auspices of international organizations (Abuelafia et al., 2019; Amnesty International, 2010; IOM, 2018). Last, some lines of research highlight the importance of the respect for the human rights of temporary foreign workers (Bonnici 2009; Breedy 2011; Martínez 2008).

From a classic security policy perspective, there has been an increase in migration management policies. As described above, while traditional studies connect migration with security from an international relations viewpoint, others link it with conflicts and refugee policies (Zolberg et al. 1989). In 1994, Cornelius, Martin and Hollifield formulated the control gap thesis, referring to the wide breach between the goals of national immigration policy, such as laws, regulations, and executive actions, and the policy outcomes in this area (Cornelius et al. 2004). The apparent incapacity of states to control immigration flows has been discussed as part of a broader debate regarding the challenges of the nation-state in a globalizing world (Castles 2004c; Freeman 1994; Hollifield 1986; Joppke 1998; Sassen 2000).

In this regard, Bimal Ghosh was one of the first to propose the idea of migration management. According to the author, international migration should be manageable and predictable. Thus, he proposed a three-pillar model aimed, first, at attracting the attention of all interested states in migration, second, at creating a new international framework agreement on global mobility; and third, at strengthening the role of different actors, which would become more influential in migration policymaking (Ghosh 2000). According to Kron (2011), the main categories of thought and action can be summarized in pairs of terms: migration and security, migration and development, migration and labor market, programs of readmission and return, and border management as crosscutting migration concerns.

One of the most recent policy trends comes from the discourse of international organizations like the International Organization for Migration (IOM) and refers to the migration-development nexus. This body of research has focused on migrant networks and organizations that emerged as development agents. Their actions are analyzed from their interaction with state institutions and the flows of economic remittances, knowledge, and political ideas. In the discursive dimension, the new interests of OECD countries and IOs are on migrant families engaged in entrepreneurial activities, migrant remittances, and migrant associations abroad,[15] and their role in development. According to Faist (2007), the migration-development nexus approach is a sign of two coinciding trends. First, the community as a principle of development has come to supplement principles of social order, such as the market and the state. Second, states and IOs see migrants and transnational collective actors as significant development agents.

---

15 In the academic literature and policy briefings, migrant associations abroad are referred to as Hometown Associations (HTAs), the term used in this study as well.

Development actions involve migration policy in the following areas: first, remittance mobilization (aimed at enhancing remittances, this may vary depending on the degree of the country's financial, economic, and institutional development); second, steering monetary remittances towards official channels (remittance transfer through regular banking channels enables government to exercise control over the use of foreign exchange); third, facilitating remittance and other investments in community aid, business investments, tourism, and nostalgia trade; and fourth, diasporas as agents of development (essential to sending countries if they are to mobilize remittances for development). IOs promote the involvement of diaspora networks through active policies in order to convince resident migrants abroad and their offspring to support development projects in their countries of origin (A. I. López, 2018; Østergaard-Nielsen, 2003b, 2016). These networks are seen as a potential source of ideas, finance, and qualified labor, among other actions.

There are some critics of the "productive use of remittances" approach. De Haas, for instance, criticizes current policy and scholarly discourses because they naively celebrate migration, remittances, and transnational engagement as self-help development "from below," while also shifting attention away from the relevance of structural constraints and the important role that states and other institutions play in shaping favorable conditions for social and economic development to occur (Haas et al., 2019). In line with this thought, Castillo & Palma (2003) argue that migration policy would have a meaningful impact on development if the aim were to create more work opportunities and alternative productive models in the sending state, so that migration would not have to be the main strategy to find a job.

2.6 The Literature on the Case Studies: Central America

This section provides an overview of the studies and trends related to migration in Central America since the end of the 1990s. Research on Central America has ranged from the cultural impact of migration to the social, economic and, to a lesser extent, political consequences in the region. Central America has been analyzed as a region of origin, transit, destination, returned, and deported migration. However, little research has been done to date on the institutional aspects of migration policymaking in the region, specifically on the topics of temporary labor migration, migrants' human rights, and the migration-development nexus. Similarly, there are few academic studies about regional initiatives and their process and impact on the regulation of emigrant policies. Most of the work done on these subjects in the region is not academic, but comes from civil society or international organizations. Some countries in the region, such as El Salvador, show evidence of the increasing interest in migration research. Conversely, in Honduras there is still limited knowledge about the implications of migration.

Before the 21st century, a number of studies were done on refugee migration in North America, particularly on Guatemalans and Salvadorans fleeing to Mexico in the 1980s at the time of the civil wars in El Salvador, Guatemala, and Nicaragua, and the returned migration during the postwar phase in the 1990s. Thus, policy and research trends of that time were generally related to refugees and internal migration (Aguayo 1985; Castillo & Palma 1996; García 2006; Stepputat 1999; Torres-Rivas & Jiménez 1985; Worby 2002). These approaches are important to understand the context of migration in the region. In this regard, a pioneer article by Torres-Rivas & Jiménez (1985) showed that although there have been important changes derived from internal armed conflicts and the subsequent migration, the national authorities did not pay enough attention to the international migration of Central Americans during that period. Migration has been traditionally considered a matter for foreign affairs. Fundamentally, governments did not take responsibility for their citizens abroad in the 1980s (Stanley, 1993).

According to Castillo & Palma (2003), governments initially started to adopt political measures to control and contain mobilization in response to the migration of temporary foreign workers in the Soconusco region in the Chiapas border area of Mexico and the settlement of asylum seekers in that country. After the events of September 11, 2001, a number of Central American countries instituted or modified their emigrant policies. Several studies have analyzed the impact of regional policies like "Plan Sur" and the rise in migration control, especially at the southern Mexican border and "Plan Coyote 2000." Particular attention has been paid to how these plans helped fuel a migration industry by outsourcing services and promoting the business of the several private actors who benefit from the informality of migration, paving the way for so-called coyotes, migrant smuggling, and trafficking in persons (Gammeltoft-Hansen & Sørensen, 2013; Hernández-León, 2013; Kaye, 2010; Naylor, 2004; Rosales Sandoval, 2013; Salt & Stein, 1997; Sørensen, 2013b).

Conversely, contemporary emigrant policies in Central America have mainly focused on the mechanisms of security and control. Rocha's book (2010) *Deported from Globalization*, for instance, shows how deportations of Central Americans increased during the 2000s. Dardón (2009), in turn, has analyzed quantitative deportation data from the southern Mexican border. Another important contribution is the work by Camayd-Freixas (2009), which documents the massive deportation of Central Americans, mainly Guatemalans, from Postville, Iowa. The text *Living Illegal* is also an essential academic work in this area that helps explain the impact of deportations and security policies on the lives of Guatemalans in the United States (Marquardt et al., 2011).

Another approach analyses the impact of governance discourses on security management policies at the Guatemalan, Nicaraguan, and Costa Rican borders (Kron 2011; 2001). A major work on this topic for Honduras by Sørensen examines the risks faced by Honduran migrants on their transit through Mexico, as well as the impact of their deportation. The author argues that the vulnerability observed in Honduran migrants can be explained by the newness of their migration history compared to other Central American countries, which have a longer migration tradition because of their civil wars (Sørensen, 2013b). Consequently, these migrants have fewer social networks, an important factor if the migration process is to be successful. A report issued by the Honduran Documentation Center (CEDOH) (2005) also analyses Honduran deportations. The Central American organizations, Institute of Studies and Dissemination on

Migration (INEDIM) and the Central American Institute for Social Studies and Development (INCEDES) (2011), argue for an advocacy approach to security policy that considers the primary concerns of sending states on the political agenda. Other critical approaches to Central American deportees examine their construction as "superheroes" when they migrate and "deportee trash" when they are deported (Sørensen, 2010). These images are usually constructed by sending communities and by the migrants themselves before, during, and after their migration (Falla & Yojcom 2012; Falla 2008; González & Montenegro 2003).

Most studies of temporary emigrant policies are produced by NGOs and civil society (Caballeros & Lorenzana 2006; Breedy 2011; Martínez 2008; MENAMIG 2006) rather than academics, although with a few exceptions (Bonnici, 2009; Elizondo Breedy, 2011). Other authors look at temporary migration programs from an intraregional perspective. Such studies emphasize the role of Central American states on local employment opportunities and how this could be a determinant factor to create work opportunities for Central American migrants (Baumeister et al. 2008; Morales et al. 2011; 2007).

There are few academic studies of citizenship in the region to be found. This probably has to do with the fact that Central American countries only recently approved legislation allowing their migrants to vote abroad: Honduras in 2001 (CEDOH, 2005), El Salvador in 2013, and Guatemala in 2017. Some studies have looked at the impact of American immigration policy on Central Americans (Jonas, 2011; Mahler, 2000b; Marquardt et al., 2011; Palma C., 2004), including the political role of the emigrant population in their communities and the influence of Hometown Associations on economic development in their communities of origin (Mahler, 2000b; Martínez Rodas, 2017; Orozco, 2006; Popkin, 2003).

The social impact of migration is the area that has probably received the most attention in Central America. For instance, a large amount of research has been done on social changes in border communities, from cultural changes to perceptions of North America and the effect of migration on the everyday lives of migrants abroad and their families left behind (Andrade-Eekhoff, 2003; Andrade-Eekhoff & Silva-Avalos, 2003; Camus,

2007; Falla, 2008; Lungo & Kandel, 1999; Palma, 2004; Puerta, 2008; Williams, 2009).

In sum, there are significant gaps in the research on migration in Central America. As far as the migration-development nexus, little research has analyzed the impact of remittances on development in the region (Orozco, 2006, 2012), although there have also been some critiques of the subject (Rocha, 2011; Sørensen, 2004). Very few works have examined policies at a regional level or provided an account of bilateral or multilateral treaties (Abuelafia et al., 2019; Rosales Sandoval, 2021; Rosales Sandoval & Marvic García, 2021; Sørensen, 2019). Lastly, there is a lack of comparative research on emigrant policymaking in the different phases of the policy cycle.

2.7 Concluding Remarks

A review of the state of research on emigrant policy and sending states in Central America reveals gaps in both political science and in the body of migration research. First, the impact of migration has primarily been examined from a social, cultural, and economic viewpoint, disregarding the political aspects of the mobilization of people. However, when the political elements of migration are considered, it is usually from an international relations approach, leaving institutions, interest groups, advocacy, policymaking, and the policy process under-researched. This can be explained by the security paradigm that rules the international system and that tends to view mobilization as a threat to security and a violation of the sovereignty of receiving states. Nevertheless, because migration has traditionally been seen as a problem of the receiving states' sovereignty, the actions and interests of sending states have been minimized, both in the political realm and in academic research. Policy questions to a large extent follow the security and development interests of the receiving states. Lastly, although Central America is a region of geopolitical importance, migration studies have traditionally focused on the receiving communities in the United States. Another shortcoming of the studies is that most researchers limit themselves to single case studies, producing little information about sending states in Central America as a region or about its subregions.[16] The question remains: which factors account for the differences and similarities in the actions taken by sending states to reach out to their citizens abroad?

The following chapter discusses the theoretical and conceptual approaches that help explain state actions. Using the concept of state-led transnationalism, this writing analyzes different emigrant policies in order to conceptualize the sending state using a transnational lens, as well as the factors that account for its role in emigrant policy, such as its interaction with domestic and international actors.

---

16 There are some exceptions; migration researchers in the region include Manuel Ángel Castillo, Abelardo Morales Gamboa, Irene Palma, and José Luis Rocha, all of whom have published studies with a regional approach.

Chapter 3
Theoretical Framework

3.1 Introduction

To answer this research's question of why and how sending states adopt policies to engage with their emigrant communities abroad, this chapter discusses the theories and concepts applied throughout the work in three sections. The first discusses how origin states are increasingly engaging with their populations abroad, thus redefining the relationship between the state and its territorial boundaries. One of the main gaps found in the existing literature is that origin state institutions dedicated to the emigrant community and their leading transnational role have been largely overlooked in mainstream political science studies, perhaps because they fall into the gray area between domestic and international politics. However, international relations scholars have studied this topic and analyzed it through a transnationalism lens.

The second section describes how the dependent variable, state-led transnationalism (SLTN), is measured. SLTN provides explanations about how far states are willing to go to ensure that their emigrant community maintains a stable long-distance membership. This study elaborates on two mechanisms used by sending states to engage their emigrant community. The first is designed to build relationships with the emigrant community and encompasses two policy categories: 1) recognizing the emigrant community through the creation of institutions; and 2) cultivating loyalties in the emigrant community through symbolic policies. The objective of the second mechanism is to integrate the emigrant community and includes the following policy categories: 1) extending emigrant rights; and 2) extracting resources by incorporating migrants into the national economy. This section provides a description of state involvement and the actors playing a role in setting the emigrant policy agenda, such as the government, civil society, private sector, international organizations, and non-governmental organizations. Particular attention is paid to the degree of state participation in setting the agenda for emigrant policy, and the means of influence it has, including funding, consensus, and interinstitutional coordination.

In the third section, this study provides empirical support for three theoretically grounded explanatory factors: the importance of the size and potential impact of the emigrant community; party system competitiveness; and the state's institutional capacity to implement policies. These explanatory factors are clarified and operationalized at the end.

3.2 Sovereignty and the State

The research on states using emigrant policy to engage with their citizens living abroad sheds light on how migrant-sending states are redefining the relationship between the state and its territorial boundaries and reconfiguring the conventional understanding of sovereignty, citizenship, and membership in a nation-state. The book *Forced Migration and Global Politics* by Betts (2009) explains how states respond to forced migration and argues that when the field of international relations tries to provide explanations for state behavior, it has done so by using theories of neo-realism, liberal institutionalism, and liberal constructivism. These theories usually analyze world politics at the system or inter-state level, thereby diminishing the role of domestic politics. The question of how to conceptualize the relationship between domestic and international politics is still one of the main challenges for international relations. Neo-realism argues that states either see migration through a security lens or seek to contribute to migration for the purpose of fulfilling their own interests. The other motivation that will make a state act, from a neo-realist perspective, is when an hegemon has a sufficient and strong interest in addressing forced migration-related issues (Betts, 2009). Liberal institutionalism, on the other hand, starts from the legacy of idealism and classical liberalism, and its main contribution is to reintroduce domestic politics into international relations while not leaving inter-state relations completely out (Betts, 2009). The national interest comes from the sum of domestic claims or preferences. Foreign policy also results from interest-group lobbying within the state. In other words, the domestic character of the state and politics matter, irrespective of whether the state is liberal, authoritarian, capitalist, or socialist (Betts, 2009).

Within migration studies, some scholars have argued that the rise in transnational actors and international institutions regulating the movements of people has reconfigured or even eroded the sovereignty of the state (Appadurai, 1996). Other scholars like (Soysal, 1994) call this the emergence of a "post-national citizenship" and argue that it has encouraged rights claims based not on national membership but rather on a universal code of human rights. This is contrary to neo-realist international relations assumptions that look at migration through an international or domestic lens, and to scholars from different disciplines within migration studies who argue that state sovereignty has been eroded (both approaches view migration as a "two-level" dynamic). This investigation argues that the engagement of migrant-sending states with their emigrant community abroad reveals that these relations are not dichotomist (international or national) but rather a simultaneous interplay between the state and its citizens, no matter the territory, or in other words, beyond the nation-state boundary. States are increasingly extending their boundaries to those living outside the borders of their nation-state. Migrant-sending states are creating economic, political, and social mechanisms that enable migrants to participate in the different political, economic, social, and cultural processes of the nation (Levitt & de la Dehesa, 2003). The processes of involvement between the emigrant community and the sending state go beyond the national level, and can be observed at the community and family level as well. These dynamics call into question longstanding assumptions about the nation-state (Onuf, 1991; Weber, 1992). The increase in globalization has enabled some—and pushed other—migrants into maintaining strong ties to their countries of origin, even if they are integrated into the receiving country (Levitt, 2001). Growing globalization has translated into an increase in the movement of people across borders and new ways of communication and transporting technologies, as well as an increase in ways of regulating such movements (be it people, merchandise, or drugs). Thus, this study builds from Levitt's argument that even if boundaries are becoming porous and participatory channels are changing, states are not fading, but rather reinventing themselves to actively encourage emigrant participation in national politics from abroad (Levitt, 2001).

3.3 Migration Governance

Both non-state and state actors use mechanisms to engage their emigrant community through practices of identity formation as a means of generating economic and political support in an increasingly global economy. State interests are a product of identities that emerge from their interaction with other actors. This idea implies that states can be persuaded to view issues differently and so change their behavior over time on the basis of holding different perceptions. In his book on forced migration and global politics, Betts (Betts, 2009) observes that countries that have had to deal with refugees and asylum protection have internalized those norms over time, institutionalizing them within domestic legislation in ways that have then shaped their behavior and interests in relation to refugee and asylum issues. Furthermore, the emergence of norms related to refugee protection, for instance, has begun to change states' perceptions of these polices and led to a gradual acceptance that refugees and asylum seekers have a right to a legal status, thus making states feel obligated to protect these citizens.

Governance has two central features. First, it opens the door to non-state actors—such as IOs, NGOs, and academics—to exert some degree of influence on politics. One example of this is the United Nations High Commissioner for Refugees (UNHCR), which can be viewed as having an independent influence over state behavior through persuasion and moral authority. Governance can shed light on how states have responded and used their autonomy to shape the politics of migration. Migration governance has given NGOs and transnational civil society an important role in contributing to raising awareness about refugees, asylum, and emigrant policies. Governance involves the interaction of a diverse array of traditional and non-traditional actors. Nation-states are important actors, but they are not the only ones. NGOs, corporations, and various networks and "communities" also play an increasingly important role. Second, governance includes actors looking to self-organize, interact, and engage with a certain policy.

Enabling engagement with a policy refers to the design of specific governance arrangements. In her paper, Suhari, (2016) defines governance as coexisting forms of the collective regulation of social issues, from institutionalized civic self-regulation to various forms of interaction between state and private actors, also taking into account the sovereign actions of state actors. The author analyzes the promotion of civil society initiatives in the context of the development of wind energy as an important design element of governance practices in the countries she examines. In her study, although wind farms are largely operated by private, cooperative, and agricultural actors, new forms of organization and actors within the energy sector have emerged and become established, such as energy cooperatives and municipalities. According to Anita Engels, the climate governance regime has changed the architecture of the climate agreement from top down to bottom up, with a proliferation of actors, forms, and levels of governance (Engels, 2016, 2018). What is observed with energy can be applied to the development of migration practices. For emigrant policies, the state is perceived by civil society as being deficient. However, as part of this new architecture of governance, states, IOs, and NGOs are increasingly directing their efforts towards the cooperative management of transnational flows and networks in the hope of promoting development for all. Gamlen & Marsh (2011) argue "that unlike other global flows, migration lacks a dedicated multilateral institutional framework, but this is not to say that it lacks global governance *per se*" (Gamlen & Marsh, 2011, p. xiv). Rather, as Betts (Betts, 2011) puts it, "migration is governed by a fragmented tapestry of overlapping, parallel and nested institutions at the global level." Some issues related to migration offer more fertile ground for international cooperation than others. For instance, while state and other actors may prefer to tackle security issues alone, they might be prone to collaborate if the policy is linked to development.

In their anthology *Migration and Global Governance*, Gamlen and Marsh (2011) suggest three related but distinct "modes" of governing migration: national, international, and transnational. The national mode operates through boundaries maintained by borders and citizenship regimes. As seen above, the failure of this model has to do with the need for more migration-related cooperation among nation-states, and it is here that the second, international, mode comes in. The international mode of governing migration calls for more formal agreements at the bilateral, regional, and multilateral levels. However, because the creation of formal institutions and binding norms tends to go very slowly in some regions of the world, it is not as effective everywhere. Moreover, states are generally cautious about losing sovereignty over migration. There is, however, a middle way proposed by some scholars (Levitt & de la Dehesa, 2003; Margheritis, 2007), namely, the transnational alternative. Here, not only is the governance of circular migration, remittances, and diaspora engagement promoted, but other categories of emigrant policies are governed as well. Gamlen & Marsh (2011) define the transnational mode of governance as:

> A policy programme informed by neoliberal reassessments of migration and development thinking, and that the rise of this programme can be explained as a process of compromise between two fundamentally different views of migration: one which sees migration policy as the sole preserve of sovereign nation-states (the 'national' mode), and another which sees migration as a cross-border issue that must be addressed through international cooperation (the 'international' mode). In between these two fundamentalist positions, both of which centre on the territorially sealed nation-state, we chart the emergence of a 'transnational' mode of migration governance (Gamlen & Marsh, 2011, p. xiii).

This analysis employs a combination of the transnational mode and regional governance as a middle way to frame the compromise arising from the tensions between the national and international modes of migration governance. This interdependence challenges the capacity of states to autonomously contain and govern such flows, thus emphasizing the importance of global scale governance.

Within the international mode of governing migration are three subcategories: bilateral, regional, and multilateral governance. For this study, regional governance is most helpful to explain the regional efforts that have been made towards governing migration because, for instance, certain policies like labor migration occur within a region. Regional governance helps explain how agreements are more easily made within a small number of geographically or culturally connected neighboring states. However, regional cooperation may not actually result in more open or effective emigrant policies. Regional consultative processes on migration are initially attractive to states because they do not pose a challenge to sovereignty, as they operate on a voluntary, non-binding, and confidential basis with low administrative costs. Nevertheless, these processes help diffuse shared policy tools, which then transform state practices and produce a common emigrant policy agenda in some regions (Gamlen & Marsh, 2011). Thus, regional agreements can become regional practices over time.

Regional governance is a broad concept that reveals interaction patterns between different regional organizations. Since regions usually feature more than one organization working towards a policy goal, some of these institutions will often overlap regarding their mandates. According to Detlef Nolte, this can lead to either conflict or cooperation. Based on (Biermann et al., 2010), Nolte has developed an analytical scheme and taxonomy to differentiate between various types of regional governance: synergistic, cooperative, conflictive, and segmented (Nolte, 2016, p. 1). The concept is useful for the study of state-led transnationalism since it explains how public and private institutions are valid and active in each area of world politics, where migration is a very important subject. In Nolte's taxonomy, synergistic governance refers to a cooperative situation, where all the governments support the same organizations, including a central regional organization and project. While some smaller actors might be outside of the central organization, they still cooperate with it. In cooperative regional governance, core norms are supported and not contested, thus members support the central organization and may even divide tasks. Conflictive regional governance, on the other hand, is characterized by a constellation of actors, where the central organization can be challenged and contested, because the major state actors involved support different regional organizations and promote different projects. Finally, segmented regional governance refers to a situation in which major state actors support different regional organizations. This concept is particularly applicable when actors are fragmented. (Nolte, 2016, p. 10).

In sum, together with other actors such as civil society, international organizations, and religious and political institutions, states can potentially play an important role in creating and reinforcing lasting transnational engagements. How, though, are these engagements defined? I argue that they can be observed through the concept of state-led transnationalism, which explains how much of the emigrant policy process is led by the state and how the state collaborates with the other actors involved in the governance of migration. To that end, this study takes into account, on the one hand, the emigrant policy mechanisms that sending states adopt to promote the engagement of its citizens abroad, and on the other, state involvement in each emigrant policy.

3.4 Measuring the Dependent Variable: State-led Transnationalism

The relationship between transnationalism and migration has generated a fair amount of research on the processes and actors that develop and work at the social level across borders, linking origin and destination countries. Nevertheless, state engagement in those processes has been less explored, particularly when it comes to sending state responses to emigration. In most cases, state involvement is understood as a response to migrants' demands and their increasing capacity to organize and lobby, and is more likely to occur in the cases of mass migrations that can have a significant political impact (e.g., Mexicans in the United States). In such cases, emigrants are encouraged to engage through political campaigns to promote voting for a certain political party or the promotion of remittances and investments. These and other policies make emigrants more visible on the political landscape, not only in the migrants' states of origin, but also on the international stage (Gamlen, 2008). To coordinate and support these policy mechanisms and initiatives, a growing number of sending states have established formal institutions to engage with the emigrant community. Some scholars call these "diaspora institutions," and they can take a variety of forms, ranging from state-funded quasi-governmental organizations to councils, committees, and units within origin state legislatures and executive bodies, to fully-functioning emigrant political departments, some with ministerial-level importance (Gamlen et al., 2019).

To explain these state initiatives and their willingness to engage their emigrant communities, the concept of state-led transnationalism is central to this work because it provides possible explanations for why and how migrant-sending states adapt policies for citizens beyond their territory. SLTN explains how far states are willing to go to make sure that their emigrant community remains engaged, even from a long distance. State-led transnationalism is defined as: "institutionalized national policies and programs that attempt to expand the scope of a national state's political, economic, social, and moral regulation to include emigrants and their descendants outside the national territory" (Goldring, 2002:64). Emigrant policies serve as a good case of how state-led transnationalism is reconfiguring the relations between the state and its territorial boundaries, hence redefining the traditional understanding of sovereignty, citizenship, and membership (Levitt & De la Dehesa, 2003).

This work draws on the analytical framework of diaspora mechanisms from Gamlen (2008) to determine which emigrant policy mechanism certain sending states use to engage their emigrant communities. Moreover, based on the concept of state involvement developed by Margheritis (2011), it defines the extent to which a sending state leads the process of reaching out to its emigrant community.

Figure 1   Measuring the Dependent Variable: State-led Transnationalism

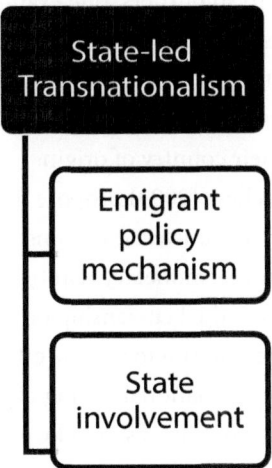

Note. Prepared by the author.

3.4.1 Emigrant Policy Mechanisms

This section examines how a migrant-sending state engages with its emigrant community living abroad through the shifting policies and actions it promotes. These policies, designed to recognize and cultivate loyalties among the emigrant community, as well as to extend rights and extract economic or political resources from the emigrants, are redefining the relationship between the state and its territorial boundaries.

In theory, migration should be a win-win situation. Increasingly, migrant-sending states want to know who is leaving, and to ensure that migrants return with skills that might be useful for the economic and local development of the country. Some scholars have made some important inroads in describing the types of policies a sending state can implement. For instance, Smith (1998) compared what he calls "homeland policies" and "global-nations policies." The former encourages the state to maintain contact with its temporary emigrant workers abroad to ensure and facilitate their return after a working season. The latter policies are devised to help states maintain contact with the emigrant community permanently residing in the receiving state, to ensure a sense of belonging and membership towards the sending state. Goldring (1998), who made a similar comparison, called these "policies of introversion," extending protection and services from the state to sojourners, one example being the Bracero program for guest workers enacted between Mexico and the United States in mid-20th century. Another type of policy is the so-called "policy of extension," which extends protection to already settled citizens, to help them maintain bonds with their country of origin.

Levitt and de la Dehesa (2003) propose five types of policies adopted by the sending states: 1) ministerial or consular reforms; 2) investment policies to attract or channel monetary remittances; 3) the extension of political rights in the form of dual citizenship or nationality, the right to vote from overseas, or the right to run for public office; 4) the extension of state protections and services to nationals living abroad beyond consular services; and 5) the implementation of symbolic policies designed to reinforce the emigrant's sense of enduring membership. Some policies are designed to control and channel remittances, create incentives to invest, support migrant cultural activities and organizations, or enact legislation regarding dual citizenship, political representation, or voting rights (Margheritis, 2011). These policies usually include a political discourse that recognizes emigrants as part of the nation (Gamlen, 2008), aiming to enhance pride in nationhood. Below is a novel categorization of emigrant policies developed for this book that provides an analytical framework to explain sending states and emigrants beyond diasporas.

Policies to Build Relationships with the Emigrant Community: Some policies formally recognize existing emigrant communities, while others build and cultivate the migrant identity and community structures, and include the following aspects:

   a) *Recognizing the Emigrant Community:* States can recognize their emigrant community by, for example, treating them as unitary populations to be discovered and described through aggregate statistics. Commissioning new studies or improving statistical procedures is often the first step that governments take when deliberately seeking to engage the emigrant community.
   b) *Cultivating Loyalties in the Emigrant Community:* States often encourage non-residents to identify with their national communities by publicly taking responsibility for them or creating symbolic holidays.

Policies to Integrate the Emigrant Community: These are the rights that sending states extend to their emigrant community and the obligations or resources they attempt to extract from them. Sending states grant political and social rights to emigrants strategically, so they can make a case for legitimately extracting political and economic benefits in return

   a) *Extending Emigrant Rights:* These can be political, civil, or social rights. Although these policies vary from state to state, the basic right that states extend to emigrants is the right to retain citizenship. In principle, this confers a right of abode in the country of origin, unimpeded travel, the right to do business, the right to pass on citizenship to children, and the right to vote. States also extend rights to assist the arrested, missing, and emigrants in transit and appoint programs to receive the deported.

b) *Extracting Resources by Incorporating Migrants into the National Economy:* These are policies through which states instill or capitalize on feelings of responsibility, loyalty, or obligation in their emigrant communities.

Table 2 State Emigrant Policy Mechanisms to Engage with the Emigrant Community

Mechanisms	Policy Category
Policies to Build Relationships with the Emigrant Community	a) Recognizing the Emigrant Community • Creating institutions, foreign affairs actions, the expansion of consular services • Promoting work opportunities abroad b) Cultivating Loyalties in the Emigrant Community • Creating symbolic days, districts, and the celebration of national holidays • Declaring responsibility for migrants
Policies to Integrate the Emigrant Community	c) Extending Emigrant Rights • Out-of-country voting and citizenship • Legislative representation • Support for Hometown Associations • Regional institutions and agreements • Providing education, health, and labor protection services abroad • Assisting the arrested, missing, and emigrants in transit • Receiving the deported d) Extracting Resources • Facilitating investment services, the productive use of remittances, matching fund programs

Note. Prepared by the author.

3.4.2 State Involvement

In June 2013, the world's first Diaspora Ministerial Conference took place in Geneva, Switzerland. Organized by the International Organization for Migration (IOM), the event drew 548 high-level government participants from 143 states, along with 40 representatives from several international organizations that focus on migration. As noted by Gamlen et al. (2019), diaspora institutions are now found in more than half the member states of the United Nations, and they are increasingly recommended by expert international organizations in the field. Many UN members states now appear to be seeking some level of involvement with their emigrant communities; hence the efforts to formalize the process at the international and national levels.

The reasons behind and forms of state involvement vary (see: Levitt, 2001; Levitt & de la Dehesa, 2003; Østergaard-Nielsen, 2003b). However, there is clear prominence in the literature on states that require economic and political motivations to adopt transnational emigrant policy. To measure state involvement, this study uses indicators from studies of policy analysis (Fischer et al., 2007; Jann & Wegrich, 2003). These indicators show how different key actors influence the setting of a policy's direction, specifically, who is leading the political agenda, what role public institutions play in each policy, and how the influence is exerted (i.e., funding, lobbying, the incorporation of business sectors, etc.). In this respect, the first action shows the actors involved in each policy. The second indicates whether a state works together with other actors (civil society, political parties, international organizations, or non-governmental organizations, whether national or international), while also determining whether state involvement is a) high and leading the political agenda; b) medium; or c) low, a situation in which other actors limit the state's leadership. Finally, the third action looks at the influence exerted, showing the resources that states and other actors must bring to set the policy agenda.

Table 3 Variation of State Involvement

Actions	Indicators
Key actors involved in each policy[17]	a) Public institutions: executive branch, legislative branch b) Civil society organizations: scholars, NGOs, the Church, migration boards, community organizations, business groups, HTAs c) International organizations: International Monetary Fund, IOM, UN, World Bank d) Private sector
Degree of state participation setting the agenda for emigrant policy	a) High role of governments, leading the political agenda b) Medium role of government (civil society organizations and international organizations) c) Low role of government (state is not seen as a source of policy leadership)
State influence is exercised via	a) State creates consensus b) State allocates funding for the policy c) State invites international organizations d) State promotes interinstitutional coordination e) State invites the private sector

Note. Prepared by the author.

State-led transnationalism has two sides, as it is about the interaction between the sending states, on the one hand, and the emigrants on the other. State involvement, then, is one of the two faces of this relationship (Margheritis, 2011). This study analyzes only one side of the relationship: how the political authorities of a state reach out to their emigrant community. The other side of the relationship, the agency of the emigrants, is a broad enough topic for another study.

---

17 Not all these actors are public. This study looks at how states engage with civil society and international organizations in formulating policy.

3.5 Selection and Measurement of Three Explanatory Variables: Conditions for a Higher Degree of State-led Transnationalism in Emigrant Policy

This study asks what types of policies states are adopting and why. Some researchers have made important discoveries towards answering these questions. Scholars argue, for instance, that sending state motivation to engage their emigrant community depends on the characteristics of the emigrant community (Margheritis, 2007). Guarnizo (1998) argues that the structural position of the sending states in the global economy makes it more eager to adopt emigrant policies. Itzigsohn (2001), in turn, claims that the important variables for a sending state to engage with its emigrant community are the geopolitical position of the peripheral sending states, their degree of democratization, or the racial barriers migrants encounter in the receiving states. The cases analyzed in this study do not fit neatly into existing categorizations. Thus, this research tests three explanatory factors and identifies differences among the sending states examined. These factors are summarized in the following table and explained below.

Table 4 Conditions for a Higher Degree of State-led Transnationalism in Emigrant Policy

Perspectives, Theories, and Assumptions	Variable Name	Indicators	Data Sources
Transnational Migration; Economic Development; Institutionalism	Size and potential impact of emigrant community	a) Emigrant community size b) Emigrant community history c) Degree of organization of emigrant community d) Current remittances from emigrant community e) Out-of-country voting rights of emigrants	a) (IOM, 2019) b) Author's calculation c) (Orozco, 2006) d) (World Bank, 2019) e) Author's calculation based on each country's laws
Institutionalism; Party Systems	Party system competitiveness	a) Fragmentation (effective number of parties at the electoral level) b) Polarization (party ideological distance)	a) (Gallagher, 2019) (Laakso & Taagepera, 1979) b) (Alcántara Sáez, 2008a)
Institutionalism	State's institutional capacity to implement policies	a) Adaptability b) Stability c) Coordination d) Implementation and enforcement e) Efficiency f) Public regardedness	Adapted from Stein, Tommasi, Echebarría, Lora, & Payne (2005)

Note. Prepared by the author.

These three explanatory factors are grounded in broader international relations theories and relevant previous studies. As argued by Gamlen et al. (2019), international relations research on the emergence of diaspora institutions is still in the early stages of inquiry, and the topic can be best explained using an eclectic approach, combining perspectives grounded in rationalism and institutional state theories.

3.5.1 The Size and Potential Impact of the Emigrant Community

H1: If the importance of the size and potential impact of the emigrant community in the origin country is high, sending states will reach out to it because of the possible economic or political benefits it may represent.

Emigrant Community Size: The size of the emigrant population is the percentage of emigrant citizens from the origin country living in destination country. Previous research highlights how small, densely populated island states in the Caribbean have greater incentives to engage their diasporas (Glick Schiller & Fouron, 2001). The need to coordinate emigrant policies through an institution in the receiving state is greater if the emigrant community size is important. A larger emigrant community indicates a larger constituency to be served by a sending state.

Emigrant Community History: The sending state will have a different type of engagement with the emigrant community related to the mode of migration, length of stay, and migrant or refugee status in the receiving country (Østergaard-Nielsen, 2003b). The relation may also vary depending on when the emigrant community started migrating. Emigration has received increasing political attention in the last few decades, especially since the 1990s when the numbers rose and the flow characteristics changed. While in the past emigration was considered a temporary phenomenon largely linked to political instability and persecution, it is now seen as a steady, heterogeneous trend related to the deteriorating political and economic situation of the Global South (Margheritis, 2007; Novick, 2008; Oteiza, 2010).

Degree of Organization of the Emigrant Community: An organized community will make it easier or more difficult for the sending state to reach out to the emigrant community. According to Orozco (2006), although diaspora philanthropic organization is not a new phenomenon, projects and interests in local community development in the countries of origin have spread through the visible activism of Hometown Associations.

Current Remittances from the Emigrant Community: Some studies emphasize the economic motivation behind state involvement (Guarnizo, 1998). Many states have copied Mexico's famous remittance-capture initiatives, such as the 3x1 (*Tres por Uno*) program, where local governments, states, and federal governments match remittances sent from emigrants with public funds to invest in development projects in their communities of origin (Gamlen et al., 2019). State-led transnationalism is more or less likely to emerge when states have a greater ability to extract resources from emigrant income and as origin state dependence on emigrant remittances increases or decreases.

Out-of-Country Voting Rights of Emigrants: State-led transnationalism will be more likely to succeed when emigrants have channels to express their views on policies and politics in their country of origin (Gamlen et al., 2019). One key example in this respect concerns out-of-country voting rights.

3.5.2 Party System Competitiveness

H2: The degree of engagement of political parties is important for creating debates over emigrant policies.

Beside governments, other sending country actors, such as political parties, seek out economic and political support among emigrants (Itzigsohn & Villacrés, 2008; Khagram & Levitt, 2008). In Turkey, for example, parties with dominant religious values frequently send their leaders to Western Europe to rally support (Østergaard-Nielsen, 2003b). These parties have a close relationship with emigrant organizations whose leaders, in several instances, have stood as candidates for the party in Turkish elections (Østergaard-Nielsen, 2001).

This study defines political parties as the functioning framework of political systems and, even though there are no global definitions, the conceptualizations that matter within this framework refer to issues such as representation and interest articulation, legitimacy, and ideology (CAPEL, 1989). In other words, one way to define parties is related to the functions that they fulfill in the political system, such as representation, which makes parties channel certain sector interests. Political representation is a significant concern, both for democracies with a long history and for democracies in consolidation. Representation is the way to ensure that the citizens' preferences are taken into account in the elaboration of laws and public policies, even if they are not living in their country of origin (Algazi, 2009). Political parties have an impact on the form, timing, and effectiveness of policies toward the emigrant community (Levitt & de la Dehesa, 2003). This study takes fragmentation and polarization as key indicators, because the number of parties fighting for the vote of emigrants abroad can have an impact on the degree of state-led transnationalism. Moreover, if there is a clear ideological distance between parties, they may also try to earn the loyalties of the emigrants abroad based on their ideology.

Fragmentation (Effective Number of Parties at the Electoral Level): Party systems have long been classified into types defined by their number and relative size (Coppedge, 1998; Duverger, 1974; Sartori, 1992). This study adopts Laakso and Taagepera's "Effective Number of Parties" approach based on shares of the vote (Laakso & Taagepera, 1979).

Polarization (Party Ideological Distance): This study bases its understanding of the ideological distance of a political party based on where its electors place themselves on a scale from left to right, making it possible to place opposing parties at the extremes (Ajenjo, 2004; García Montero, 2009). When using the term "ideological distance," it is important to gather certain relevant common characteristics that shape the electoral competition and therefore determine the placement of the parties on an ideological spectrum. This study uses the indicators of ideology proposed by the Latin American Elites Project at the University of Salamanca in Spain (Alcántara Sáez, 2008a).

3.5.3 The State's Institutional Capacity to Implement Policies

H3: If a state has strong institutional capacities, it will be more active in the implementation of emigrant policy to engage with its emigrant community. A state with low institutional capacities will delegate its functions to other actors such as civil society or international actors.

Some scholars argue that the two main factors that can lead a sending state to engage with its emigrant community are a) the costs of implementing policies; and b) the state's ability to cover those costs. A comparison of Brazil, Haiti, Mexico, and the Dominican Republic shows that poorer states are likely to converge on low-cost policies like symbolic policies, while states with larger budgets, like Brazil and Mexico, are more likely to extend state services to emigrants (Levitt & de la Dehesa, 2003). This provides a better understanding of how institutional capacities to adopt emigrant policies can block effective responses to emigrant needs. In order to give an operative definition of a state's institutional capacity to implement policies, this study draws on the indicators proposed by Stein, Tommasi, Echebarría, Lora, & Payne (2005):

Adaptability: the extent to which policies can be adjusted when they fail or when circumstances change;

Stability: the extent to which policies created by a state with high capabilities are stable over time;

Coordination: the degree to which policies are consistent with related policies, and result from well-coordinated actions among the actors who participate in their design and implementation;

Implementation and Enforcement: the degree to which the state ensures effective implementation of public policies. To an important degree, the quality of policy implementation and enforcement in a country will depend on the extent to which policymakers in that country have incentives and resources to invest in their policies;

Efficiency: the extent to which policies reflect an allocation of scarce resources that ensures high returns; and

Public Regardedness: the degree to which policies pursue the public interest.

3.6 Concluding Remarks

This chapter set out, first, to discuss how origin states are increasingly engaging with their population abroad, thus redefining the relationship between the state and its territorial boundaries. It did so by relying on an analytical framework that takes elements from international relations, new institutionalism, and policy analysis, which together hold a greater explanatory power. This analytical framework is explained with a discussion of state sovereignty and migration governance.

The chapter also explained how the dependent variable of state-led transnationalism is measured, by operationalizing the emigrant policy mechanisms used by sending states to engage their emigrants and by analyzing state involvement. The chapter also provided an analytical framework to measure the degree of state participation in setting the agenda for each policy, as well as the means of influence at their disposal, like funding, consensus, and interinstitutional coordination. Finally, the third section provides possible explanations for how to achieve a higher degree of state-led transnationalism in emigrant policy, by operationalizing three explanatory variables (the importance of the size and history of the emigrant community, party system competitiveness, and the state's institutional capacity to implement policies).

Chapter 4
Methodology

4.1 Introduction

This chapter explains the research design, a Most Similar Systems Design (MSSD) employed in this work. The investigation presents a comparative case study using three sending states, and how they have both contextual similarities and differences regarding the degree of state-led transnationalism. The chapter sets out to delimit the scope, conditions of space, and time. Finally, the chapter describes how the data was collected, including during in-depth interviews and document analysis.

4.2 Research Design: Case Study Methods

A case study can be defined as an "in-depth study of a single unit (a relatively bounded phenomenon) where the scholar's aim is to elucidate features of a larger class of similar phenomena" (Gerring, 2004, p. 241). This case study belongs to the confirming or infirming sub-theory. Such studies are used to assess or test theories or hypotheses involving a small number of cases. The theories are either strengthened (confirmed) or weakened (infirmed). A case study method includes both a within-case analysis of single cases and comparisons of a small number of cases. "There is a growing consensus that the strongest means of drawing inferences from case studies is the use of a combination of within-case analysis and cross-case comparisons" (George & Bennett, 2005, p. 18). Thus, this research engages in two levels of analysis. First, it makes a within-case comparison by examining the emigrant policy of each of the three selected sending states. Second, at a cross-case level, the study compares the policies and actions of the three case studies and analyzes their actions regarding emigrant policies. This makes it possible to observe the differences between the states. The study uses a Most Similar Systems Design (MSSD) to achieve a systematic comparison of a few countries. An MSSD is designed to control for factors that are similar across the countries in the study, while focusing only on those factors that are different and account for the different outcomes (H. E.; Brady & Collier, 2004). The aim is to find the factors that differentiate the actions of sending states related to emigrant policy.

This research design is based on a small number of cases (small N) with a high number of variables. The empirical findings from the case study provide lessons from the Salvadoran, Guatemalan, and Honduran emigrant policy processes, to augment the existing theory within the subfields of state-led transnationalism and emigrant policy studies. This choice of research design and number of cases will contribute to the analysis of sending states and their reasons for fashioning emigrant policies, and advance general research in Central America, an understudied region in Latin America. In short, the objective is to shed light on the sending state cases that have received the least attention.

4.3 Case Selection: El Salvador, Guatemala, and Honduras; Similiar Features

This work analyzes three sending states in Central America: El Salvador, Guatemala, and Honduras, known as the Northern Triangle of Central America (NTCA). The three countries share a common history, contemporary, social, and economic characteristics that include widespread poverty, illiteracy, inequality, and a stunted health system. Migration has changed many aspects of these societies. For instance, there have been social changes in the human capital of communities, security tensions at the borders, and economic changes due to the value of remittances to both the countries' Gross Domestic Product and to family incomes.

4.3.1 Convergences

Historically, there have been three types of migration within the NTCA region: internal, regional, and international. During the 1970s and 80s, wars in El Salvador and Guatemala and varying degrees of repression culminated in the displacement of approximately 1.5 million people to Mexico and the United States. Unlike El Salvador and Guatemala, Honduras did not suffer the high costs of internal military conflict. However, the country received more than 30,000 refugees fleeing the conflict in El Salvador. Honduras also served as a U.S. military base to fight against the Contra insurgency fighting the Sandinista government in Nicaragua, and therefore shared some post-war characteristics.

Despite the Peace Accords signed in the region during the 1990s, which brought many people back from their asylum in Mexico, undocumented migration continues to be one of the main survival strategies for the population in the region. Recently, migration has been driven by economic rather than political factors and is largely focused on the United States. The causes for this are related to, among other things, a crisis in the agricultural sector, declining coffee prices, an increase in unemployment rates, some devastating natural disasters, and high levels of post-war violence.

4.3.2 Divergences

Regarding levels of state-led transnationalism in emigrant policy, El Salvador has made more advances in its attempts to establish closer ties with its diasporas than the other two countries. It is, for instance, the sending state with the most signed agreements on labor migration with Canada, Spain, and the United States. It has also created institutions and policies to provide state services and protect its emigrant community. Guatemala, on the other hand, was the first of the three countries to create a public institution to formulate and implement emigrant policies; however, migration has never been part of the government's political project. Compared to the other two countries, Honduras has fewer institutions, although the available statistical data related to its emigrant population indicates more legislative activity. Many policies are nonetheless making little difference in the lives of the country's emigrants.

4.4 Scope

Space: This study compares the three NTCA countries, where migration is currently one of the most important issues on the political agenda. This study does look at some of the migration policies in a transit country (Mexico) and two receiving countries (Canada and the United States) in various chapters, because of the many regional agreements made. However, the focus of this publication is on sending states and their emigrant policies to manage migration involving North America. Although Mexico is traditionally a sending state to the United States, it does not share the same social, political, and economic conditions of the Central American countries. In other Central American countries like Nicaragua, migration occurs mostly to Costa Rica, while Panamanians traditionally migrate to Colombia or Costa Rica. On the other hand, far from being a sending state, Costa Rica is usually a receiving one. In the case of Belize, although some migration takes place to the United States from that country, the context is also very different when compared to the NTCA countries, given the fact that Belize shows more postcolonial, contextual, and systemic similarities with the Caribbean countries; therefore it was not selected for this analysis.

Time: This is a comparative policy study that analyzes over 20 years of emigrant policies in Central America, from 1998 to 2021. The focus of the research is on contemporary policies in the postwar period beginning in 1998, after Hurricane Mitch devastated the region and brought about a new wave of migration from the NTCA to the United States. The study period ends in 2021, with presidential elections in El Salvador and Guatemala, which coincided with the final days of the Trump administration and the transition to the new government of President Biden in the United States, the main migrant receiving state for the NTCA sending states.

During the wars, migration in the region had a different meaning and policies had other aims, oriented more towards the reintegration of refugees. However, post-war policies in the region are strongly related to changes in civil society and political parties, as well as the regional security context created by the hardening of American immigration policies after the terrorist attacks of September 11, 2001. With the rise in remittance flows, it is no surprise that governments started to recognize the importance of their migrant population abroad and its political and economic implications, and that states started to modify their transnational emigrant policies in the early 2000s.

4.5 Data Collection and Management

This work builds upon three detailed case studies that trace the sources of emigrant policies. I conducted 70 in-depth interviews in El Salvador, Guatemala, Honduras, and Mexico between 2011 and 2021 with former and current high-ranking public officials in various areas of the public administration; scholars in the field; leaders of migrant organizations; congressional representatives; and members of civil society organizations. I also drew on data from my own database of 400 official reports, laws, bills, and academic and civil society publications collected from the NTCA countries. Both the interviews and collected data were analyzed using ATLAS.ti, a qualitative research software program, to code the database and analyze the interview transcripts and field notes.

4.5.1 In-depth Interviews

I conducted 70 in-depth interviews with:

a) public officials from state institutions such as the Directorate-General of Migration, Foreign Affairs Ministries, Supreme Courts and Consulates;
b) civil society organizations and individuals, migration scholars, human rights organizations, migrant association representatives, national forums, and journalists;
c) political parties, specifically with representatives from Grand Alliance for National Unity (GANA), the National Unity of Hope (UNE) and the Patriotic Party (PP) in Guatemala. In El Salvador with party members of Farabundo Martí National Liberation Front (FMLN) and Nationalist Republican Alliance (ARENA). In Honduras I interviewed members of the Honduran National Party (PNH) and the Honduran Liberal Party (PLH); and
d) international organizations such as the International Organization for Migration (IOM), the United Nations Development Program (UNDP), NGOs, and international political foundations.

Generally speaking, the civil society organizations stressed how much more the governments could do for the emigrant community in all three countries. In the case of public officials, I observed that they notably emphasized the importance of some aspects or events over others (possibly because some public officials seek acknowledgment when a policy is approved or implemented). Therefore, the evidence obtained from the interviews was carefully cross-checked with other written sources as well as with other actors.

4.5.2 Document Analysis

I examined a number of source documents, including the following:

- a) law reform projects and political party initiatives;
- b) regional policy documents and bilateral and multilateral treaties;
- c) the US Homeland Security database;
- d) intergovernmental organization policy recommendation documents;
- e) civil society policy proposals and press releases;
- f) bills on the political agenda; and
- g) legislative and executive decrees.

I also used additional documents such as press releases because I discovered in the field that many national actors prefer to go public about their policy preferences when they feel they are not being listened to by the governments. Therefore, policy preferences are more likely to be found in statements published in newspapers and other media outlets or informational printouts to raise emigrant awareness about the dangers along the route. Likewise, think tanks and international actors tend to channel their demands through policy proposals and workshops, where they invite public officials and civil society organizations and distribute internal papers, magazines, and memoirs to the participants.

4.6 Concluding Remarks

This chapter has explained and justified the choice of research design and the use of a comparative case study, discussing the adoption of the Most Similar Systems Design to compare the three case studies of El Salvador,

Guatemala, and Honduras, which are similar in their migration contexts, but have different outcomes in their overall degrees of state-led transnationalism. Finally, the chapter describes how the data was collected and where the sources and information were obtained, with particular emphasis on the 70 in-depth interviews conducted and the 400 documents that now make up the novel, author-created database that support Parts II and III of this study.

Part II

Describing and Comparing State-Led Transnationalism in Central America

Chapter 5
Policies to Build Relationships with the Emigrant Community

5.1 Introduction

So-called sending states are emigration states that can influence ties with their citizens, even beyond the reach of their coercive territorial powers. They do this through mechanisms that exist outside their borders and operate on a transnational scale in accordance with external policies (Gamlen, 2019; Østergaard-Nielsen, 2016). The three Central American sending states examined in this chapter have gone from having no policy at all to playing a major role in migration policy. Together with political, social, religious, and international organizations (IOs), sending states create and reinforce transnational ties.

This chapter analyzes the two ways in which states build a relationship with their emigrants: 1) policies aimed at recognizing the emigrant community through institutional procedures; and 2) policies whose purpose is to cultivate loyalties in the emigrant community through symbolic measures. For each country, the chapter describes the emigrant policy mechanisms implemented by the sending states and how different actors participate in each policy (if the states are leading the actions, this is defined in the study as "state involvement").

5.2 Recognizing the Emigrant Community: Institutional Policies

The aim of some emigrant policies is to recognize or reify existing emigrant communities. Gamlen (2008) describes the recognition of the emigrant community as follows:

> They [states] can treat diasporas as unitary populations to be discovered and described through aggregate statistics. Commissioning new studies or improving statistical procedures is often the first step taken by governments deliberately seeking to 'engage diaspora' [...] Formally recognizing diaspora communities involves

> dedicated bureaucratic structures. The consular service provides one set of such structures: for example, Mexico's network of around 50 consulates is crucial to its relations with Mexicans in the USA. Diaspora programs or offices are also common—typically within labor secretariats, foreign services, and other agencies with an interest in emigration. These programs often coalesce into permanent units or dedicated ministries. (p. 844)

One notable example is the Institute of Mexicans Abroad. In this respect, Délano (2009) has described how the Mexican state moved from limited to active engagement. For a state to recognize a segment of its population means creating the conditions for that part of the population to feel a sense of belonging and institutions that assert and support this recognition are needed to that end. Consequently, to recognize the emigrant community, states have created new institutions, expanded their consular network and services abroad, implemented actions through their Ministry of Foreign Affairs, and sought to promote labor opportunities abroad.

5.2.1 Creating Institutions, Foreign Affairs Actions, the Expansion of Consular Services

Many states have implemented bureaucratic reforms in response to the heightened importance of emigrants to policymakers. Consulates in the Northern Triangle of Central America (NTCA) countries (El Salvador, Guatemala, Honduras) have taken on an increasingly important role in their emigrant communities, either in transit or working temporarily in Mexico or the United States, becoming a sort of "mini-embassy." Whereas twenty years ago the work done by consulates was limited to the standard issuing of documentation, today each consulate has a section in charge of providing protection and legal advice to emigrants. In addition to overseeing political rights, several states are engaged in delivering services to emigrant communities that go beyond consular services. These include the creation of institutions or directorates within some ministries help meet the needs of emigrants abroad.

El Salvador

El Salvador's government has done the most to provide a number of institutions and services abroad. For this state, the incorporation of the emigrant community into local politics started with the creation of a unit in the Ministry of Foreign Affairs under the Farabundo Martí National Liberation Front (FMLN) administration (Ríos, 2011). The Vice-Ministry for Salvadorans Abroad created in 2004 oversees emigrant policies and is organized into three Directorates-General. The tasks of the first, the Directorate-General of External Services, include diplomatic and consular matters as well as legal aid. The second, the Directorate-General of Migration and Development, is responsible for coordinating activities for Salvadorans abroad and for the exchange of innovation, trade, and business activities. Finally, the Directorate-General of Human Rights is in charge of guaranteeing the rights of the emigrant community, ensuring that international treaties comply with human rights stipulations. "The directorate is also in charge of monitoring missing migrants in coordination with international organizations" (L. Aguirre, personal communication, February 12, 2012).

The Vice-Ministry for Salvadorans Abroad organizes activities to strengthen cultural ties between emigrants and their home countries (MRE El Salvador, 2018). In an interview with the Director of the Ministry of Foreign Affairs Directorate-General of Migration Policy in El Salvador, he stated:

> We created the Vice-Ministry for Salvadorans abroad in 2004; before that, it was not such an important topic for the state. What made the state wake up was the fact that remittances were increasing in relation to the country's Gross Domestic Product. Before the creation of the Vice-Ministry, we had an unwritten policy. (D. Rivas, personal communication, February 20, 2012)

In 2011, the government created the Salvadoran National Council for the Protection and Development of the Emigrant and their Family (CONMIGRANTES), created by the Special Law for the Protection and Development of Salvadoran Migrant Persons and their Families. This group is an interinstitutional body designed to guarantee the protection of emigrants and to advance development policies. Its main objective is to serve as a link between the state and Salvadoran emigrants ("Ley Especial ..., Sec. 6").

The institution contains both government and a number of non-governmental delegates: three delegates from emigrant associations, one from the Salvadoran non-governmental organizations (NGOs) that handle migration concerns, one from a private university, one from the public University of El Salvador, and one from a small and mid-size enterprise association (Reglamento de Ejecución de La Ley Especial Para La Protección y Desarrollo de La Persona Migrante Salvadoreña y Su Familia, 2015). Importantly, the statute appoints the Vice-Minister of Foreign Affairs for Salvadorans abroad to lead the CONMIGRANTES plenary. The law also states that it is the duty of the Ministry of Foreign Affairs, through the Vice-Ministry of Salvadorans Abroad, to guarantee that the selection procedure of emigrant representatives for CONMIGRANTES is transparent and balanced regarding equal geographic, regional, and sexual orientation (Ley Especial Para La Protección y Desarrollo de La Persona Migrante Salvadoreña y Su Familia, 2011). Karina Sosa, former President of the Congress Committee on Foreign Affairs from El Salvador, and in charge of policy for emigrants abroad, summed up the goals of the law:

> The Special Law for the Protection and Development of Salvadoran Migrant Persons and their Families is a law that has two main aims: first to protect all migrants' human rights, and second to provide development opportunities for them and their families so that they do not have to leave their country if they do not want to. (K. Sosa, personal communication, February 15, 2012)

Another institution—though not created by the Salvadoran state—is the Salvadoran Migrant Institute (INSAMI), an NGO in which one state delegate also participates. INSAMI's aim is to ensure that the rights and obligations of the emigrant community are respected (Ríos, 2011). According to César Ríos, INSAMI's director, this institution has been critical of the role of the state due to its lack of commitment to endorsing migration policies to develop the country and its weak interinstitutional coordination skills (C. Ríos, personal communication, February 23, 2018). Finally, El Salvador's diplomatic network comprises 18 consulates in the United States and four in Mexico (MRE El Salvador, 2019a), which provide legal aid through mobile consulates and offer special weekend working hours (MRE El Salvador, 2019b).

Guatemala

After an internal restructuring in 2003, the Ministry of Foreign Affairs created the Directorate-General of Consular and Migration Matters, followed two years later by the Vice-Ministry for the Assistance of the Guatemalan Migrant, a body charged with creating an emigrant strategy. In 2006, the Migrant Services Center was established (Maldonado Ríos et al., 2010) to provide services to Guatemalan emigrants and their families. Part of the Ministry of Foreign Affairs, this facility provides free Internet, a conference room with computers, legal counselors, an employment office, a health office, and an investment counseling desk. Additionally, consultations can be made on Guatemalans who are missing, deceased, or detained abroad (Altolaguirre Larraondo, 2006). The Migrant Services Center also serves as the headquarters of the National Council for Guatemalans Abroad (CONAMIGUA), a cabinet-level office created in 2007 (Ley Del Consejo Nacional de Atención al Migrante de Guatemala, 2007). An autonomous institution, part of the Ministry of Foreign Affairs, the Council is the government's voice on emigration-related matters. In terms of creating institutions, CONAMIGUA is one of the Guatemalan state's great achievements. This institution formulates emigrant policies and coordinates appeals from civil society, while also representing emigrants in their home countries (Maldonado Ríos et al., 2010). However, it is only a consultative body and must answer to the Ministry of Foreign Affairs. When the CONAMIGUA advisory council gives recommendations, there is no right to response as established by law, as they are invited as observers (Reglamento Interno Del Consejo Asesor de CONAMIGUA, 2009). According to the Vice-Chair of the Migrant Rights Commission of the City and County of San Francisco, an elected member of CONAMIGUA:

> In Guatemala this institution was created in part as a response to demands made by Guatemalans abroad. While its formal goals are fostering links and mutual understanding between the government and Guatemalans abroad, in practice, CONAMIGUA has become the agency in charge of state involvement with Hometown Associations and with implementing state services offered to emigrants. It has also become a tool of formal participation channels where Guatemalans abroad can be elected in the state where they are living in the United States and represent their community there on the board of CONAMIGUA. (F. Fuentes, personal communication, May 24, 2012)

Guatemala had intended to have a policy to protect and assist Guatemalans abroad since 2007 (MRE Guatemala, 2007). However, almost 10 years had to go by before the Migration Code was finally passed in 2016. This regulation repealed Decree 95–98, enacting the Migration Law. The code is divided into three books, the first of which establishes the right to migrate and the rights of migrants, the rights of migrant workers and their families, the rights of trafficked persons, and rights to the recognition of refugee status asylum and humanitarian assistance, among others. One of the major achievements of the Migration Code was the creation of the Guatemalan Institute of Migration, which replaced the Directorate-General of Migration (Código de Migración, 2016). The new institution is no longer under the Ministry of the Interior, which makes it less punitive towards migrants. The main criticism of the Code is that, even though it is a major improvement for the country, in its intention to be very specific, it also ends up being quite bureaucratic. In addition to the institution itself, the Guatemalan Institute of Migration has two boards: the Guatemalan Immigration System and the National Immigration Authority. Both boards have needed to create their own regulation codes, some of which require many high-ranking public officials to meet every three months, in addition to other complex provisions that may be hard to comply with in the near future. For example, one of the new regulations states that public officials working in institutions created by or related to the code must have a "career in Migration Studies," when Human Rights and Social Sciences majors are sufficient for the work required. Although the intention is to professionalize public officials, the result is a most extensive bureaucracy, for example in order to create a school or university major for these public officials. However, it is a complete piece of legislation that required three years of effort on the part of several public officials and members of civil society.

Regarding the consular network, given the increasing size of the undocumented emigrant population in Mexico and the United States, the Guatemalan Ministry of Foreign Affairs took steps to be able to provide services to emigrants abroad. However, due to insufficient capacity to provide services to such a large population, they decided to, first, share offices to reduce the costs of renting space, creating an initiative called A Single Consulate that started in Mexico with El Salvador and Guatemala through bilateral agreements. The ministry then launched the Mobile Consulates, designed to bring consular services to the emigrant community abroad by periodically offering office hours at convenient venues where there are no consulates in the United States. With these actions, it has been able to improve some of the functions and extend the reach of the consular network to meet the increasing demand. As of 2019, Guatemala had 17 consulates in the United States and 10 consulates in Mexico (MRE Guatemala, 2020). Since 2006, the Guatemalan consulates have issued the Consular Identification Card. While this document does not replace passports, it allows Guatemalans access to certain services in the United States, such as opening a bank account and obtaining a driver's license, depending on the state where they reside (Creación de La Tarjeta de Identificación Consular, 2005).

Figure 2 Consular ID card Issued by a Guatemalan Consulate to an Undocumented Emigrant

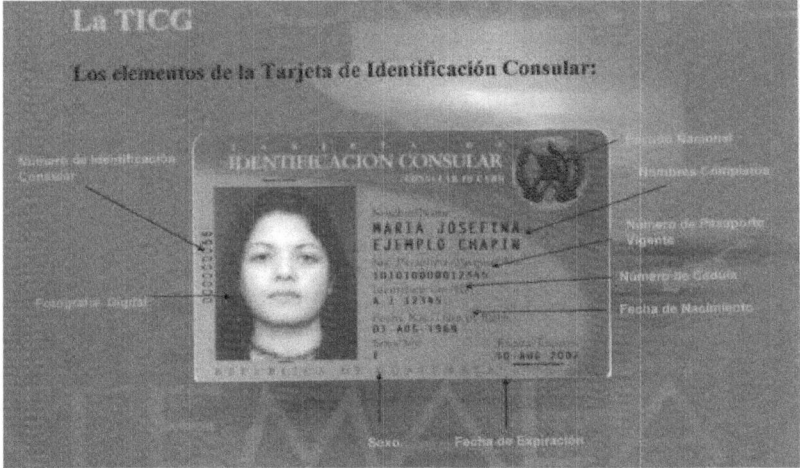

Note. Altolaguirre Larraondo, M. (2006, November). El Ministerio de Relaciones Exteriores y la Atención al Migrante. Guatemalan Foreign Affairs Vice Ministry Meetings with Emigrant Community in the US, United States. Retrieved June 9, 2022, from <http://www.crmsv.org/sites/default/files/Presentaciones/guatemala_-_encuentro_con_el_migrante_nov._2006.ppt >.

Guatemalan consulates offer legal advice through two programs. The first is the Global Justice program, which puts Guatemalans in the United States in touch with lawyers from different branches of the law through the general consulates. The second is the online Guatemalan Migrant Assistance Platform, which allows migrants to submit legal questions to the consulate in different formats, e.g. written, videoconference, or chat. The idea behind the program is to help Guatemalans know their rights and prevent abuse by unscrupulous lawyers (Rodas Melgar, 2010).

Honduras

In 2013, the Honduran Congress passed the Law for the Protection of Honduran Migrants and their Families, which set a trend in the Central American region in that it provided guidelines for comprehensive policy-making in matters of emigrant policy. Nevertheless, it did not enter into force until 2014, and various secondary regulatory laws required for its full implementation have not yet been passed (Pedroza et al., 2016). Its implementation would entail important changes and consequences for the institutional framework of Honduras. The Law for the Protection of Honduran Migrants and their Families establishes a significant number of institutions and consultative bodies. Its main body in charge of emigrant policy is the Directorate-General for the Protection of Honduran Migrants, created within the hierarchy of the Ministry of Foreign Affairs and divided in two offices, one for protection and one for return (Ley de Protección de Los Hondureños Migrantes y Sus Familiares, 2013).

To protect the emigrant community, the law created the National Council for the Protection of Honduran Migrants (CONAPROHM), a consultative body for emigrant issues under the Ministry of Foreign Affairs. CONAPROHM engages in interinstitutional coordination with that Ministry and over a dozen other public administrative bodies (ministries, institutes, directorates, and the Directorate for the Protection of Honduran Migrants). To execute all the policies created by the Law for the Protection of Honduran Migrants and their Families, the law also created the Office for the Protection of Honduran Migrants (OPROMH), also within the Ministry of Foreign Affairs. This Office is an interinstitutional committee for the administration of emigrant policies, with the participation of five ministries. Although it is unclear how OPROMH differs from CONAPROHM, they have both a role in the protection of emigrants (Pedroza et al., 2016).

Regarding the return of emigrants, the Law for the Protection of Honduran Migrants and their Families created the Office for the Assistance of Returning Migrants, while the Honduran state also created the National Institute for Migration in 2014 to address the migration of unaccompanied minors. Nonetheless, this body is also responsible for regulating other migration issues, and is mostly concerned with immigration and transit migration (Ley de Protección de Los Hondureños Migrantes y Sus Familiares, 2013). In order to improve the statistics on migration, the Honduran state created a consular migration observatory under the coordination of the Sub-secretary of Consular and Migration Matters. The Observatory, which opened in 2015, provides statistical data and monitors the consular and migration system in the country (SRE Honduras, 2017). Honduras has 10 consulates in the United States (SRE Honduras, 2011) and three in Mexico (INM, 2016), a number very low in contrast to El Salvador and Guatemala, particularly considering the large number of Honduran who set out for the United States each day.

5.2.2 Promoting Work Opportunities Abroad

El Salvador

El Salvador has taken a leading role in promoting safe migration to Canada, Brazil, and Italy through its Seasonal Agricultural Worker Program (SAWP). In 2006, a Cooperation Agreement was signed between the Ministry of Foreign Affairs, the Ministry of Labor, and the International Organization for Migration (IOM) in El Salvador to join forces to promote and administer the SAWP for Salvadorans. In 2012, the Salvadoran authorities signed an agreement with the Canadian Maple Leaf Foods company to create positions for Salvadorans seeking to go to Canada. Throughout the process, the authorities at the Ministry of Labor looked closely at the recruitment and selection process (Periódico Equilibrium,

2012). Negotiations extended to working programs beyond agricultural activities; in 2018, for instance, the bilateral Temporary Foreign Worker Programs between Canada and El Salvador offered more jobs in the restaurant industry in British Columbia (Miranda, 2018). The Salvadoran authorities also started a pilot SAWP (with H-2A visas) in 2019 with the United States, in which Salvadorans are guaranteed a weekly salary of $527, plane tickets, food, and lodging and allowed to remain in the United States for four months (Aleman, 2019).

Guatemala

In 2015, 4,275 Guatemalans were hired to work in Quebec, representing 45% of all temporary agricultural foreign workers in that province (Gesualdi-Fecteau et al., 2017). However, there is no bilateral agreement between the Canadian and the Guatemalan governments with regard to seasonal workers. A large number of Guatemalans also temporarily migrate to farms located on the southern border of Mexico, primarily to work in the agricultural sector. In 1997, the governments of Mexico and Guatemala established a temporary work visa agreement following the Fifth Mexico-Guatemala Binational Meeting on Migration Issues held the year before, where it was agreed to establish a documentation program for the legal and migratory security of Guatemalan agricultural workers. This program allowed temporary Guatemalan agricultural workers on farms in southern Mexico the option of being accompanied by their families if they filled out a migration form for agricultural visitors (Bustamante, 2008). Finally, in 2019, the governments of Guatemala and the United States signed the first agreement for a temporary agricultural workers program, designed to provide thousands of employment opportunities to temporary migrant Guatemalan workers through H-2A (temporary agricultural workers) visas (Ministerio de Trabajo y Previsión Social de Guatemala, 2019).

Honduras

Honduras is the state that has made the greatest attempt to reach cooperation agreements in order to send its nationals to work abroad, having done so with Canada, the United States, and Spain. The IOM has played a large role in many of these agreements. In 2007, the Ministries of Labor, Foreign Affairs, and the Interior in Canada and Honduras signed an operational and technical cooperation agreement for a temporary agricultural workers program with the IOM (Gillivray Mac, 2009). One year later, an Addendum to that agreement was signed between the Honduran state and the IOM.

Figure 3   A Canadian Job Opportunity Announcement, Published by the Ministry of Labor in the Main Newspapers in Honduras

Note. Gillivray Mac, J. (2009, 23–24). Programa de Migración Laboral Temporal: El Salvador, Honduras, OIM. Taller sobre los Programas de los Trabajadores Migratorios Temporales, San Salvador, El Salvador. Retrieved June 9, 2022, from <http://www.crmsv.org/es/eventos/taller-sobre-los-programas-de-los-trabajadores-migratorios-temporales>.

Since 2008, when the Directorate-General of Migration, the Ministry of Labor in Spain, and the Honduran government signed a bilateral agreement for temporary foreign workers in Spain, the Latin American country has been sending highly qualified migrants upon request for specific development projects in the European country. The Honduran state is so eager to send its nationals to work in Spain that in 2019, the president himself flew to the country to explore the possibility of creating a seasonal agricultural worker program, and is actively trying to position Honduras as a provider of skilled labor in the agricultural sector (EFE, 2019b). With regard to the United States, in 2019, a new temporary agricultural workers program was signed for Hondurans to work in that country (EFE, 2019a). At least three attempts have been made to establish this initiative. In 2008, for instance, the Honduran Ministry of Labor, in alliance with the National Association of Industrialists, the United States Embassy, the Honduran Advisory Center for Human Resources Development, the Zamorano Panamerican Agricultural School, and the Covelo Microfinance Foundation (now a bank) jointly promoted a program to send Honduran farmers to California (R. Puerta, personal communication, February 27, 2012).

5.3 Cultivating Loyalties in the Emigrant Community: Symbolic Policies

Many states have implemented a number of symbolic measures to reinforce emigrants' sense of enduring membership in their culture and to generate loyalty from the emigrant community towards their country of origin. These relatively low-cost policies are, in many ways, an extension of traditional consular actions and efforts to promote national culture abroad. Such policies range from cultural festivals to sporting events in communities in the destination country (Levitt and de la Dehesa 2003). Some policies include the creation of special days, weeks, or an extra symbolic district for those living abroad, as well as communicating the concept of responsibility towards a country's emigrants abroad.

5.3.1 Days, Districts, and the Celebration of National Holidays

El Salvador

In 2005, the Salvadoran state declared that November 26 would be The Day of the Salvadoran Abroad in recognition of the efforts of Salvadoran migrants and their contributions to the country (Declárase El 26 de Noviembre de Cada Año Como Día Nacional de Los Salvadoreños En El Exterior, 2005). Additionally, YouTube has a video from 2010 where the Ministry of Foreign Affairs greets and recognizes the emigrant communities abroad (MRE El Salvador, 2010). In several annual reports, the Vice-Ministry for Salvadorans abroad has announced its policy of *arraigo* (a sense of "rootedness") to cultivate attachment. Mechanisms have also been put in place to link the emigrant community abroad with their communities of origin, a clear government priority. The intention is to encourage the social, cultural, and economic participation of emigrants (MRE El Salvador, 2015a).

Guatemala

As part of the country's outreach to its emigrants, the Guatemalan Congress's Committee on Migration created an award for emigrants in the United States. They can be nominated by any fellow countryman for their outstanding work in a cultural, social, political, professional, or athletic activity. In that regard, the former president of the Committee on Migration published a statement on his Facebook page: "For many years, our compatriots residing abroad have excelled in different areas. Because of this, the Committee on Migration wants to recognize this effort, and thus calls for nominees to be awarded the recognition of 'Outstanding Migrant of the Year'" (Briere, 2016). The recognition of work done in the Guatemalan community overseas received broad coverage in community organizations and the social media read by the public in the both countries (Curruchich, 2016). The award ceremony in California was attended by the Minister of Foreign Affairs, the president of the Committee on Migration, the executive director of CONAMIGUA, and a representative of the IOM.

On his visit to the emigrant community in Trenton, New Jersey in 2015, the mayor of Salcajá, a town in southwest Guatemala, said: "I am very happy to have the opportunity to meet Guatemalan *Salcajenses*, honest people who come to make a contribution to Trenton with their work." He also proposed that the mayor of Trenton officially declare Salcajá and Trenton "sister cities," with the support of the Guatemalan general consulate in New York. The mayor of Trenton accepted the initiative, declaring Salcajá and Trenton sister cities to seal their friendship (MRE Guatemala, 2015b).

In 2015, former Minister of Foreign Affairs Carlos Raúl Morales met with Guatemalan children studying in a secondary school in Queens, New York, where the consulate general of Guatemala, with the support of the school authorities and the Center for Education Innovation, initiated the "Boost Project" designed to provide students with academic and cultural experiences, including visits to museums, theaters, the United Nations, universities, and the consulate itself. During the last meeting, the consulate selected the winning students and gave them the honorific titles of consul and vice-consul for a day. At this event, Vice-Minister of Foreign Affairs Ana María Diéguez addressed the young people: "seize the opportunities that the society you live in now is bringing you, but never forget your country of origin, Guatemala" (MRE Guatemala, 2015a). With these actions, the government aims to generate loyalty towards the home country among these children's parents and grandparents in addition to the children themselves.

The Guatemalan consulate has also sponsored cultural events through the "Guatemalan Fair" (although this fair is fully described in the section on investment policies, this event also has a symbolic component). Every day, different Guatemalan artists with a cultural agenda perform on the fair's stage. It is not uncommon for public officials to travel from Guatemala to the fair as a form of the state's symbolic interest in the emigrant community. Other events for the Guatemalan emigrant community include, for instance, the Los Angeles "*La Feria Chapina*," (*chapina* being a slang word for a Guatemalan), a fair that has been held 13 times, 11 in Los Angeles and 2 in New York, and has brought more than 5,000 Guatemalans together (Expofer Guatemala USA, 2018). Many of these activities are organized by the emigrant community abroad through Hometown Associations (HTAs), and some have the support of the Ministry of Foreign Affairs, which send consuls or diplomats to participate. Mayors, first ladies, congressional officials, and political candidates have all visited the emigrant community abroad, although there is no official policy to do so. A proposal was submitted to Congress to declare December 18 of each year—which the UN has declared International Migrants Day—National Migrants Day in Guatemala (Iniciativa Que Dispone Declarar El 18 de Diciembre de Cada Año "Día Nacional Del Migrante", En La República de Guatemala, 2013), but this has not yet been passed by legislative decree.

Honduras

The Law for the Protection of Honduran Migrants and their Families was conceived to strengthen a sense of belonging among emigrants and to spread Honduran culture. This law also commits to providing state support for emigrant associations and reinforcing cooperation (Ley de Protección de Los Hondureños Migrantes y Sus Familiares, 2013). Along these lines, the Honduran state has sought to legally recognize the emigrant community as the "19th Department" (Honduras currently has 18 departments, or regional administrative units) (M. A. Barahona, personal communication, March 14, 2012).

5.3.2 Declaring Responsibility for Migrants

The implementation of measures to protect the human rights of emigrants comprises part of cultivating the relationship between the emigrant community and the home country. Whether through the National Institute for Migration or the Ministry of Foreign Affairs, the three NTCA countries have been increasingly outspoken in condemning human rights abuses committed against undocumented emigrants transiting through Mexico, or missing or arrested in the United States. In one particularly gruesome example, on August 22, 2010, 72 emigrants, mainly from El Salvador, Guatemala, and Honduras, were kidnapped and killed by Los Zetas, a drug cartel in San Fernando, Tamaulipas, Mexico. These migrants, who were fleeing the violence in their villages, became victims in one of the biggest migrant massacres in the last 10 years. In the following years, the Mexican state joined efforts to locate missing migrants by creating a forensic commission, the Migrant Unit of the Attorney General's Office, and a transnational mechanism for access to justice for migrants. In contrast, the NTCA states did nothing beyond announcing their responsibility for those migrants.

El Salvador

During a visit to Los Angeles, Deputy Minister of Foreign Affairs Liduvina del Carmen Magarín said: "Today we began a series of meetings with our citizens in different cities in the United States, in which I am the representative for El Salvador's recognition of the country's children abroad, for their effort, their identity, and their solidarity with our people and our country" (MRE El Salvador, 2015b). This is one way in which the state has attempted to generate loyalty through a public speech. In this respect, former Vice-Minister of El Salvador's Ministry of Foreign Affairs, Juan José García, stated in an interview that:

> The great strategic objective of our migration policy is to revert the migration dynamic that our country has had in the last 30 years. We cannot continue having 300 people leave our country every day, according to the United States census, certainly underestimated numbers, because you cannot account for the undocumented population. If El Salvador continues like this, it will become a country with no viability. (J. J. García, personal communication, February 27, 2012)

This is consistent with what is contained in several annual Ministry reports, which emphasize that the main focus of the Salvadoran state regarding migration policy is to provide state services and protect emigrant's rights and to cultivate a sense of "rootedness," so that people will not want to leave their home country (MRE El Salvador, 2015a, 2017).

Guatemala

In 2014, the former president of the Committee on Migration (2014–18) wrote a text that he put on a plaque in commemoration of the death of 72 Central American emigrants in the Mexican state of Tamaulipas. He published a picture of the plaque on his Twitter account to publicize his discontent with the case of yet another deceased Guatemalan migrant, Claudia Gómez, an unarmed, 20-year-old indigenous woman who was shot and killed by a United States Border Patrol agent near Laredo, Texas, in May 2018; she had been crossing the state while in search of work to pay for her education. The commemorative plaque reads:

> In memory of those who left and cannot come back. To the families that yearn to see them again. To those dreams they want to reach, and for those who started a journey they were not able to end. Especially to those who lost their lives on August 22, 2010 [the day of the Tamaulipas massacre]. We promise that this will never happen again. Guatemala, 2014. (Briere, 2018)

In other such cases, public officials from the NTCA have made statements accepting their responsibility for their emigrants, but without sending financial support to their families, taking care of the expenses to repatriate the deceased, or helping the Mexican authorities or the Argentine Forensic Anthropology Team locate the missing emigrants in Mexico.

Honduras

In contrast to El Salvador and Guatemala, the Honduran government has not been eager to take responsibility for its migrant citizens. One clear example is the position it has taken with the so-called migrant caravans. On October 12, 2018, a group of about 160 Hondurans set forth from the town of San Pedro Sula, which during the first half of the decade was often referred to as the "murder capital of the world," in hopes of applying for asylum in Mexico or the United States. By October 15, the Associated Press estimated that around 1,600 Hondurans had gathered at their country's border with Guatemala (Pradilla, 2019). On January 15, 2020, another caravan left Honduras for the United States. In both cases, the caravans fueled the debate in the northern country over immigration policy, with American President Donald Trump using the migrants to try to secure backing for his plan to build a wall along the country's southern border with Mexico, all while threatening the NTCA states with withdrawing aid (Trump, 2018). In response, the conservative government of Honduran President

Juan Orlando Hernández denied all support for the Honduran migrants, and accused Bartolo Fuentes, a former leftist legislator, and his activist wife, Dunia Montoya, of organizing the caravan to embarrass the Hernández administration and promote instability (Lind, 2018). This hypothesis was supported by some members of Mexican civil society as well, in particular the prominent priest, Alejandro Solalinde, who in various declarations blamed journalists and human rights activists of organizing and supporting the caravans (C. Martínez, 2019). In summary, neither the Honduran state nor civil society organizations have taken responsibility for these migrants. The governance of migration is polarized, without any agreement among the traditional actors on how to proceed.

5.4 Concluding Remarks

Most of the measures implemented by Central American states analyzed in this chapter and discussed above are symbolic, such as the reminders to their emigrant communities that they have a home country. More than a sense of national belonging, such measures seek to promote a sense of national identity beyond borders. If governments cannot extend citizenship or guarantee the access and protection of emigrants' rights abroad given a lack of financial resources or political will, at least they can create some sense of loyalty by promoting the concept that the government cares for its citizens abroad.

Even though Guatemala approved the Migration Code at the end of 2016, it was the last NTCA state to have a law that directly addressed the emigrant community and the government's policy still lacks coherence. In Guatemala, although it is possible to find documents of different kinds, from laws to protocols, that define the tasks and functions of the bodies that are supposed to handle emigrant issues, these organizations only exist on paper at this time (Pedroza et al., 2016). In contrast, El Salvador appointed Vice-Minister for Salvadorans Abroad Liduvina Magarín to act as president of CONMIGRANTES, as well. This was a clever way to save resources, minimize meetings and lost time, and reduce the possibility of duplicating institutional functions.

Despite the fact that Honduras lags far behind with regard to emigrant human rights protection, development, and democracy, the state was the first in the region to begin political efforts to recognize Honduran emigrants' rights and to create programs for their protection. However, even though the Law for the Protection of Honduran Migrants and their Families was passed in 2013, it was not until 2015 that the state started to put some of its planned programs into action. Moreover, emigrant policy in Honduras focuses largely on urgent issues. With the cooperation and influence of NGOs, international organizations, and foreign state institutions, the state has worked to improve the protection of Honduran emigrants in transit, providing services to migrants in a number of difficult circumstances, ranging from injury to death during migration, human trafficking, and recently, the reintegration of the deported population. Unfortunately, the institution responsible for implementing emigrant policies in Honduras, the Ministry of Foreign Affairs, is severely limited and weak in its reach and powers. This challenges the degree to which the policies envisaged by the Law for the Protection of Honduran Migrants and their Families are applicable by the state (Pedroza et al., 2016). This and the position of the country's conservative President Hernández with regard to not providing safer conditions for the emigrant population may explain two things: on the one hand, why the few existing policies have only advanced thanks to the cooperation of NGOs and IOs and second, why migrants have started to migrate in caravans, because they feel safer in groups, knowing that their state is not going to be there to help them.

In all three cases in this study, the authorities seem to have plans for how emigrant policies should work, but they lack legal engagement, due either to insufficient financial resources, no institutional capacity to implement them or, in some cases like El Salvador, an absence of political willpower related to political party interests. Even so, the large number of institutions that have been created in the region has sparked a change in all three administrations regarding state services for emigrants, even if many of the changes involve taking advantage of traditional consular services in order to function.

Regarding the caravans of October 2018 and January 2020, none of the three NTCA states have made a public declaration of responsibility for the causes that drove their citizens to migrate. Some scholars argue that the phenomenon itself is not new; what is new is group migration motivated by a feeling of safety in numbers and the political nature of the act (Aristegui, 2020). Instead of offering these emigrants protection or expressing concern about their safety, the reaction of the NTCA states towards the caravans has been to offer to contain the flows, all to make a good impression on former President Trump and respond to his threat to cut United States aid.

Chapter 6
Policies to Integrate the Emigrant Community

6.1 Introduction

This chapter presents existing integration policies for emigrants either abroad or who have returned to their home countries. As the chapter shows, there has been an excessive focus on integration policies for immigrants in receiving states and less on what migrant-sending states do to integrate their own citizens. As observed by Pedroza (2020), this focus on immigrant integration is only part of the story in any migration journey. The chapter examines the rights that origin states extend to their emigrant community abroad and the resources they attempt to extract from them. Sending states grant political and social rights to emigrants strategically, so they can make a case for legitimately extracting political and economic benefits in return, such as votes and financial remittances, respectively.

6.2 Extending Emigrant Rights

This section explains policies regarding out-of-country voting and legislative representation; support for Hometown Associations (HTAs); regional institutions and bilateral agreements; how states provide education, health, and labor rights protection services abroad; and aid for arrested, missing, and in-transit emigrants. Finally, it sheds light on the process of receiving emigrants deported to their home countries. All these aspects are part of the sending state's efforts to extend rights to their emigrant community abroad.

6.2.1 Out-of-Country Voting and Citizenship

The extension of political rights is usually examined by scholars in the form of dual citizenship or nationality, the right to vote from overseas, or the right to run for public office (Gamlen, 2008; Ragazzi, 2014). Although they have different meanings, the terms "nationality" and "citizenship" are often used interchangeably. Nationality refers to the formal legal status of state membership, while citizenship delineates the character of a member's rights and duties within the national polity. According to Bauböck (2006), dual nationality allows individuals to hold membership in two or more states. It does not, however, necessarily guarantee access to all the rights and benefits of national citizenship, such as voting or holding office.

By 2000, 10 countries in Latin America had passed some form of dual citizenship, including Brazil, Colombia, Costa Rica, the Dominican Republic, Ecuador, El Salvador, Mexico, Panama, Peru, and Uruguay. Other countries had recognized dual membership selectively, with specific signatories. Such is the case of Guatemala with the Central American countries and some Central American countries with Spain. Of the case studies presented here, only El Salvador and Guatemala allow dual citizenship. The Honduran state decided against this, and Articles 24 and 42 of the country's Constitution state that Hondurans lose their nationality upon acquiring citizenship in another country (Constitución Política de la República de Honduras, 1982). The extension of dual nationality, rather than dual citizenship, in the cases of El Salvador and Guatemala means that these governments retain some rights vis-à-vis the home country, but they do not include the political rights of citizenship, such as the right to be elected to a public position. The approval of dual nationality is only a stepping-stone along the road to acquiring the right to vote from abroad. However, dual nationality and out-of-country voting by NTCA citizens abroad have little or no impact on undocumented emigrants, because few have voted in past elections, perhaps due to suspicions about what they will encounter in their consulates when they go to vote.

El Salvador

For El Salvador, out-of-country voting was the focus of a controversial campaign in the 2009 election between the Nationalist Republican Alliance (ARENA) and the Farabundo Martí National Liberation Front (FMLN) parties. As noted by Karina Sosa, a FMLN legislator and former president of El Salvador's Congressional Committee on Foreign Affairs:

> For the 2014 election, we are trying to get approval for Salvadorans abroad to run for office, because it is fair and necessary. Migrants have always sustained the country's economy; they have rights and obligations. (K. Sosa, personal communication, February 15, 2012)

To that end, the Special Law for the Exercise of Voting from Abroad in Presidential Elections (Ley Especial Para El Ejercicio Del Voto Desde El Exterior En Las Elecciones Presidenciales, 2013) was passed in 2013. When asked why this law was not approved earlier, the FMLN legislator stated:

> There was no political will. The FMLN has always supported civil society and those who asked for a law, but they never brought a proposal, so we presented one that allows Salvadorans to vote by correspondence. (K. Sosa, personal communication, February 15, 2012)

The FMLN took office in 2009 after 20 years of ARENA governance. From 2009 until they left in 2019, the FMLN concentrated on putting migration reform in charge the Ministries of Justice and Foreign Affairs instead of the Ministry of Interior, in order to shift the focus from security to human rights. After all the reforms implemented by the FMLN during the party's first term, they decided to pass a bill on out-of-country voting, afraid that they could lose the election to ARENA (they did not). In January 2013, with 82 votes, the Salvadoran Congress approved the Special Law for the Exercise of Voting from Abroad. Article 4 of this law enables Salvadoran citizens residing outside of El Salvador to exercise their right to vote from wherever they are via postal vote (Ley Especial Para El Ejercicio Del Voto Desde El Exterior En Las Elecciones Presidenciales, 2013). The party also proposed a project allowing municipalities to create specialized units to provide advice to migrant families (K. Sosa, personal communication, February 15, 2012).

The El Salvador Supreme Electoral Court registered 350,638 Salvadorans abroad for the 2019 election. Although this is a low figure considering that the estimated number of Salvadorans abroad for that year was 1.6 million (IOM, 2019), it does not diminish the importance of granting the right to vote to Salvadoran citizens abroad.

Figure 4 Number of Registered Emigrants and their Votes in the 2014 and 2019 Elections in El Salvador

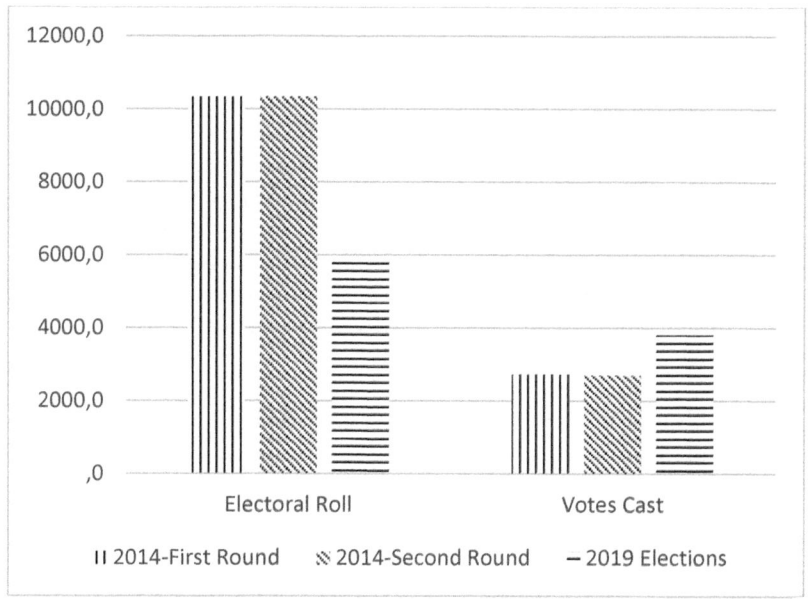

Note. Prepared by the author based on data from (TSE El Salvador, 2020).

According to the Electoral Observation Report for the 2019 presidential election, postal voting procedures must be reviewed and alternatives for the exercise of suffrage explored in order to guarantee greater electoral participation. This is due to the low number of registered Salvadorans living abroad and of voters in the 2014 and 2019 presidential election, compared to the number of registered voters on the electoral rolls (FUNDAUNGO et al., 2019). The FUNDAUNGO et al. report (2019) also highlights the importance of allowing Salvadorans abroad to exercise suffrage for legislative and municipal elections as well. Even though the Constitutional Chamber in 2016 decided that Congress should create a regulation that would allow voting for legislative and municipal elections abroad, because of unconstitutionality ruling 156-2012, both Congress and the Supreme Court agreed to postpone voting until the election of 2021, instead of implementing the regulation for the upcoming 2019 election. However, there is no regulation to date, except for a proposal presented by deputies from the National Concertation Party to the Congressional Electoral and Constitutional Reform Commission, which was not enacted for the 2021 legislative and municipal elections in El Salvador (Campos & Huete, 2020). The challenge entailed by this new regulation is no small thing, since the Latin American countries have no comparative experiences related to the exercise of suffrage abroad for municipal elections (only legislative elections in seven countries). Likewise, it is necessary to clarify the legal and political links that will allow a Salvadoran abroad to vote in each electoral district in their home country, so that the representative-represented link is clear.

Party offices abroad are neither explicitly permitted nor prohibited according to Salvadoran law. However, unofficial "party houses" exist where informal political activity takes place, financed by the emigrants themselves (Pedroza et al., 2016). Political campaigns are also not legally regulated. If they take place, they are unofficial and privately funded and organized. Emigrant membership in political parties is equal to the membership of resident citizens, according to the statutes of the political parties.

Guatemala

Regardless of the large number of remittances Guatemalan emigrants send to their home country, the importance of out-of-country voting has received little attention in the sending states compared to El Salvador and Honduras. Despite the pressure from the emigrant community abroad to have access to out-of-country voting, for one decade in the 2000s, there was no discussion in Congress to approve this amendment to the Electoral and Political Parties Law. In contrast to Honduras in 2001 and El Salvador 2014, out-of-country voting was only approved by the Guatemalan government in 2016, without any conflict on the part of the political parties (Reformas al Decreto Número 1-85 de La Asamblea Nacional Constituyente, Ley Electoral y de Partidos Políticos, 2016). The first time that emigrant Guatemalans voted abroad was, then, in the election of 2019. However, migrants described the result as a "failure," since only 734 emigrants voted, a mere 1.18% of the total number of registered citizens. Emigrants strongly criticized the fact that only four voting centers were open in the United States, requiring anyone with the intention to vote to travel enormous distances. However, the president of the

Supreme Court argued that the exercise of the vote abroad should not be qualified by the number of voters, but by the fact that it modernized the Guatemalan electoral system (S. Morales, 2019).

Guatemalan law does not explicitly regulate political competition abroad. Though funding by foreigners or foreign organizations is forbidden, the Electoral Law makes no mention of campaigns abroad (Reformas al Decreto Número 1-85 de La Asamblea Nacional Constituyente, Ley Electoral y de Partidos Políticos, 2016). There have been reports of Guatemalan politicians campaigning abroad. For instance, in Los Angeles, a presidential candidate, now President Alejandro Giammattei, held meetings with the Guatemalan community and invited them to vote in August 2019 (Macías, 2019).

In Guatemala, the statutes of the various political parties do not generally regulate emigrant membership. Only two parties (out of dozens), the now nonexistent National Development Action and the Patriot Party, have had a secretary in charge of migrant issues, indicating that migrants are eligible for membership and that they are also, at least symbolically, considered a constituency by some (Pedroza et al., 2016).

Honduras

Honduras was the first NTCA country to allow out-of-country voting, passing it in 2001. The Law for the Exercise of Suffrage for Hondurans Abroad is now included in the Electoral Law as amended in the 2004. Out-of-country voting is only allowed for presidential elections and only in the cities determined by the Supreme Court by a simple majority of votes. The selection criteria for the cities is not clearly stipulated in the law, beyond the mention that these must be the cities abroad with the highest concentration of Honduran emigrants (Ley Especial Para El Ejercicio Del Sufragio de Los Hondureños En El Exterior, 2001). This law was passed in the context of debates and opposition between the Honduran Liberal Party (PLH) and the Honduran National Party (PNH), with the former party in favor of the project and the latter party opposed. Some politicians from the PNH, including former President Ricardo Maduro, argued that out-of-country voting is not a priority for emigrants abroad and that it costs an excessive amount of money to win only a few votes (Meza, 2011). As argued by a judge from the Honduran Supreme Court:

> Ironically, to transport ballots to Miami costs less than to transport the ballots to some local communities in Honduras. However, the available budget (around $600,000) is not enough to cover all the states in the United States, which is why the law determines a certain number of cities there where the Honduran vote is valid. One of the issues that has led to criticism about out-of-country voting in Honduras is the low participation rate. (D. Matamoros, personal communication, March 14, 2012)

Out-of-country voting in Honduras has taken place five times since it was enacted in the seven cities[18] in the United States designated by the law in 2001. However, for the 2021 election, Hondurans abroad are going to be able to vote from any of Honduras's 50 consulates, not only in the United States, but also from other countries with a significant number of Honduran citizens, including Costa Rica, El Salvador, Guatemala, Mexico, Nicaragua, Panama, and Spain (El Heraldo, 2020). Out-of-country voting has been taken advantage of by 13,627 Hondurans abroad in the five elections since the law was passed, an average of 2,725 voters in each election (TSE Honduras, 2020).

6.2.2 Legislative Representation

El Salvador

The legislative committee working for the emigrant community in El Salvador, the Committee on Foreign Affairs, Central American Integration, and Salvadorans Abroad, was led by congresswoman Karina Sosa (FMLN) for seven years (2011–18). Her primary efforts to support the emigrant community included the Law for the Protection and Development of Salvadoran Migrants and their Families, which entered into force in 2011. Together with the participation of representatives from all the legislative benches, she also made around a dozen visits to North America to lobby in favor of the emigrant community (Serrano, 2019). This legislative committee is known for its efforts to engage emigrants abroad. In an interview with Sosa, she explained that:

---

18 Atlanta, Houston, Los Angeles, Miami, New Orleans, New York, and Washington.

We are looking to implement all the legislation needed for emigrants to come back to El Salvador, to feel at home. One of the policies we plan to discuss is how to benefit migrants once they have retired in the United States. We want to offer them a discount to buy property, to travel here, to send money, and to have access to health care. (K. Sosa, personal communication, February 15, 2012)

In short, these kinds of policies are designed to extend rights to the emigrants, even when they have been away for years.

Guatemala

In 2012, the Guatemalan Congress created the Committee on Migration, which promotes the recognition of both the Guatemalan emigrant community and the immigrant community in the country. In the picture below, the former president of the Congress Committee on Migration, Jean Briere, recognizes Guatemalan citizens in Los Angeles, California for their work at the Guatemalan Emigrant Union.

Figure 5   President of the Congressional Committee on Migration Recognizing the Emigrant Community in Los Angeles

Note. Briere, J. P. (2017, October 22). De parte del Congreso se reconoció a varios Guatemaltecos residentes en Los Angeles, gracias a la labor de Doña Rosita y Dip. Ovidio Monzon. [Twitter]. *@PAULBRIERE*. Retrieved June 9, 2022, from <https://twitter.com/PAULBRIERE/status/922185713470251008>.

Regarding the priorities of the Congressional Committee on Migration, Congressman Mauro Guzmán stated in an interview that:

> The priorities of the Congressional Committee on Migration include the creation of a regional strategy to request support for Central American migrants, which is framed within the Central American Integration System. The strategy includes a request to the Mexican government to respect migrants' human rights and to demand the investigation of the murdered migrants in Tamaulipas. Another priority for our Committee is to request Temporary Protected Status for Guatemalan migrants, due to the damage caused by Tropical Storm Agatha [in 2010], which left thousands of people homeless and did millions of dollars of damage to the infrastructure. (M. Guzmán, personal communication, January 24, 2012)

The Guatemalan government, which has always had serious annual budget problems during the winter, announced they would find it difficult to assist the victims of storms, and that they would have even fewer resources to serve migrants if continued deportations are not stopped. Their strategy has always been to request Temporary Protection Status for Guatemalan migrants from the American authorities, which is denied year after year.

Honduras

Like El Salvador and Guatemala, Honduras has a legislative committee working on behalf of the emigrant community, in this case the Committee on Foreign Affairs, which was responsible for introducing the Law for the Protection of Honduran Migrants and their Families, discussed above, in 2013. According to the former president of the Committee on Foreign Affairs, "the law was passed in one day by Legislative Decree 106-2013" (M. A. Barahona, personal communication, March 14, 2012). As Honduras will hold primary elections in 2021, the Congress approved six new articles to include in the new Electoral Law. One Hometown Association presented a proposal to include the novel figure of the "migrant deputy" to represent Hondurans residing in the United States in the draft of the new law. However, it was not considered by Congress in 2020. The reason behind having a migrant deputy is to build a communication bridge between Washington, the Honduran Ministry of Foreign Affairs, and Congress, as well as to advocate and create laws in favor of the emigrant community.

6.2.3 Hometown Associations

Since the late 1980s, the number of Latino NGOs—known as Hometown Associations (HTAs)—in the United States has grown substantially. In Chicago alone, groups with ties to Mexico increased from around 20 in 1994 to more than 100 in 1998, and now account for nearly 70% of all the associations in the city. Like most nonprofits, Latino organizations predominantly focus on charitable work and tend to rely on government funding or support from individuals (Orozco, 2000). HTAs, which are dominated by first-generation immigrants in the United States, are composed of migrants from the same town or state in their home country who endeavor to retain a sense of community as they adjust to the new country. The HTA not only promotes social exchange, but pursues small development goals by using family remittances as a form of economic aid in home countries.

El Salvador

Many Salvadoran HTAs, which emerged in the 1990s and are growing rapidly in number, pursue structured development agendas for their hometowns and are among the most organized of all the Central American associations. According to a study by Orozco, one example of how Salvadoran HTAs work is the United Community of Chinameca. This HTA began operating after the 1992 Chapultepec Peace Accords, which brought an end to the Salvadoran Civil War. After visiting the war-ravaged area, members began providing small donations to the local Chinameca parish for reconstruction. The Chinameca association has engaged in various forms of fundraising and obtained the support of companies like United Airlines, which made donations to the community in exchange for the possibility of acquiring new customers (Orozco, 2000).

Hometown Associations are eager to engage with their sending states, but this relationship goes both ways. Sending states also aim to engage HTAs. Examples of this include Presidential Forums, when in 2004 and 2006, the Salvadoran government made an effort to build a connection between Salvadoran migrants and the country's national institutions, with the participation of prominent Salvadorans around the world. Unfortunately, there is no record of any Forums being held on a regular basis after 2006 (Pedroza et al., 2016, p. 200). In contrast, the International Convention of Salvadoran Communities Residing Abroad, which was founded by emigrant associations, has taken place annually since 2003 (Pedroza et al., 2016).

Guatemala

Guatemalan HTAs have a long history of participation, but on a lower scale than the other two countries. Most Guatemalan HTAs are active in the United States, specifically in Los Angeles and Houston, although they have kept a low profile. Following the 1996 Guatemalan Peace Accords that put an end to 36 years of war, HTAs established by Guatemalans in the United States gathered support for their country. For instance, the New York committee, a group usually concerned with cultural affairs, managed to raise $5,000 for their fellow countrymen affected by Hurricane Mitch in 1998.

The sending state has also made efforts to engage with its HTAs in the United States. One example of this is the work of the Guatemalan consulate in Los Angeles, which has sponsored a Guatemalan Fair since 2004. Their webpage describes the event as one "of a commercial and cultural nature, which aims to unite Central American families in the US. Held in the city of Los Angeles, at this event, businessmen exhibit, sample, and report on their products or services" (Feria Chapina, 2021). Over twenty sponsors, the majority from Guatemala—including the Guatemalan government—and some from the United States, organize this event annually, and there are stands offering a wide variety of services and selling all sorts of nostalgic products. The products offered at this fair include real estate, construction materials, and appliances to build or equip a home in Guatemala. The services offered are related to education, medical insurance, funeral services, travel, and rental cars for emigrants in the United States or their family back home. Financial services such as banking and financial remittances through exchange houses or by telephone are offered as well.

Honduras

Honduran Hometown Associations have been involved in campaigns to foster the bond between the Honduran community in the United States and their home country. For instance, a decade ago, the Florida Honduran Unity group organized a voter registration drive for immigrants wishing to vote in the Honduran presidential election (Orozco, 2006). Another example is the New Horizon Investment Club, founded in 2000 by 10 immigrants from the Honduran Garifuna indigenous community in New York City. The founding members had the idea to combine their resources, learn how to invest in the stock market, and then assist in the economic development of the Honduran community in New York. New Horizon, which aims to empower the Garifuna community and Afro-Latinos in general with investment knowledge, has reached over 100 members (Orozco, 2006).

6.2.4 Regional Institutions and Agreements

The Central American Integration System

The Central American Integration System (SICA) has several regional platforms, one that brings together Foreign Affairs ministers, another with Interior ministries and one at the executive level with the presidents of the region, the highest mechanism for the discussion of migration in the region. According to the president of the Central American Court of Justice, all these platforms have their origin in the Tegucigalpa Protocol, the framework treaty for the SICA. The International Organization for Migration supported the SICA in its efforts to design a regional migration program, the Comprehensive Migration Policy, which focuses on labor and human rights protection (C. Salazar Grande, personal communication, April 12, 2012). The policy is to be implemented by the Ministries of the Interior and Foreign Affairs.

The Central American Parliament, also known as the PARLACEN, is a political body within SICA charged with planning, analysis, and making recommendations. As its representatives are freely elected by universal suffrage in all the member countries (SICA, 2021d), it has the status of a legal entity and is democratically legitimate. While the PARLACEN does not have a specific strategic plan for migration, it addresses the topic in statements and recommendations at the regional and international levels. One recent example is the Parliament's outreach to United States authorities to solicit support for the undocumented Central American migrant population living in the country, given its extreme vulnerability to the COVID-19 pandemic; the emigrants lack services and are afraid to ask for help because of their undocumented status (PARLACEN, 2020).

SICA Commission of Migration Directors (OCAM)

The Central American Commission of Migration Directors (OCAM) branched off from the SICA in October 1990 in Costa Rica, at the request of the Central American presidents. The OCAM was initially created to facilitate the transit of people between the countries in the region and to recognize the importance of migration for Central American integration. However, at this time, OCAM also promotes actions to obtain and process migration information, train public officials from the migration institutions of member countries, modernize migration management, implement common migration instruments and procedures, fight against migrant smuggling and human trafficking, work towards the homologation of entry requirements for foreigners, and design agreements for the dignified, safe, and orderly return of regional and extra-regional immigrants (further described in this chapter under "Bilateral Agreements").

As of 1999, the IOM has carried out the role of OCAM Technical Secretariat to support regional activities related to migration (SICA, 2021b). OCAM participates and coordinates with civil society and governments in the following regional and international forums: the Regional Conference on Migration (RCM), Ibero-American Forum on Migration and Development, Central American Forum on Migration and Development, Global American Forum on Migration and Development, Ibero-American Network of Migration Authorities, Community of Latin American and Caribbean States, and Interstate Consultation Mechanisms on Migration (SICA, 2021b).

COPAREM

The Regional Parliamentary Council on Migration, or COPAREM, is a political influence forum without any implementing capacity. Instead, it sets the agenda among congressional representatives from Central America. COPAREM was created in 2009 as a coordination council between legislators to strengthen migration governance in the Mexico, Central American and Dominican Republic region. "This council is a regional space where Central American legislators can contribute to drafting, revising, and approving legal frameworks that make it possible to institutionalize public migration policies that apply a human rights and development approach" (A. D. Rivera, personal communication, August 2, 2012). In short, this regional coordination and dialogue body of legislators provides a valuable space to bring migration matters to the legislative table.

The Regional Conference on Migration

The Regional Conference on Migration (RCM), based at the IOM offices in Costa Rica, has a technical secretary. It is a regional initiative, also known as the Puebla Process, established in 1996 as a result of the Tuxtla II Presidential Summit. The RCM is a multilateral mechanism for coordinating policies and actions related to migration in the eleven member states: Belize, Canada, Costa Rica, the Dominican Republic, El Salvador, Guatemala, Honduras, Mexico, Nicaragua, Panama, and the United States. Its primary objectives are to exchange information, experiences, and best practices, as well as to promote regional cooperation on migration.

In addition to providing a space for dialogue and information exchange between governments, a vast array of actions have been implemented within the framework of this regional process: cooperation projects, projects to assist the return of migrant women and children, training workshops and seminars on topics related to migration, and technical and institutional assistance for immigration authorities from member states. In recent years, the member states have come together to guarantee a response to the migration of unaccompanied migrant children from Central America to the United States by creating ad hoc groups (RCM, 2020).

Regional Network for Civil Organizations on Migration
The Regional Network for Civil Organizations on Migration (RROCM) was created in 1998 to strengthen dialogue between the state and civil society on topics related to migration. The RROCM participates in seminars hosted by the Regional Conference on Migration, with the participation of groups like the Regional Consultation Group on Migration and a variety of vice-ministers (RROCM, 2021). In 2013, an ad hoc group was created between the RCM and RROCM to establish a common agenda and a coordination mechanism between civil society and the state. During its meetings, the ad hoc group discussed fundamental topics such as human trafficking, integration, and providing services to vulnerable groups of migrants.

El Salvador

El Salvador is home to the Migrants Forum, an organization comprising several members from civil society organizations such as the Central American Resource Center (CARECEN), the Human Rights Institute of the Central American University, the Independent Monitoring Group of El Salvador, and the Salvadoran Health Initiative for Migrants and their Families Joint Initiative.

Guatemala

The first organizations that gathered to discuss and advocate for migrants in Guatemala were the Migrant Houses in Guatemala City and Tecun Uman, the Central American Institute for Social Studies and Development (INCEDES), and Catholic Relief Services (CRS). Other coalitions in the country include the National Committee on Migration in Guatemala and the Guatemalan Civil Society Migration Board, made up of more than 15 civil society organizations, whose most recent action was the issuance of a statement during the visit of United States Vice-President Kamala Harris to the country, arguing for the creation of mechanisms for dialogue regarding American cooperation in Central America, urging the country to work closely with civil society organizations for the protection and guarantee of human rights and during the entire process of formulating, implementing, monitoring, and evaluating emigrant policy in the region (Grupo Articulador, 2021).

Honduras

The National Forum for Migration in Honduras (FONAMIH) is made up of more than 30 organizations and focuses on political advocacy, research and institutional strengthening, and public policy. Its observer members include the IOM, United Nations High Commissioner for Refugees, and the National Human Rights Commissioner. Organizations such as Casa Alianza and the Committee of the Families of Disappeared Migrants of El Progreso also participate. FONAMIH has promoted the creation of a committee for returned migrants in the cities of Tegucigalpa and San Pedro Sula. It also works together with state institutions such as the Directorate-General of Migration and requests temporary permits to work in the United States (K. Valladares, personal communication, March 12, 2012).

Mexico-Guatemala Binational Commission initiative

One of the first binational civil initiatives was the Guatemala-Mexico group, Migration and Development, promoted by the College of Mexico, the Latin American Social Studies Institute in Guatemala, and INCEDES with the support of the CRS, Ford Foundation, and George Soros's Open Society Foundation. The governments of Guatemala and Mexico assembled the Binational Group on Migration Affairs, part of the broader Mexico-Guatemala Binational Commission initiative. An ad-hoc committee was created to improve the employment situation of seasonal agricultural workers through access to economic and social benefits and to encourage oversight and the enforcement of labor laws in both countries. Participants in this group include members of the institutions of the Mexican and Guatemalan executive branch, e.g., the Ministries of Foreign Affairs, the Interior, and Labor, and the National Migration Institute.

Central America-4 Free Mobility Agreement

This agreement was created and incorporated into the SICA in 1991 and is often called upon to play a significant role in migration matters. It was enacted by executive agreements signed between the presidents of El Salvador, Guatemala, Honduras, and Nicaragua, with the objective of allowing passport-free regional transit for the nationals of the member countries with expedited immigration instruments (SICA, 2021c).

Memorandum for the Return of Migrants in a Dignified, Orderly, and Safe manner

This memorandum was signed by the governments of El Salvador, Guatemala, Honduras, Mexico, and Nicaragua in 2006. Repatriation procedures include specific care programs for vulnerable individuals, such as minors, those over 60 years old, pregnant women, people with disabilities and victims of human trafficking (RROCM, 2021).

Central America Regional Security Initiative

The United States Department of State's Central America Regional Security Initiative, or CARSI, was created in 2008 as a joint strategy between the United States and Belize, Costa Rica, El Salvador, Guatemala, Honduras, Nicaragua, and Panama to address the increase in migration from the region to the United States. CARSI was designed to strengthen regional security by reinforcing the security apparatus of Central American countries and, consequently, to reduce national crime rates. The goals of CARSI are to respect human rights, protect vulnerable populations in the region, overcome impunity, and to facilitate access to justice and the rule of law. To that end, the American government allocated $361,5000,000 to the initiative between 2008 and 2011 (Meyer & Seelke, 2015).

Northern Triangle Alliance for Prosperity Plan

It is estimated that between October 2013 and May 2014, approximately 50,000 unaccompanied and undocumented children and adolescents migrated from Central American countries to Mexico and the United States (RELAF et al., 2015). This circumstance produced a regional migration crisis that reinforced the premise that migration is a phenomenon that must be addressed jointly. Up to that point, each NTCA government had set its own mid-term objectives related to migration, but the humanitarian crisis involving children and adolescents opened the door to an inevitable regional conversation, which included the United States, as the destination country.

The Plan of the Alliance for Prosperity in the Northern Triangle, or PAPTN, was agreed on between the governments of El Salvador, Guatemala, Honduras, and the United States, with advice from the Inter-American Development Bank. This regional initiative, which provided a joint approach to the migration crisis, was presented and approved in Washington in 2014, with the attendance of the three presidents of the NTCA countries and Vice-President Joseph Biden representing President Barack Obama. The objective of the PAPTN was to improve security and economic conditions in the countries of origin in order to prevent undocumented migration to the United States. To that end, each government developed its own goals, objectives, and programs and the administration of President Obama negotiated with the U.S. Congress to obtain one billion dollars for the NTCA countries in 2015, and 750 million the next year (Villafuerte, 2018).

According to the proposal presented by the PAPTN, more than 22 billion dollars would be required for activities and projects. An official document prepared by the governments of El Salvador, Guatemala, and Honduras and published by the United Nations stipulated that obtaining funds would be a joint effort engaged in by the NTCA governments, national and international private actors, multilateral organizations, and partners in the region. From the outset, the countries proposed that most of the funding for the plan come from their own budgets (Gobiernos de El Salvador, Guatemala y Honduras, 2015).

Mexico-Northern Triangle Consular Consultation Program

In 2015, the consulates of the NTCA countries signed a joint declaration with Mexico to create a consular coordination group in McAllen, Texas to promote collaborative actions related to protection, consular assistance, and the exchange of best practices: TRICAMEX. The aim of TRICAMEX is to address urgent, day-to-day migration situations affecting migrant communities in the United States, and the initiative has served as a useful tool to facilitate communication with local authorities on issues such as education, health, legal advice, and protection. It also allows the consuls of Mexico and the NTCA to share their best practices to the benefit of their nationals in the United States. TRICAMEX was formalized in several American cities where the four countries have a consular presence: Washington D.C., Houston, New York, Chicago, Atlanta, Los Angeles, San Francisco, McAllen, Miami, and Seattle. The most common actions carried out are tours with the Rio Grande Valley Sector Border Patrol, rescue drills for lost migrants, visits to shelters to follow up on family situations, high-level meetings, diplomas in psychological aid for migrants, cultural events, and health fairs (MRE El Salvador, 2016).

One of the most recent and important actions performed by TRICAMEX involved following up on the policy of separating and detaining migrant families implemented by former President Trump in July 2018. As part of this initiative, TRICAMEX helped consulates maintain regular communication to assist the families involved, coordinated with American authorities, exchanged information, and supported family reunification processes (Bosques, 2018). TRICAMEX also contributed to information exchanges that took place during the period of the migrant caravans from October 2018 to January 2019 heading from Honduras, El Salvador, Guatemala, and Mexico to the United States (Rosales Sandoval & Marvic García, 2021).

Mexico-Northern Triangle Comprehensive Development Plan
In 2018, when Mexican President López Obrador took office, the presidents of Guatemala and Honduras and the vice-president of El Salvador met with him in Mexico City to sign the El Salvador-Guatemala-Honduras-Mexico Political Declaration. In this declaration, the countries expressed their willingness to build a new relationship, promoting actions to generate development and opportunities at the local level in order to stop undocumented migration by attacking its structural causes and, thus, producing safe, orderly, and regular migration. The Executive Secretary of the

Economic Commission for Latin America and the Caribbean, Alicia Bárcenas, participated as a witness of honor for the signing of the political declaration, as a sign of the support that this institution would provide in the design and implementation of the Comprehensive Development Plan, or PDI.

The PDI was the first official instrument to propose a comprehensive development scheme for the region, with a specific focus on addressing the growing migration flows from the NTCA to the United States from a perspective based on human security and the rights of migrants. The document, Towards a Comprehensive Development Plan between El Salvador, Guatemala, Honduras, and Mexico, was released and presented in Honduras by the foreign ministers of the four countries. Its stated priorities are social protection, education-employment-income, productive integration, and adaptation to climate change (CEPAL, 2019).

A declaration made by the United States government welcomed the PDI and committed a total of 5.8 million dollars for institutional reforms and economic development in the NTCA and to generate more employment opportunities in southern Mexico (SRE México, 2018). Mexico, in turn, would invest 25 billion dollars over the next five years, and the United States will increase its cooperation by 4.8 billion dollars, of which 2 billion dollars will be for projects in southern Mexico. In December 2020, Bárcenas presented a progress report on the PDI and its ability to generate synergies with multiple actors, both public and private, particularly in the context of the COVID-19 crisis and Hurricane Eta and Hurricane Iota, both of which strongly impacted Mexico and Central America (CEPAL, 2020). The final document is expected to be presented in 2021.

The Biden Plan for Central America

After the Trump administration left office in 2020, a new plan was presented by the administration of President Biden for the development of Central America, originally unveiled in 2019 on his campaign page (Biden, 2021). In June 2021, United States Vice-President Harris, appointed by President Biden to handle the border crisis, made her first international trip to meet with the presidents of Guatemala and Mexico to learn more about the causes of migration in the region. The five aims of Biden's project are: 1) to give 4 billion dollars to address the drivers of migration from Central America to the United States; 2), to find private sources of investment; 3) to improve security and the rule of law; 4) to address endemic corruption; and 5) to prioritize poverty reduction and economic development (Puerta, 2020). Although Biden's plan does not claim to be an extension of the Comprehensive Development Plan, it has the same aims, but with the difference that the United States is now included.

6.2.5 Providing Education, Health, and Labor Protection Services Abroad

Although only a scarce number of programs in the NTCA sending states focus on health, education, and labor rights protection, these states are making an effort to send their nationals abroad to work. Proof of this is the meeting held in 2013, when 38 consular officials from Belize, Costa Rica, the Dominican Republic, El Salvador, Guatemala, Honduras, Mexico, Nicaragua, and Panama met in Tegucigalpa to receive training and discuss strengthening the regional dialogue to protect labor migrants' human rights in migrant receiving states. The two-day workshop, organized by the IOM's regional project, Improving Labor Migration Management in Central America and the Dominican Republic, and funded by the Canadian Ministry of Labor, focused on promoting regional dialogue to expand the consular officials' knowledge about protection and the human rights of migrant workers (IOM, 2013). The meeting may have been a reaction to the increased demands from civil society to protect the rights of seasonal agricultural workers in Canada, because there have been several accusations of human rights violations in Canadian hiring companies (Gesualdi-Fecteau et al., 2017).

El Salvador

There is currently no possibility for Salvadoran emigrants to maintain their healthcare coverage once in another country. However, El Salvador's government offers social insurance benefits through the Health Windows model, and it has signed and ratified the Multilateral Ibero-American

Social Security Agreement, which is a fundamental tool for the protection of migrant workers and their families (Pedroza et al., 2016). Regarding protection services, in contrast to Guatemala and Honduras, El Salvador has few working programs abroad. Nonetheless, the country has established itself as a leading actor by carefully negotiating all programs with foreign contractors and recruiters. As stated by the Minister of Labor: "We are the only institution authorized to provide information about the Labor Migration program, and the American Embassy is responsible for granting work visas. We will not allow acts of fraud" (Noticiero Lourdes, 2019).

Guatemala

Since 2007, through an agreement with the Ministry of Education, the Ministry of Foreign Affairs, and the consular missions of Guatemala abroad, CONAMIGUA has collaborated in literacy programs and schooling for adults aimed at Guatemalans abroad through its consulates and has sent literacy material to the consulates (S. Cuc, personal communication, January 26, 2012). While emigrants do not have access to healthcare in Guatemala, Guatemalan consulates have begun to offer healthcare counseling. There are plans for the Guatemalan Institute of Social Security to start offering emigrants health insurance packages to cover their families in Guatemala (Álvarez, 2010). Some Guatemalan consulates have also participated in Bi-National Health Weeks (BHW). This program aims to promote and foster the health of the Hispanic migrant population living in the United States and to increase access to medical services available in the area to expand health care coverage. The BHW's main partners include the Secretariats of Health and Foreign Affairs of Mexico, the Ministries of Foreign Affairs of Guatemala, Honduras, and other Latin American ministries, as well as the Centers for Disease Control and Prevention, several public health departments, the Council of Mexican Federations in North America, the Health Initiative of the Americas, and a program at the University of California, Berkeley, School of Public Health (Osorio, 2019).

Guatemala has been the most controversial state with regard to promoting programs for working abroad. This is due to the fact that the state is not the primary body tracking the process of worker recruitment.

Instead, private recruitment has proliferated to the point that many workers go abroad without the knowledge of the Ministry of Labor or Ministry of Foreign Affairs. This situation makes workers prone to human and labor rights violations once in the destination country. One of the main recommendations from the Guatemalan Civil Society Migration Board was that the Guatemalan and Canadian governments sign an agreement and that the Ministry of Foreign Affairs and Ministry of Labor become involved in the protection of emigrant labor rights (Grupo Articulador, 2010).

Although the IOM states that it provides technical assistance to the Guatemalan government (IOM, 2010b), neither the Ministry of Foreign Affairs nor the Ministry of Labor were involved in a Memorandum of Understanding signed in 2003. This gave a wide margin of action and control to the IOM in the process of recruiting migrant workers. The state was only involved in providing the necessary documentation for traveling, i.e., a passport. Regarding state protection and services, Guatemalan consulates in Canada make periodic checks on farms to make sure that the rights of the workers are being respected. Nevertheless, there are clear limitations to the protections offered by the consulates, as there is no real agreement signed between the two states beyond what is in effect a private contract.

Section 34 of the Labor Code provides the Guatemalan government with the legal authority to regulate the recruitment of temporary workers and specifically charges the Ministry of Labor with their protecting their rights. This section also establishes the Ministry's power to authorize the recruitment and departure of workers for the Seasonal Agricultural Worker Program and explicitly prohibits contracts without the Ministry's authorization (Código de Trabajo de Guatemala, 1961). Since 2014, Guatemala has been involved in plans to issue regulations for intermediaries who recruit temporary foreign workers.

According to the Labor Code, the contract must establish that all expenses will be covered by the recruiter or the employer, including transportation, housing, and border crossing expenses. Workers should not incur any expenses for the placement services offered by the recruiting intermediary. Nevertheless, a fieldwork trip in 2012 produced the recruiting call made by the IOM and the Foundation of Foreign Agricultural Workforce Recruitment Companies, an employment association in Quebec during which migrant workers were threatened that they would have to pay for their flight tickets if they did not comply with the work contract. Additionally, there are some concerns about the respect for the human rights of the migrants once in Canada, since some companies take away workers' passports until the end of their stay (PTAT-C, 2010). In 2019, however, the first agreement was signed by Guatemala and the United States in which the Labor Minister of Guatemala established that the principles of this agreement are the respect for the human and labor rights of temporary Guatemalan migrant workers in the agricultural sector (Ministerio de Trabajo y Previsión Social de Guatemala, 2019).

Honduras

The Safe Honduran program, which began in 2011, seeks to offer medical assistance and the possibility of maintaining employment and retirement benefits for all Honduran emigrants and their families residing in the United States cities where most Hondurans live. The program seeks, above all, to facilitate the integration of returnees (La Prensa, 2011). The Law for the Protection of Honduran Migrants and their Families plans for the same kind of program (Ley de Protección de Los Hondureños Migrantes y Sus Familiares, 2013). However, none of these initiatives are currently operational and many programs provided for by this law lack implementing regulations.

Regarding education, the Law for the Protection of Honduran Migrants and their Families created an online study program in 2015, the Online Highschool for Emigrants (Tiempo Digital, 2015). This program targets Hondurans abroad who did not finish their primary or secondary education and offers them the chance to conclude these studies online. Concerning the protection of rights, in 2005 the Honduran state ratified the UN International Convention on the Protection of the Rights of all Migrant Workers and Members of their Families, although the state has not adequately adjusted its own regulations accordingly. There is poor coordination when it comes to the actors involved in the process of recruiting, employing, and returning migrant workers in the Seasonal Agricultural Worker Program. Currently the Directorate-General of Migration, the Ministry of Foreign Affairs and the Ministry of Labor have a limited role in processing Honduran emigrant workers.

One clear example of the Honduran state delegating its functions to private actors is the Special Regime of Legal Migration of Honduran Workers for seasonal workers programs in the United States and other countries, approved by Decree 69-2010 (Régimen Especial de Migración Legal de Trabajadores Hondureños Para Trabajar En El Sector Agrícola de Estados Unidos y Otros Países, 2010). This decree is an exceptional mechanism that provides the National Association of Industrialists of Honduras and private companies with the possibility of recruiting Honduran farmers to go abroad without having to obtain the government's approval. One disadvantage of this mechanism is that it puts Honduran migrant workers at a high risk of human rights violations.

6.2.6 Assisting the Arrested, Missing, and Emigrants in Transit; Receiving the Deported

State services for deported nationals start with a visit from the Guatemalan, Honduran, or Salvadoran consul general to a United States prison upon the detention of one of their citizens. Then, through interinstitutional coordination, the consul verifies that the detained person is truly a citizen of the country they say they come from. Last, the consuls provide documentation to emigrants caught without any. El Salvador was the first state to have a systematized database containing information on deported nationals. Consulates are part of Ministries of Foreign Affairs and are located where there is a considerable number of their citizens. Among the services offered by mobile consulates is the issuance of a Consular Identification Card.

El Salvador

El Salvador's Special Law for the Protection and Development of Salvadoran Migrant Persons and their Families incorporates a few initiatives for the reintegration of deported nationals into the country, for example, the

Productive Cooperation and Technical Cooperation Project (Ley Especial Para La Protección y Desarrollo de La Persona Migrante Salvadoreña y Su Familia, 2011). As soon as migrants arrive in their home country, they are provided with a snack (*pupusa*, a type of stuffed corncake, and coffee), allowed to make a phone call, and given some money for the bus ride back home. The facilities have an official work database for which deported migrants must provide information—including the skills they learned while abroad—to encourage the incorporation of the deported nationals into the economy. The Directorate-General of Migration offers services for deported nationals (E. Olán, personal communication, February 20, 2015). The Directorate for Migrant Services (DGM) operates a Return Reception Center, where deported nationals from Mexico arriving by land and those deported from the United States arriving by air are received daily in the neighborhood of Colonia Quiñónez in San Salvador. The commitment of the Salvadoran state has produced an exemplary model at the regional level for the reception of returned Salvadorans, based on a state-led coordination effort between various government institutions and the support of NGOs, foundations, and IOs to focus on the needs of the deported citizens upon their return to the country. Priority is given to caring for people in vulnerable conditions, always guided by respect for human rights (Dirección General de Migración y Extranjería de El Salvador, 2020). Once in El Salvador, the deported migrants are received by the DGM. When the "Welcome Home" program started, it was administered by Catholic Relief Services (CRS), an agency run by the American government. The program was then handed to a local NGO called the National Development Foundation. However, since 2008 El Salvador's Directorate-General of Migration has been in charge of the program.

The Salvadoran state took several valuable steps related to the protection of emigrants in vulnerable situations in 2019 when it reformed the Special Law for the Protection and Development of Salvadoran Migrant Persons and their Families. Article 7 sets out the purpose of the law:

> To provide services to emigrants who have been victims of accidents, terminal illnesses, victims and survivors of human trafficking, victims of sexual abuse and exploitation, or are missing; as well as other situations that threaten personal integrity.

> It gives medical, psychological, psychiatric, and rehabilitation assistance to returned people with a focus on unaccompanied children and adolescents. For the latter, the care is specialized. In addition, it provides psychological assistance to relatives of victims (Reforma a La Ley Especial Para La Protección y Desarrollo de La Persona Migrante Salvadoreña y Su Familia, 2019).

Article 8 of the reform states that El Salvador's "Institute of Legal Medicine has a bank of genetic profiles comprising DNA samples of the relatives of missing persons in order to facilitate identification" (Reforma a La Ley Especial Para La Protección y Desarrollo de La Persona Migrante Salvadoreña y Su Familia, 2019).

In this line, the Social and Labor Reintegration Program is being promoted by the Salvadoran Migrant Institute (INSAMI), with the support of the Ministry of Labor, Vice-Ministry for Salvadorans Abroad, and CONMIGRANTES. This initiative has implemented activities to provide counseling to deported citizens regarding financial matters. INSAMI, in turn, created the National Network of Returned Entrepreneurs of El Salvador, as well, to grant seed funding to deported Salvadorans (C. Ríos, personal communication, February 23, 2018).

There have been several campaigns in El Salvador regarding policies for missing and in-transit citizens, some to prevent or discourage emigration, others to promote it in a safe way, and some campaigns to provide information about emigrants' rights in transit. For instance, the "If you are thinking of migrating, the first step is to inform yourself" (*Si estás pensando migrar, el primer paso es informarte*) program was promoted by the Ministry of Foreign Affairs to address the consequences of undocumented emigration. Another example is the campaign "Do not Risk their Lives" (*No Pongas en Riesgo sus Vidas*), which was released to address the migration of unaccompanied minors in 2014 (Pedroza et al., 2016). In 2017, El Salvador created, by legislative decree, the Fund for Special Activities to Support Salvadorans Abroad and for Deported Nationals, which only Honduras had implemented before (Fondo de Actividades Especiales Para La Atención de Los Salvadoreños En El Exterior y Para Las Personas Retornadas, 2017).

Guatemala

According to the 2011 report on Actions and Achievements in Consular and Migration Matters: "The Ministry of Foreign Affairs welcomes deported citizens by providing a snack, free national and international calls, as well as currency exchange in a private national banking system" (MRE Guatemala, 2011). Guatemalan authorities have arranged a place at the airport with plastic chairs to receive deported migrants, in addition to a reception area at the Military Air Force facilities (F. Reynosa, personal communication, January 30, 2012).

In Guatemala in 2019, approximately three to five flights from the United States arrived weekly with 300 deported Guatemalans aboard (Gutiérrez & Manzanedo, 2019), a higher number than any other Central American country. The Human Rights Ombudsman visits the Air Force several times a month to interview deported nationals. During this process, a confidential survey is conducted with each deportee to profile and identify trends related to age, gender, place of origin, and whether the migrant was abused at the hands of organized criminals, whether Mexican or American. When human rights violations appear, the Ombudsman opens a file and sends it to the Ministry of Foreign Affairs, which then files a report against Mexico or the United State. However, none of the reports filed against these countries' authorities are known to have been resolved.

In addition to some private initiatives to provide employment options to deported nationals, there is one state program designed to facilitate the economic reintegration of deported citizens. A strategy called "Migrant Footprint," its main goal is to facilitate the labor insertion of deported citizens by building a database of the skills learned by migrants in the United States (Gándara, 2017). The work is done jointly with the Ministry of Foreign Affairs and the former Directorate for Migrant Services. The Migrant Footprint Program has two other strategic focuses: an alliance with the Technical Institute for Training and Productivity to provide training and to certify the competencies of the deported emigrant; and granting seed money to deported nationals for entrepreneurship projects, coordinated with the Ministry of the Economy. While the program was designed to guide returned emigrants to investment through micro and small businesses, the deported emigrants received more counseling than seed capital.

Policies for undocumented Guatemalans in transit do not go beyond providing legal assistance or basic documents, helping them while detained, or assisting with the process of returning minors. Even though it is quite recent, one important achievement is the Migration Code, which establishes measures for immigrants and emigrants in vulnerable conditions such as trafficking victims, unaccompanied minors, and missing persons. Before the Migration Code was approved in 2016, the Guatemalan government had intended to distribute a manual with information about possible organizations to contact in case of danger when in transit across Mexico or in the United States. Rather than a manual, however, this turned out to be merely a list of phone numbers (Pedroza et al., 2016). In 2020, the International Organization for Migration launched an information campaign on migration and COVID-19 in the Mayan languages in order to prevent stereotyping and discrimination against returned migrants in the NTCA (OIM, 2020b). In this context, the IOM is aiding governments with deported citizens from the United States and Mexico by delivering humanitarian assistance in shelters established for quarantine (OIM, 2020a).

"Don't be one more number! Don't travel illegally to the North" (*¡No seas un número más! No viajes ilegal al norte*), is an awareness-raising campaign promoted by the United States Embassy in Guatemala and released in 2016 to discourage undocumented migration. This campaign can be seen on Twitter and Facebook as well as on the back of public transportation vehicles in Guatemala City.

Figure 6   "Don't Be One More Number, Don't Travel Illegally to the North!"

Note. Photograph taken by the author, November 10, 2016, in Guatemala City.

Likewise, the United States Agency for International Development (USAID) financed a new online soap opera in Guatemala called "Stay Here" (¡*Quédate aquí!*), designed to convince Guatemalans not to migrate. All of these efforts are reflected in the comments made by Vice-President Harris in a joint briefing with Guatemalan President Giammattei on her first visit to the country on June 7, 2021, when she said: "I want to be clear to folks in this region who are thinking about making that dangerous journey to the US-Mexico border: Do not come. Do not come" (Sardiña, 2021). Finally, with regard to emigrants missing in transit, the former president of the Congressional Committee on Migration sent out a tweet announcing that a legislative initiative had been submitted that contains a procedure for emigrant families to search for their missing family members (Briere, 2019). However, the initiative has not made it past the initial bill stage to a first reading in Congress.

Honduras

In 2013, the IOM worked with the Law for the Protection of Honduran Migrants and their Families to create and later finance, in 2015, the Honduran Migrant Solidarity Fund to provide immediate assistance to deported nationals (Reforma al Artículo 29 de La Ley de Protección de Los Hondureños Migrantes y Sus Familiares, 2015). That same year and under the same law, a policy was implemented for the return of Hondurans abroad to set up centers for deported migrants, facilitate access to social security systems and the job market, provide in-kind support for returning single wage-earning women, and to offer traineeships to teach the skills necessary to find a job. To date, the Protection Law has only been valid for Hondurans in Spain, and depends on the support of the IOM, the European Fund for Return, and the Spanish Ministry for Employment and Education. It includes flights home, a one-time transfer of money upon return, and up to 20 hours of training on how to open a small business, as well as information about return conditions and psychological and employment counseling (Pedroza et al., 2016).

In Honduras, the Center for Returned Migrants (CAMR), an NGO that receives deported migrants, was founded in Tegucigalpa in 1999 on the initiative of the Pontifical Council for the Pastoral Care of Migrants and is supported by the volunteer work of some Scalabrinian missionaries. Through its DGM, the Honduran government has delegated some of its functions to civil society, allowing the Catholic Church to manage reception and care programs for deported migrants. "What we need is basic government services. Local governments need to understand what is happening and help their communities. We need small-scale businesses, training for women, so they do not just subsist on remittances. We need group therapy for deported migrants" stated Sister Valdette Willeman, a nun who directs CAMR at the airport where the deported migrants arrive (V. Willeman, personal communication, June 3, 2012). Finally, Honduras was the first sending state to implement a fund to cover the expenses for the repatriation of the deceased (O. Solís, personal communication, March 13, 2012).

6.3 Extracting Resources: Incorporating Migrants into the National Economy

The NTCA states also use policies that instill or capitalize on feelings of responsibility, loyalty, or obligation in their emigrant communities. This approach is more difficult than extending rights, because the coercive power of the origin state is severely restricted and usually relies on the cooperation of authorities in the host state.

6.3.1 Facilitating Investment Services, the Productive Use of Remittances, Matching Fund Programs

In many cases, a number of the policies geared toward emigrants are part of a broader effort to attract or channel remittances from emigrants. Leaders at the local, national, and international levels are all acutely aware of the potential economic engine represented by emigrants. To attract money from their citizens abroad, governments have adopted policies ranging from investment funds that pay higher-than-normal interest rates to matching funds for investment in public works.

El Salvador

A few administrative activities have been put in place to pursue the emigrant community and encourage them to invest in their home countries. The Investment Attraction Project for Salvadorans Abroad, for example, both offers incentives to small and medium-sized enterprises and provides advice about how to link remittances with businesses by putting emigrants in touch with financial institutions (Pedroza et al., 2016). The Investment Attraction Project offers advice to the families of Salvadorans abroad, mainly those in the United States, who hope to open a business at home with the remittances sent.

In 2011, El Salvador created the Technical and Productive Cooperation Project to decrease the cost of sending remittances to the country from abroad. In an interview with the director of INSAMI, César Ríos, he explained how this works:

Another way of sending remittances is using telephones. Someone owes someone else $50 and he sends it over the phone. Then, the one receiving the payment can go to a store and buy products for the same amount, but they cannot get the money in cash. The problem with this transaction method is that it works against the production of local farmers. Local farmers will find it even more difficult to sell their products, because the migrant's family is going to have to buy at the supermarket if the money is transferred via telephone. This is a business chain, because the money is being spent in supermarkets such as Walmart, an American chain, so the money is returning in a way to the same country. Money is also sent through credit cards from emigrants. Then the local banks are not receiving the money. This might result in scams or a lack of control by the national bank over how much money is actually entering the country, because these cards are from the United States (C. Ríos, personal communication, February 23, 2018).

In 2015 former Salvadoran Vice-Minister of Foreign Affairs, Liduvina Magarin, visited Los Angeles for a week to speak with emigrants, the private sector, scholars, and other important representatives of the Salvadoran community abroad in the framework of the celebration of the Day of the American Salvadoran. While there, she also took part in a tourist caravan, encouraging emigrants to spend their vacations with their families in El Salvador. Magarin took advantage of the opportunity to present options for the purchase of housing in the country. Finally, the Vice-Minister explained that it is especially important to recognize the importance of the Salvadoran emigrant community to the government of President Salvador Sánchez Cerén (MRE El Salvador, 2015b).

To date, many of the services offered to emigrants by the Salvadoran government do more to promote their continued participation in life in their home country than to ease their lives in their new home. For example, El Salvador's government has worked with private banks to revise its customs policies so that emigrants who want to move back to the country can import their belongings, including one car per household, without paying taxes and apply for low mortgage rates if they buy a house. Finally, Salvadorans who plan to return to live in El Salvador will pay no, or reduced, taxes upon retiring. (K. Sosa, personal communication, February 15, 2012).

Guatemala

In terms of policies to extract resources, Guatemala has lagged behind the other countries. Even with the large amount of remittances—almost 11 million dollars were sent to the country in 2019 (World Bank, 2019)—the state has been inactive, apart from just one program to promote the use of remittances for investment in small businesses. The Migrant Encounter program, part of the National Competitiveness Program led by the Ministry of the Economy, provides incentives for investment and the creation of productive businesses, using family remittances for sustainable projects (Pedroza et al., 2016). While some private initiatives direct remittances sent by emigrants for collective purposes, as of yet, there are no other public programs to incentivize remittances or to improve the channels used to transfer money.

There is an exemption from import duties for Guatemalans who reside abroad permanently that applies to the value-added tax (VAT) on their belongings, importing a car every five years, and cashing their retirement pension in Guatemala. This tax incentive also applies to foreigners who move to Guatemala for retirement and is part of a general migration policy, rather than a policy developed specifically for Guatemalan emigrants (Pedroza et al., 2016). Although Guatemalan officials clearly see the economic potential represented by Guatemalans living abroad, the country does not have many programs aimed at extracting those resources, probably because of its low institutional capacity.

Honduras

While not going as far as the Salvadoran state, Honduras has begun to make similar efforts. A number of Honduran mayors have visited the emigrant communities in the United States, looking for both political and financial support for their projects in local communities (La Prensa, 2019). Existing programs aim to reduce the costs of sending remittances, to improve financial services, and to promote investment in human capital, productive activities, and social infrastructure. Imitating the Mexican 3x1 Program, which helps Mexicans living abroad in the development of social infrastructure and productive projects, the Honduran state, in collaboration with the United Nations Development Program (UNDP), started Solidarity and Productive Remittances in 2010 to promote the investment of remittances in productive projects. The program matches remittances with an equal contribution from the government, the municipality, and the migrant. The program, however, was shut down, although the UNDP, the Vice-Ministry of Foreign Affairs, and the Secretary of Development and Social Inclusion from Honduras signed an agreement to reactivate the program in 2014 (Proceso Digital, 2015).

6.4 Concluding Remarks

As seen in the many projects related to the extension of rights in the preceding section, even though out-of-country voting has been implemented in all three countries, none of the governments have passed a law that allows emigrants to vote for legislative and municipal elections abroad, and only Honduras has approved the right to run for office. Honduras was the first sending state to approve this specific type of policy, while El Salvador—usually a pioneer—was the last of the three (something explained by the fear on the part of ARENA, the right-wing party that held power for over 20 years in the country, that the party would lose the election if out-of-country voting was approved for Salvadorans living in the United States). Dual nationality and out-of-country voting by NTCA citizens living abroad have little or no impact on undocumented emigrants, because very few have voted in past elections, perhaps due to some degree of wariness associated with having to go to their consulates to vote.

Regarding Hometown Associations, El Salvador, followed by Guatemala, has the most organizations of this type. This could be explained by the internal armed conflicts in these two countries that led a larger part of the population to seek asylum in the United States than Hondurans. The connections between the sending states and the HTAs in the United States indicate a desire to draw on human capital abroad and show that emigrant communities have a potential that goes beyond cash transfers.

There are more than enough regional institutions, plans, and projects, both at the multilateral and bilateral levels, in addition to state and non-state mechanisms and platforms to propose bills and set an emigration-based agenda. However, even though they may look good on paper, many of these policies have little or no impact in the region because the states lack the ability to enforce them. With specific regard to labor protection and migrant rights, all three countries ratified the International Convention on the Protection of the Rights of All Migrant Workers and Members of their Families in 1990 (United Nations, 2020b), a treaty devised to protect the human rights of international workers and their families. Even so, there are many concerns about the conditions in which migrants work abroad. Several programs promote migrant work abroad in Canada, Mexico, the United States, and even Spain, but the states fall short when it comes to protection programs. Before 2019, only Guatemala had ratified Convention No. 97 of the International Labor Organization concerning Migration for Employment; there is no sign that the Salvadoran or Honduran governments ratified the agreement.

All the Foreign Affairs Ministries in the three countries offer help with repatriating sick or deceased emigrants. Even though these are fairly common tasks provided by any state for their citizens abroad, the number of undocumented migrants who are missing, found dead in transit in Mexico, or who need legal aid because they were detained has grown out of proportion in the last two decades, particularly with the emigrant caravans. This has made it untenable for NTCA states to meet all the needs of their emigrants and their families. Although public officials from the NTCA have made several statements accepting their responsibility for their emigrants, they have not sent financial support to the families, paid for the repatriation of deceased, or helped the Mexican authorities or the Argentine Forensic Anthropology Team locate the missing emigrants in Mexico. Even so, the Salvadoran state has increased efforts to integrate its emigrant community. Proof of this is the Special Law for the Protection and Development of Salvadoran Migrant Persons and their Families, a piece of legislation that reflects the annual reports issued by a number of ministries asserting that the focus of the Salvadoran state regarding migration policy is to provide state services and protection for emigrant rights and to foster a sense of "rootedness" so that people will not want to leave the country.

Regarding the extraction of resources, in contrast to El Salvador and Honduras, as of 2019, the Guatemalan government had not yet implemented a program to attract funds, in part because officials felt that the government had to earn the trust of its emigrants before approaching them for support. However, even though Honduras has some programs and the fact that remittance inflows represent 21% of their Gross Domestic Product (INE Honduras, 2019), the country nonetheless falls short in the development of policies for its emigrant community.

Most of the measures implemented by the NTCA states analyzed in this chapter and discussed above are symbolic, such as, for instance, the reminders sent to their emigrant communities that they have a home country. More than a sense of national membership, such measures seek to promote a sense of national identity beyond national borders. If the governments cannot extend citizenship or guarantee access to and protection of rights abroad due to a lack of financial resources or political will, at least they can foster some loyalty by promoting the image that the government cares for its citizens abroad. However, as seen in the case of the migrant caravans, instead of offering these emigrants protection or making public the state's concern about their safety, the reaction of the NTCA countries has been to offer to contain the flows in order to make a good impression on the United States, without fully taking into account the fact that their citizens have started to migrate in caravans because they feel safer in groups and, most importantly, because they know that their state is not going to be there for them when they need it.

Part III

Explaining State-Led Transnationalism in Central America

Part XII

Chapter 7
The Conditions for a Higher Degree of State-Led Transnationalism

7.1 Introduction

In the Northern Triangle of Central America (NTCA), it does not seem possible to talk about a single migration public policy with clear macro orientations and common long-term institutional goals. This study, instead, has focused on policies beyond the normative idea of a public policy. In the countries under study—El Salvador, Guatemala, and Honduras—public policies are divided between different institutions that, most of the time, operate in an isolated, uncoordinated, and inconsistent way. This happens when policies are oriented at mitigating short-term needs, instead of planning for the long run. In this chapter, I argue that states have not only led the policy, plan, and program process, but that states—along with some non-state actors—have also managed to put the topic on the political agenda.

According to existing categories analyzed by a number of scholars (Gamlen, 2008; Levitt & de la Dehesa, 2003; Østergaard-Nielsen, 2003b), NTCA states adopt the following types of measures: 1) recognizing the emigrant community through the creation of institutions; 2) cultivating loyalties in the emigrant community through symbolic policies; 3) extending emigrants' rights; and 4) extracting resources by incorporating emigrants into the national economy. These categories were described thoroughly in Chapters 5 and 6.

To explain the motivations that lead migrant sending states to reach out to their emigrant community, this study uses an analytical framework that combines elements from international relations, new institutionalism, and policymaking which, together, hold a greater explanatory power.

As seen in Part II of this work, the three migrant sending states have taken different paths when it comes to emigrant policies. To explain why that is, this chapter presents an analysis of the different mechanisms that

NTCA states use to engage with their emigrant communities. The policy mechanisms used to classify the categories described above are: emigrant community building, which encompasses recognizing and cultivating the relationship with emigrant community; and emigrant community integration, which includes extending rights and extracting resources from emigrants.

Table 5   State Policy Mechanisms to Engage with the Emigrant Community

Sending State	Emigrant community building		Emigrant community integration	
	Recognizing the emigrant community	Cultivating loyalty among the emigrant community	Extending rights	Extracting resources
El S	X	X	X	X
GT	X	X	X	
HON		X	X	X

Note. Prepared by the author, based on fieldwork data.

This chapter elaborates on three explanatory variables for why states adopt certain policy packages and the different degrees of state-led transnationalism: 1) size and potential impact of the emigrant community in the country of origin; 2) party system competitiveness; and 3) the states' institutional capacity to implement policies.

Table 6   Explanations for State-led Transnationalism in the NTCA

Country	State-led transnationalism (Y)	Importance of the size and potential impact of the emigrant community in the origin country (X1)	Party system competitiveness (X2)	State's institutional capacity to implement policies (X3)
El Salvador	High	High	High	High
Guatemala	Low	High	Low	Low
Honduras	Moderate	Low	High	Low

Note. Prepared by the author.

Finally, I suggest some possible explanations both for the repertoire of policies that states employ and for how far states are willing to go to ensure that migrants remain enduring long-distance members. To that end, I propose the degree of state-led transnationalism as the dependent variable, which I operationalize as: 1) emigrant policy mechanisms and why a migrant-sending state engages with their emigrant community, either through policy building mechanisms or policy integration mechanisms; and 2) the variation in state involvement, which consists of analyzing three aspects: a) the key actors involved in each policy; b) the degree of state participation setting the agenda; and c) how states exercise their influence to set the agenda.

7.2 Size and Potential Impact of the Emigrant Community in the Country of Origin

7.2.1 The Emigrant Community Size

While migration is one of Central America's enduring livelihood strategies, the volume and dynamics have changed tremendously during recent decades. While armed conflict, political instability, human rights violations, and natural disasters drove Central Americans to migrate in the 1980s and early 1990s, continuing socioeconomic problems and widespread violence are the main factors behind the present movements (Sørensen, 2013a). However, migration has not affected the different Central American countries in the same way and to the same extent. The armed conflicts in El Salvador, Guatemala, and Nicaragua have produced larger migration flows from those countries than from more stable countries such as Costa Rica and Panama, and within each country the conflict zones have generated more migrants (Morales, 2007). When new conflicts occur—like the 2009 overthrow of Honduran President Manuel Zelaya— migration flows are instantly affected (Sørensen, 2013b), as is currently occurring with the Nicaraguans fleeing from President Daniel Ortega's regime and heading to Costa Rica. The distinction between earlier refugee movements (motivated by fear) and post-conflict migrations (economically motivated) is difficult to uphold in Central America. More recent migrants no longer qualify for refugee status according to the country of reception, although they often share several experiences with earlier pioneer refugees regarding exposure to regime instability and increasing levels of insecurity and extensive violence (Sørensen, 2013a).

Table 7   Number of Emigrants from Mexico and the NTCA Going to the US (2000–2019)

Country	2000	2005	2010	2015	2019
El Salvador	949,300	1,100,000	1,300,000	1,500,000	1,600,000
Guatemala	583,000	737,100	925,300	1,000,000	1,200,000
Honduras	343,300	449,300	587,900	731,100	800,700
Total NTCA	1,875,600	2,286,400	2,813,200	3,231,100	3,600,700
Mexico	9,600,000	10,800,000	12,400,000	11,900,000	11,800,000

Note. Prepared by the author with data from (United Nations Population Division, Department of Economic and Social Affairs, 2019).
The number of emigrants that appear each year are accumulated.

As shown in the following table, 11% of the total NTCA population was living in the United States in 2019 and for countries like El Salvador, 25% of its population lives there.

Table 8 NTCA Population by Country and Estimated Emigrant Population in the US in 2019

Country	Total population (millions)	Estimated population in the US
El Salvador	6.5	25%
Guatemala	16.3	7%
Honduras	9.2	9%
Total NTCA	32	11%

Note. Prepared by the author based on total population data from El Salvador (DIGESTYC, 2017), Guatemala (INE Guatemala, 2019), and Honduras (INE Honduras, 2019). NTCA emigrant population in the United States from (IOM, 2019).

During the 2000s, the number of international emigrants from the NTCA to the United States increased from 1.8 to more than 3.6 million in 2019 (IOM 2019b). Despite the peace accords signed in the 1990s and American pressure to impose strict migration controls in the region, undocumented migration from the NTCA continued.

7.2.2 The History of the Emigrant Community

Emigration from the NTCA to the United States through Mexico is largely a result of the political conflicts that took place in the region during the 1970s and 1980s. The wars in El Salvador and Guatemala, along with the various levels of repression, culminated in the displacement of approximately 1.5 to 2 million people to Mexico and the United States (Torres-Rivas & Jiménez, 1985). Even though Honduras did not suffer the high costs of internal military conflict, the country received more than 30,000 refugees fleeing the conflict in El Salvador. There have been four types of migration from the NTCA: internal, regional, transit and, after the mid-1990s, international migration driven by economic rather than political factors (Andrade-Eekhoff & Silva-Avalos, 2003).

After reaching record high levels in 2014, the flow of NTCA emigrants arriving at the US-Mexico border declined sharply in 2015.[19] Numerous factors contributed to the decline. First, the United States

---

19 Measured by total apprehensions at the southern United States border.

intensified its enforcement efforts at the border, targeting more resources towards investigating and prosecuting migrant smugglers and working with the NTCA governments on a public information campaign to discourage outflows (Alonzo 2015). Additionally, the three NTCA countries announced a large-scale development strategy in 2014 known as the Plan of the Alliance for Prosperity in the Northern Triangle (PAPTN) (Rosenblum & Ball, 2016). Mexico also implemented a major enforcement effort, the Southern Border Program, to secure its borders with Guatemala and Belize and block emigrant flows. Shortly afterwards, in 2015, the consulates of the NTCA and Mexico signed a joint declaration to create a consular coordination group in McAllen, Texas, TRICAMEX, to promote collaborative actions on matters of protection and consular assistance (see Chapter 6). Thus, while the drop in the number of migrants from the region in 2015 led some to believe that the regional migration "crisis" had been resolved, recent data shows that undocumented migration continues to increase. The table below illustrates how the number of apprehended migrants from the NTCA came to surpass those from Mexico in 2018.

Table 9   US Apprehensions of Central American and Mexican Migrants, 2012–2019

Country	2012	2013	2014	2015	2016	2017	2018	2019
El Salvador	38,976	51,226	79,321	51,200	78,983	59,687	42,132	99,750
Guatemala	57,486	73,208	97,151	66,982	84,649	81,909	135,354	285,067
Honduras	50,771	64,157	106,928	42,433	61,222	60,169	91,141	268,992
Total NTCA	147,233	188,591	283,400	160,615	224,854	201,765	268,627	653,809
Mexico	468,766	424,978	350,177	267,885	265,74	220,138	252,267	254,595

Note. Prepared by the author using data from (Guo, 2020).

Hondurans have become the second largest migrant group from the NTCA apprehended and deported by American authorities, after Guatemalans. Behind the numbers, the deportees consist of a diverse group of migrants, from settled migrants who have lived and worked in the United

States for 10, 20, or 30 years, to new arrivals apprehended during their first attempted unauthorized entry.

Table 10   US Deportation of Central American Migrants by Country, 2012–2019

Country	2012	2013	2014	2015	2016	2017	2018	2019
El Salvador	18,910	21,130	26,671	20,298	20,264	18,448	14,877	18,190
Guatemala	38,885	47,013	54,405	33,379	33,886	33,049	49,135	53,180
Honduras	31,724	31,724	40,877	20,298	22,015	22,163	28,451	40,751

Note. Prepared by the author using data from (Guo, 2020).

These numbers need to be multiplied by at least two to estimate how many more Central Americans have been deported by land from Mexico. The socio-political ramifications of current mass deportations remain very much under-examined and insufficiently explored in the region, but they definitely play an important role in every country's emigration history.

Those deported by air are most likely transported by New Mexico-based CSI Aviation Services Inc., which—due to American privatization of its detention and deportation operations—makes huge profits on the so-called removal business (Gammeltoft-Hansen, 2009). In fact, the company has become the largest provider of American deportation flights to Central America, with million-dollar contracts awarded by the Department of Homeland Security's Bureau of Immigration and Customs Enforcement (Kaye, 2017).

Despite the hardening of immigration policies in North America, NTCA emigrant flows have been steady. If increased regional enforcement explains falling emigrant arrivals in 2015, what accounts for the resurgence of flows beginning in 2016? Powerful push factors in the region and pull factors in the United States appear to be overwhelming the regional enforcement efforts.

In general, the underlying drivers of migration from Central America remain in place and have intensified. The region suffered a crisis in the agricultural sector and was hit by severe disasters such as Hurricane Mitch in 1998 and Hurricane Stan in 2005. In a survey asking recent NTCA migrants residing in the United States about their motivations for leaving, the main reason was economic. Almost 90% of Guatemalan migrants report economic reasons as the main reason for leaving their country of origin. The economic motivations reported include unemployment (43%), lack of sufficient work to cover needs (22%), and low wages (15%) (Abuelafia et al., 2019). Economic growth in the NTCA countries is below their peers in Latin America, with the three countries having some of the highest poverty rates in Latin America and the Caribbean. In 2017, 53% of Hondurans, 49% of Guatemalans, and 29% of Salvadorans lived on less than $5.50 per day (International Monetary Fund, 2019).

The region also has high levels of post-war violence. For several years, El Salvador, Guatemala, and Honduras have accounted for the highest murder rates in the world, with deaths frequently connected to drug trafficking and organized crime (UNODC, 2019). In El Salvador, a truce between rival gangs led to a reduction in homicides in 2012–13. However, violence intensified when the truce collapsed in 2014, and the country's homicide rate climbed in 2015 to the highest monthly total since the country's civil war (which ended in 1992); there was one murder every hour in El Salvador that year (Lakhani, 2015; Watts, 2015).

According to a United Nations Office on Drugs and Crime (UNODC) report, in 2016 El Salvador and Honduras were the countries with highest homicide rates in the world,[20] with 62.1 and 41.7 homicides for every 100,000 inhabitants respectively (UNODC, 2019). These numbers, along with the homicide rates in Guatemala, add up to 25.9 homicides per 100,0000 people and confirm that Central America is one of the most insecure regions in the world (Dalby & Carranza, 2019; UNODC, 2019). Moreover, it is possible to find mid-sized cities with homicide rates far above the national average (e.g. San Pedro Sula, Honduras) and cities of over 1 million inhabitants with above-average homicide rates, like Tegucigalpa (Honduras) with 91 homicides per 100,0000 people and Guatemala City with 65 homicides per 100,0000 people (UNODC 2019).

---

20 Excluding some subregions of Africa that might have higher rates, but for which complete data are not available (UNODC, 2019).

The pull factors driving migration flows from the NTCA countries vary. After three decades of migration from the region, about one in five Salvadorans and one in 15 Guatemalans and Hondurans already live in the US, making the United States an obvious destination for most families fleeing the region (Rosenblum and Ball 2016). In 2014, the United States responded to the surge of unaccompanied children and family units by increasing its reception and adjudication resources to begin hearings within three weeks of their arrival. However, chronic funding shortfalls for immigration courts meant that more than half of the cases opened in 2014 were still pending in 2015. Smugglers have used these slow processing times to lie to families, telling them that they will be granted immediate permission to reside in the country (Gianopoulos, 2015).

On October 12, 2018, a group of about 160 Hondurans set forth from the town of San Pedro Sula, which has been often referred to as the "murder capital of the world," in hopes of presenting themselves for asylum in Mexico or the United States. By October 15, the Associated Press estimated that around 1,600 Hondurans had gathered at the border with Guatemala (Pradilla, 2019). On January 15, 2020, another caravan leaving from Honduras started its journey north. Despite all the regional enforcement plans in Central America (see Chapter 6), the NTCA continues to push people to leave their homes.

7.2.3 The Emigrant Community's Degree of Organization

This section analyzes civil society organized around issues affecting emigrants in the country of origin, on the one hand, and Hometown Associations (HTAs) in the destination country, on the other.

In Honduras, the organized civil society organization working on behalf of emigrant rights is the National Forum for Migration in Honduras (FONAMIH), while in Guatemala it is the Liaison Group. During my fieldwork in El Salvador, I was unable to find a network or primary association that focused on migration. Rather, in that country, a number of actors are working separately, although sometimes in collaboration. This includes the José Simeón Cañas Central American University (UCA El Salvador), through its Communications Department, and the UCA Human Rights Institute (IDHUCA), which works together with the United Nations Development Program (UNDP) in El Salvador.

Although most Central American civil society groups in the United States are not officially declared Hometown Associations, they are very organized. In September 2004, for example, the U.S. State Department organized a historic event that brought together more than 100 Central American associations, including older groups like the Central American Resource Center (CARECEN), various chambers of commerce, and HTAs like the United Salvadoran Communities of Maryland, Washington, D.C., and Virginia. The participation of these associations demonstrates that there is some level of organization and interest in working on home country affairs (Orozco, 2006). No recent scholars have calculated the exact number of HTAs from the NTCA in the last decade, but the most recent study calculated the number at 26 for El Salvador, 31 for Guatemala, and 16 for Honduras (Orozco, 2006), meaning that Guatemala and El Salvador have the highest number of migrant associations in the United States.

Like all the HTAs from El Salvador, Guatemala, and Honduras, the majority of the members are migrants from the same community in their country of origin. As a result, the international activities of these groups are focused on their municipalities, and association leaders in the United States maintain close ties to community leaders in their hometowns. Some groups have also made it part of their mission to assist the emigrant community in the United States with everything from legal to social services.

7.2.4 Current Remittances from the Emigrant Community

A comment from an interview with César Ríos, director of INSAMI, a civil society organization in El Salvador, summarizes what remittances mean to the NTCA: "Our 'oil' is the remittances sent to El Salvador from the US" (C. Ríos, personal communication, February 23, 2018). Migrants both fulfill a demand for cheaper labor in the United States and, at the same time, earn money to send to their families. Indeed, the financial impact of migration has been extremely important for these countries' economies because of their high dependence on remittances.

Across the region, the individual experiences and characteristics associated with migration include being young, living in a low-income household, being a low-skilled worker, being unemployed, being a skilled worker with at least a high school education, having an unfavorable outlook on the future economic situation, having been victimized, and having transnational ties. Most notably, young people are twice as likely to consider migrating than their older counterparts (Orozco, 2020).

Table 11   Characteristics of those Considering Migration from the NTCA, 2019

Indicator	El Salvador	Guatemala	Honduras	Total
Percentage of people who would consider emigrating	24%	18%	33%	25%
Is between 18 and 29 years old	38%	44%	42%	41%
Has at least a high school education	62%	55%	50%	55%
Has been a victim of a crime or knows someone close who has been	25%	26%	22%	24%
Believes that conditions are worse off now than before	46%	44%	65%	54%
Believes that conditions will be worse next year	17%	23%	50%	34%
Unemployed	12%	10%	14%	12%
Household lives on less than $400 monthly and cannot make ends meet	32%	36%	40%	36%
Occupation as laborer	26%	43%	38%	35%
Has a relative living in the US	66%	50%	76%	67%
Receives remittances	35%	28%	46%	38%
Has been deported	2%	1%	6%	4%

Note. Adapted from (Orozco, 2020). Copyright 2020 by the Inter-American Dialogue. Reprinted with permission.

A range of economic issues influence whether residents from these countries consider migrating. Living in a household that earns less than $400 a month and cannot make ends meet makes people 1.24 times more likely to think about migration. Believing that conditions are worse off today than they were last year makes people 1.67 times more likely to consider migrating. Labor market conditions also matter and while having a relative abroad does not make a person more likely to think about migrating, receiving remittances does. However, the statistical interaction between receiving remittances and having a relative abroad is significant, yielding a 71% chance that the person has thought of migrating (Orozco, 2020).

Despite the income that these countries earn from remittances, their governments do not do enough to provide deported migrants with a job, health, education, or reintegration opportunities once they are back in their home country. This suggests that governments are applying a "policy of no policy" by letting migrants re-emigrate so that they can continue to send economic remittances (Rosales Sandoval, 2021). The following table details what remittances represent for these countries:

Table 12   Emigrant Remittance Inflows (Million Dollars) from 2000 to 2019 and as a Share of Gross Domestic Product

Country	2000	2005	2010	2015	2019	Remittances as a share of GDP in 2019 (%)
El Salvador	1,765	3,029	3,472	4,275	5,609	20.8
Guatemala	596	3,067	4,232	6,573	10,696	13.0
Honduras	484	1,805	2,618	3,666	5,283	21.4
Total NTCA	2,844	7,900	10,322	14,514	21,588	--

Note. Prepared by the author using data from (World Bank 2019).
All numbers are in current (nominal) United States dollars.

According to activists from the National Forum for Migration in Honduras, 90% of deportees will attempt to migrate again as quickly as possible (K. Valladares, personal communication, March 12, 2012). From the perspective of the remittance-dependent states, this can mean that rather than being invested in local development, substantial sums are used on repeated migration attempts. Consequently, expectations for a developmental impact from incoming remittances may be far too high. A survey conducted with more than 1,000 United States immigrants from eight Latin American and Caribbean nations during the COVID-19 pandemic found that people continued to send remittances despite having lost their jobs, working fewer hours, or being affected by the spread of the virus. More specifically, it showed that the likelihood of sending remittances under these circumstances increased when people had children in their home country and a stronger financial base. Moreover, the continuity with which migrants sent money during 2020 and the increases already seen in the first quarter of 2021 indicates that migrants are better prepared to face adverse situations, such as a crisis that results in economic lockdown (Orozco & Klaas, 2021).

7.2.5 The Out-of-Country Voting Rights of Emigrants

During its first term in power in El Salvador, the left-wing Farabundo Martí National Liberation Front decided to enact out-of-country voting, fearing that otherwise, they would lose in the upcoming election against the right-wing Nationalist Republican Alliance, which they did not. In January 2012, with 82 votes, the Salvadoran Congress approved the Special Law for the Exercise of Voting from Abroad. Article 4 of this Law allows Salvadoran citizens residing outside of the country to exercise their right to vote from wherever they are by mail (Ley Especial Para El Ejercicio Del Voto Desde El Exterior En Las Elecciones Presidenciales, 2013). The Law also proposed a project for the municipalities to be able to create specialized units to provide advice to migrant families (K. Sosa, personal communication, February 15, 2012). The Supreme Electoral Court registered 350,638 Salvadorans abroad for the 2019 elections. While this is still a low figure considering that the estimated number of Salvadorans abroad was 1.6 million that same year (IOM, 2019), it does not diminish the importance of granting the right to vote to citizens abroad. Out-of-country voting has been taken advantage of by 9,241 Salvadorans abroad in the two electoral processes since the law was passed, which means an average of 3,080 voters in each election (TSE El Salvador, 2020).

Emigrant Guatemalans voted abroad for the first time in the most recent elections of 2019. However, migrants described the result as a "failure," since only 734 emigrants voted. Guatemalans abroad strongly criticized the fact that only four voting centers were set up in the United States, requiring some voters to travel enormous distances. However, for the president of the Supreme Court, the exercise of the vote abroad should not be judged by the number of voters, but by the fact that it modernized the electoral system (S. Morales, 2019).

Honduras was the first NTCA country to allow out-of-country voting, passing the measure in 2001. The Law for the Exercise of Suffrage for Hondurans Abroad is now in the Electoral Act as amended in the 2004. Out-of-country voting in Honduras has taken place five times in seven cities[21] in the United States since it was designated by law in 2001. However, for the 2021 elections, Hondurans abroad are expected to be able to vote from any of the country's 50 consulates, not only in the United States, but also in other countries with a high number of Honduran citizens, including Costa Rica, El Salvador, Guatemala, Mexico, Nicaragua, Panama, and Spain (El Heraldo, 2020). Out-of-country voting has been exercised by 13,627 Hondurans abroad in the five electoral processes since the law was passed, an average of 2,725 in each election (TSE Honduras, 2020).

Table 13   Out-of-Country Voting Average in each Election since it was Approved in the NTCA

Country	Average voters in each election	Number of elections since out-of-country voting was passed
El Salvador	4,621	2
Guatemala	734	1
Honduras	2,725	5

Note. Prepared by the author using data from (S. Morales, 2019; TSE El Salvador, 2020; TSE Honduras, 2020).

El Salvador has the highest average number of votes abroad, and the fact that Salvadorans living outside the country are advocating for the right to vote in legislative and municipal elections as well is highly indicative of their commitment to their country of origin.

---

21   Atlanta, Houston, Los Angeles, Miami, New Orleans, New York, and Washington.

The five indicators for the size of the NTCA emigrant community and its potential impact on sending states to propose emigrant policy are summarized in the following table.

Table 14   Size and Potential Impact of Emigrant Communities on a Sending State Proposing Emigrant Policy

Country	El Salvador	Guatemala	Honduras
Emigrant community size	High	Medium	High
Emigrant community history	High	High	Low
Emigrant community organization	High	Medium	Low
Dependence on remittances	High	Medium	High
Importance out-of-country voting	High	Low	High

Note. Prepared by the author.

In short, if the emigrant community size is high, the sending state is more likely to propose policies for its emigrants. Even though El Salvador and Guatemala score higher with regard to the history of their emigrant community because of the armed conflicts in the region, El Salvador and Honduras are the countries with a higher dependence on remittances and have a higher percentage of their population abroad. Out-of-country voting has been an option for the longest time in those two countries and has had an actual impact on electoral results. However, the fact that the Honduran emigrant community has a shorter history of migrating to the United States makes it less organized, revealing how social capital has a significant explanatory power in terms of the potential impact of the emigrant community in the country of origin.

7.3 Party System Competitiveness

In the NTCA countries, the degree to which political parties are engaged with their country's emigrant community plays an important role in the creation of disputes about emigrant policies. Here, party system competitiveness is divided into two indicators: fragmentation (the effective number of parties at the electoral level) and polarization (interparty ideological differences), both of which are analyzed in this section.

How do parties in migrant-sending countries engage with the emigrant community? Migrants exercise an increasingly important voice in electoral politics in their countries of origin. Even when they often cannot either vote legally or vote in very low numbers, the political parties attempt to leverage the influence they believe migrants have over voters at home. However, the degree and way in which parties reach out to emigrants varies widely.

Several scholars have provided some insights regarding party engagement with emigrant communities in general (Ciornei & Østergaard-Nielsen, 2020; Délano Alonso & Mylonas, 2017; Waldinger, 2013), but so far, only scarce information is available for the NTCA. With a focus on electoral participation by citizens residing abroad, Paarlberg (2017) explores outreach efforts by political parties. Unpacking the various mechanisms through which political parties try to influence potential voters (at home and abroad), he presents the emigrant community not only as voters, but as activists, fundraisers, lobbyists, candidates, influencers from afar, and symbols in party campaign messages. This section looks at how other actors beside governments, like political parties, look for economic and political support in the emigrant community and how, on the one hand, the effective number of parties affect the relationship with the emigrant community and, on the other, ideology still plays a role in the NTCA countries.

7.3.1 Fragmentation

Party systems have long been classified into types defined by the number and relative size of the party, with Laakso and Taagepera presenting the concept of the effective number of electoral parties (ENEP) based on shares of the vote. According to this concept, the number of parties equals the effective number of electoral parties only when all parties have equal strength. In any other case, the effective number of electoral parties is lower than the actual number of parties. This measure is especially useful when comparing party systems across countries.

El Salvador

Compared to Guatemala and Honduras, El Salvador is without a doubt the country where party system competitiveness plays the most important role in state-led transnationalism, that is, the degree upon which a state engages with their emigrant community.

Table 15   Effective Number of Electoral Parties in El Salvador, 2019

No.	Parties	% of votes	ENEP calculation	ENEP
1	Grand Alliance for National Unity (GANA)	53.1	0.28	
2	Nationalist Republican Alliance (ARENA)	31.72	0.10	
3	Farabundo Martí National Liberation Front (FMLN)	14.41	0.02	2
4	VAMOS	0.77	0.00	
	Total	100.00	0.40	

Note. Prepared by the author based on data from (TSE El Salvador, 2019).
Calculated using the formula: ENEP=$1/\Sigma vi^2$.

Even though new political parties have emerged in El Salvador in recent presidential elections, the ENEP has been two since 2009. The two main parties that have maintained the traditional battle for migrants' votes are ARENA and FMLN. However, in the 2019 elections, the Grand Alliance for National Unity (GANA), which had been on the scene since 2010, overwhelmingly won thanks to "punishment votes" against the poor performance of the presidency of Salvador Sánchez Cerén, making its leader, Nayib Bukele, Salvadoran president that year. Although GANA initially had the support of the emigrant population, the decision of El Salvador's "millennial president" (so called by the media) to deploy troops to the then opposition-controlled Congress during a clash between the president and Congress over an emergency loan for the coronavirus response in February 2020 lost him support among both the emigrant community and the general population in El Salvador. President Bukele's actions have, in fact, generally skewed anti-democratic. The deployment measure was harshly criticized by the international community, including American President

Trump's ambassador to El Salvador, Ronald Douglas Johnson (Pozzebon, 2021). Vinicio Sandoval, director of a Salvadoran civil society organization that works with migrants described the situation thus:

> President Bukele had great support from the emigrant community in the United States. However, due to recent events, such as restricting civic space freedoms, the support seems to have decreased. That is why for the legislative and municipal elections, the legislature did not pass out-of-country voting, which had been planned for the 2021 elections. The hypothesis is that President Bukele was afraid to lose the majority in Congress he achieved without the emigrant community, which is now more critical of his government (V. Sandoval, personal communication, June 17, 2021).

During his presidential campaign and the first year of his presidency, President Bukele presented himself as an admirer and close ally of former President Trump, who praised the young leader in tweets for working well with the United States on migration matters. Nevertheless, the American relationship with President Bukele appears to be cooling under President Joseph Biden, although El Salvador remains a strategic partner for the country in Central America, particularly as Washington attempts to stem migration flows into the United States with the cooperation of Central American governments.

Even with President Bukele losing support from the emigrant community, the fact that El Salvador continues to have two effective parties makes the emigrant community feel both represented and important in the eyes of the parties and their candidates. In 2021, legislative and municipal elections are taking place and even if the emigrant community will not be able to vote, the question is on the agenda and out-of-country voting for non-presidential elections may have been enacted by the next time voters go to the polls. This is no small accomplishment, given that only seven countries in Latin America have passed out-of-country voting for legislative and municipal elections.

Guatemala

Guatemalan law does not explicitly regulate political competition abroad. Although funding by foreigners and foreign organizations is forbidden, the Electoral Law makes no mention of campaigns abroad (Reformas al Decreto Número 1-85 de La Asamblea Nacional Constituyente, Ley Electoral y de Partidos Políticos, 2016). There have been reports of Guatemalan politicians campaigning overseas. For instance, on August 11, 2019 in Los

Angeles, presidential candidate and current President Alejandro Giammattei held meetings with the emigrant community and invited them and their relatives to vote (Macías, 2019).

Table 16   Effective Number of Electoral Parties in Guatemala, 2019

No.	Parties	% of votes	ENEP calculation	ENEP
1	National Unity of Hope (UNE)	25,53	0,07	
2	VAMOS	13,96	0,02	
3	Humanist Party of Guatemala (PHG)	11,22	0,01	
4	Movement for the Liberation of Peoples (MLP)	10,37	0,01	
5	National Advancement Party (PAN)-PODEMOS	6,08	0,00	
6	Vision with Values (VIVA)	5,90	0,00	
7	WINAQ	5,22	0,00	
8	National Convergence Front (FCN)-NACION	4,12	0,00	
9	Commitment, Renewal, and Order (CREO)	3,75	0,00	
10	TODOS	3,13	0,00	8
11	VICTORIA	2,54	0,00	
12	Guatemalan National Revolutionary Unity (URNG MAIZ)	2,16	0,00	
13	UNIONISTA	1,43	0,00	
14	Together for Guatemala (EG)	1,15	0,00	
15	LIBRE	0,95	0,00	
16	CONVERGENCIA	0,86	0,00	
17	UNIDOS	0,61	0,00	
18	Patriotic Party (PP)	0,54	0,00	
19	AVANZA	0,48	0,00	
	Total	100	0.12	

Note. Prepared by the author with data from (TSE Guatemala, 2019).

Calculated using the formula: $ENEP = 1/\Sigma vi^2$.

The ENEP number for Guatemala increases election after election, making it impossible for migrants to stand out amid the large number of parties. The statutes of the various Guatemalan political parties generally do not regulate emigrant membership. Only two parties (out of dozens), National Development Action and the Patriot Party (PP), have a secretary in charge of migrant issues, which indicates that migrants are eligible for membership and that they are also, at least symbolically, considered a constituency (Pedroza et al., 2016).

Honduras

There is a legal vacuum on this issue in Honduras. The Electoral Law regulates political campaigns and propaganda, but there is no mention of political campaigns abroad or external political party offices. The only prohibition refers to political funding by foreign natural or legal persons. Emigrant membership in political parties is formally permitted without restrictions, thus leaving it to the parties to decide the terms of their membership. The statutes of the Honduran National Party (PNH), for example, provide an example of a party that seeks emigrant membership, while the Honduran Liberal Party (PLH) restricts membership to residents (D. Matamoros, personal communication, March 14, 2012).

Table 17 Effective Number of Electoral Parties in Honduras, 2017

No.	Parties	% of votes	ENEP calculations	ENEP
1	Honduran National Party (PNH)	42.95	0.18	
2	Liberty and Refoundation Party (LIBRE) and Party of Innovation and Unity (PINU) Coalition	41.42	0.17	
3	Honduran Liberal Party (PLH)	14.74	0.02	
4	Honduran Patriotic Alliance (APH)	0.2	0.00	
5	Anti-Corruption Party (PAC)	0.18	0.00	3
6	Christian Democratic Party (DC)	0.18	0.00	
7	Democratic Unification Party (PUD)	0.14	0.00	
8	Broad Political Front (FA)	0.10	0.00	
9	Va Solidarity Movement (VAMOS)	0.09	0.00	
	Total	100.00	0.38	

Note. Prepared by the author based on data from (TSE Honduras, 2017). Calculated using the formula: $ENEP = 1/\Sigma vi^2$.

Even though the number of effective electoral parties has risen in the last 10 years, as shown in table above, the ENEP remains low, with only three parties and a resulting political dispute over migrants, at least in the 2013 elections.

Table 18 presents a comparison of the effective number of parties in the NTCA in the countries' last three elections.

Table 18   Effective Number of Parties in the NTCA, 2009–2019

Country	Election	ENEP
El Salvador	2019	2
El Salvador	2014	2
El Salvador	2009	2
Guatemala	2019	8
Guatemala	2015	7
Guatemala	2011	4
Honduras	2017	3
Honduras	2013	4
Honduras	2009	2

Note. Prepared by the author with data from: (NDI, 2009; TSE El Salvador, 2009, 2014, 2019; TSE Guatemala, 2011, 2015, 2019; TSE Honduras, 2013, 2017).
Calculated using the formula: $ENEP = 1/\Sigma vi^2$.

As seen in the table, despite having new political parties on the scene and no longer being a two-party system—as it was during the more than 20 years that ARENA and FMLN competed with each other—the effective number of electoral parties continues to be two in El Salvador. Consequently, the battle for emigrant community loyalty continues.

Honduras is in second place, with between two and three ENEPs in a period of almost 10 years. As a result, the few parties in the electoral arena have focused on the emigrant community in their competition for votes. The main differences between El Salvador and Honduras are related to the fact, first, that the two main parties in the latter country are on the right, and second, that the country has an obstructed civic space (CIVICUS, 2021). President Juan Orlando Hernández, who won the 2013 Honduran general election, began his second presidential term in 2018 amid allegations of fraud. Thus, the battle over migrants is no longer a major concern in the country, because the elections are no longer truly free.

Guatemala's parties are those that compete the least for the migrant vote for two main reasons: first, the electoral law only passed out-of-country voting for the 2019 election with the participation of only 734 emigrants; and second, the number of effective electoral parties is high. As seen in Table 18, from 2011 to 2019, the ENEP rose from four to eight parties. The high level of party fragmentation so weakens the demands of the emigrant community that they end up not having a voice. Furthermore, the parties are not as interested in lobbying the emigrant community because they know their votes will not secure a victory.

Table 19 Evolution of Parties According to the Type of Party System

Country	Presidential Election	Parties with Majority of Votes	Type of Party System
El Salvador	1999	FMLN/Social Christian Union (USC), ARENA	Polarized multiparty
	2004	FMLN/USC, ARENA	Polarized multiparty
	2010	FMLN/USC, ARENA	Polarized multiparty
	2014	FMLN, ARENA	Polarized multiparty
	2019	Grand Alliance for National Unity (GANA), ARENA, FMLN	Moderate multiparty
Guatemala	1999	Institutional Republican Party (FRG), PAN	Moderate multiparty
	2003	UNE, Grand National Alliance (GANA), FRG	Moderate multiparty
	2007	UNE, GANA, PP	Moderate multiparty
	2011	PP, Renewed Democratic Liberty LIDER, UNE	Moderate multiparty
	2015	FCN-NACION, UNE, LIDER	Moderate multiparty
	2019	VAMOS, UNE, PHG	Moderate multiparty
Honduras	1997	PLH, PNH	Moderate two-party
	2001	PLH, PNH	Moderate two-party
	2005	PLH, PNH	Moderate two-party
	2009	PLH, PNH	Moderate two-party
	2013	PLH, LIBRE, PNH	Polarized two-party
	2017	PNH, LIBRE/PINU Coalition, PLH	Polarized multiparty

Note. Prepared by the author with data from (Alcántara Sáez, 2008b; Artiga-González, 2000; Avelar, 2019).

As noted above, although El Salvador is classified as having a moderate multiparty system, historically there have been two main political parties, along with several other minor or less influential parties. However, that changed in the 2019 election when an outsider party came into power. It remains to be seen what will happen with the emigrant community and the traditional party competition for their loyalty in the next elections.

7.3.2 Polarization

In Central America, even if a number of political parties have achieved some degree of permanence and continuity, other party formations and political coalitions in the region are volatile (Cerdas, 1995). Cerdas and Artiga-González are among the few scholars who have analyzed party systems in Central America and whose work provides a basis to examine interparty ideological distance. The following table shows the ideological self-positioning of parties in the NTCA, based on their webpages.

Table 20 Ideological Self-Positioning of Political Parties in the NTCA from 2004 to 2019

Country	Period	Party with Majority of Votes	Ideological Position
El Salvador	2006–2009	ARENA	Far Right
	2010–2019	FMLN	Extreme Left
		GANA	Right
Guatemala	2004–2011	PAN	Right
		FRG	Far Right
		GANA	Far Right
		UNE	Center
		PP	Right
	2012–2019	FCN-NACION	Far Right
		VAMOS	Far Right
Honduras	2006–2010	PLH	Center-Right
		PNH	Far Right
	2011–2019	LIBRE/PINU Coalition	Center-Left
		PLH	Center-Right
		PNH	Far Right

Note. Prepared by the author based on Alcántara, 2008; Artiga-González, 2000 and from political party webpages.

Based on interviews with Salvadoran party elites, party documents, and a historical comparison of the campaign activities of El Salvador's two major parties, ARENA and FMLN, over three presidential elections, the FMLN has considered the emigrant community more fully than the far-right ARENA or even the right-wing GANA. With a hierarchical model and a base committee structure, FMLN more effectively mobilizes emigrant community support, while ARENA, with a horizontal model and sectoral structure, finds party-emigrant coordination difficult and largely makes indirect and symbolic references to emigrant community issues (Paarlberg, 2017). Irene Palma, Executive Director of the Central American Institute of Social Studies and Development (INCEDES), explains the role of political parties in El Salvador in creating institutions and legal reform to the benefit of emigrants:

> President [Mauricio] Funes was an outsider in the FMLN party, but they were strategic, because he had characteristics the party needed to win and implement their projects. ARENA, on the other hand, unlike other parties in the region, created a program to provide services to Salvadorans abroad at the beginning of the 2000s, an institution within the Foreign Affairs Ministry, and while this was a great improvement, the FMLN made a complete reform to the Migration Law and created the National Council for the Protection and Development of the Emigrant and its Family (CONMIGRANTES) in 2011, two years after being elected. In such short time, they enacted institutional migration reform, unlike ARENA's 20 years of ruling the country, when it created only one program. The FMLN started to work with local governments as well towards improving migration conditions, such as the regularization of Nicaraguan migrant workers in El Salvador. The FMLN victory brought about great improvements for emigration regulation in El Salvador. (I. Palma, personal communication, February 8, 2012)

According to Alcántara, the polarization in El Salvador between ARENA and the FMLN has been the most extreme in Latin America (Alcántara Sáez 2008). As the two parties that have traditionally obtained a majority of the votes are always the same, there is little opportunity for the minority parties to be truly competitive.

Out-of-country voting was passed by Congress in El Salvador in 2013 after ten years of debate between the political parties. The law, which was originally proposed by the FMLN in 2010, passed along with the migration law. Out-of-country voting was accompanied by intense political struggles between ARENA and the FMLN. During the electoral campaign in 2009, ARENA accused the FMLN of attempting to break political and economic relations with the United States; consequently, migration benefits for the country, such as remittances, would be interrupted. On the contrary, during the party's years in power, the FMLN made important improvements regarding emigrant policy.

In Guatemala, struggles over the emigrant community have not been part of the political scene. During the last three legislative terms, only a few political parties have included migration initiatives in their platforms. Neither is interparty ideological distance a topic in the country. Guatemala has one of the most volatile party systems in the region, which is reorganized before every electoral event (Ajenjo, 2008). Given the extreme volatility of the country's party system and the reduction, creation, and formation of new coalition parties, the tendency is to vote for right to far right parties, except in the case of National Unity of Hope (UNE), which positions itself as centrist, social democratic party. Guatemala also has one of the least polarized systems, since there has not been a left-wing electoral party like Guatemalan National Revolutionary Unity (URNG) since the 1980s, when the coalition played a weak role in the peace process. While Guatemala has many competing parties, none are particularly different from one another.

Honduras has had two parties competing since the end of the 19th century and is a stable two-party system with a curious characteristic. Despite being a moderate two-party system for years—and now a multiparty system—the parties do not fight much over the emigrant community. This is due to the fact that the center of the political spectrum tends towards the right, so there are really no ideological differences between the parties to fight over. In short, the countries with a two-party system, such as El Salvador and, to a lesser degree, Honduras take more action on policies related to emigration.

7.4 The State's Institutional Capacity to Implement Policies

One of the explanatory factors examined in this study is the capacity that states have to implement public policy. Using a study of the Inter-American Development Bank by Stein et al., (2005), "The Politics of Policies: Economic and Social Progress in Latin America," this variable is operationalized for the NTCA countries by the key features of public policies (see Chapter 3 for the operationalization of explanatory variables):

- a) Adaptability: the extent to which policies can be adjusted when they fail or when circumstances change;
- b) Stability: the extent to which policies are stable over time;
- c) Coordination: the degree to which policies are consistent with related policies and result from well-coordinated actions among the actors who participate in their design and implementation;
- d) Implementation and enforcement: the extent to which the state ensures the effective implementation of public policies;
- e) Efficiency: the extent to which policies reflect an allocation of scarce resources that ensures high returns; and
- f) Public regardedness: the degree to which policies pursue the public interest. (Stein et al., 2005)

The table below shows the scores for each sending state according to the state's institutional capacity to implement policies.

Table 21 State Institutional Capacity to Implement Policies since 1980 in the NTCA

Country	El Salvador	Guatemala	Honduras
Adaptability	High	Medium	Medium
Stability	High	Medium	High
Coordination	Medium	Medium	Medium
Implementation and Enforcement	High	Low	Medium
Efficiency	High	Medium	Medium
Public Regardedness	Medium	Low	Low

Note. Adapted from (Stein et al., 2005) Copyright 2005 by the Inter-American Development Bank. Reprinted with permission.

This table shows that El Salvador scores the highest on most indicators related to the state's institutional capacity to implement policies, followed by Honduras. This can be explained by the relative stability of Honduras's political system. Guatemala does not score high on any of the indicators and scores low for implementation and enforcement, one of the most important policy qualities.

7.4.1 Adaptability

Given the great challenges facing the NTCA consular networks due to financial and institutional incapacity, the Foreign Affairs Ministries in the three countries have all taken actions to improve services for emigrants. They began by sharing office space in Mexico to save money in a variety of areas. Second, they established mobile consulates in the United States where none existed. Even if these changes largely entailed making traditional consular services operational, these actions, implemented ten years ago, represented the start of a change in the administration of state services for emigrants, with the NTCA states joining forces.

7.4.2 Stability

In October 2018, the Associated Press estimated that around 1,600 Hondurans had gathered at the border with Guatemala (Pradilla, 2019). Then again in January 2020, another caravan leaving from Honduras started its journey to the United States, followed by yet another one containing around 3,000 migrants in March 2021. All three caravans fueled the debate over United States immigration policy. At the time, the Trump administration entered into Safe Third Country Agreements (STCA) disguised as Asylum Cooperative Agreements with the NTCA countries—particularly Guatemala—to require people traveling through that country to seek refuge from persecution there instead of in the United States. However, critics have said that the law clearly requires that the "safe third country" is truly a safe place, where migrants are not in danger, an assurance that Guatemala cannot provide. One year later, however, the Guatemalan government declared it had not and would not sign such an agreement. Then in 2021, just days before the visit of Vice-President Kamala Harris to

Guatemala, the United States government confirmed that it would open several centers for migrants in the NTCA seeking to reach and request asylum in the United States, and that the first of them would begin to provide resources to migrants in Guatemala. The centers will offer advisory services to migrants who need legal advice to enter the United States, as well as those who need protection, asylum referrals, and refugee relocation (Arciniegas, 2021). This is a center for migrants and asylum seekers disguised as an STCA, a clear example of how unstable state policies are in Guatemala.

El Salvador, in contrast, has shown more policy stability over the years. The country's strategy has been summarized by the Vice-Minister for Salvadorans Abroad thus: "We know that in five years we are not going to solve this complex problem. What do we want to leave the country after our term of office? Institutional practices, irreversible processes" (J. J. García, personal communication, February 27, 2012). The strategy for policy stability in El Salvador, then, is to leave institutions that outlast presidential terms. This can be seen in the number of working institutions that El Salvador has created for its emigrant community, one example being the Vice-Ministry for Salvadorans Abroad, the first organization of its type in the region.

7.4.3 Coordination

The performance of all three NTCA states is rated "medium" when it comes to coherence and the coordination of public policies. A good case in point is Guatemala and its Migration Code. The main criticism of the Code is that even though it represents a major improvement for the country, in its intention to be very specific, it ends up being very bureaucratic, having created at least one institution—the Guatemalan Institute of Migration—and two boards—the Guatemalan Immigration System and National Immigration Authority. These bodies can require their own regulation codes, meetings between high-ranking public officials every three months, and other complex provisions that may be hard to comply with in the near future. At the same time, at least two other institutions were created before the Code that set regular meetings to discuss emigrant issues:

first, the Vice-Ministry for the Assistance of Guatemalans, whose purpose is to design emigration strategies (including the creation of a Migrant Service Center to manage consular issues and provide improved services to the emigrant community abroad); and second, CONAMIGUA, which was created to assist the emigrant community abroad. Many of the activities of these institutions overlap and, instead of providing support and coordination to the emigrant community, create more confusion and a dispersion of functions.

7.4.4 Implementation and Enforcement

The lack of resources—in this case the failure to provide consuls with transportation—means that these officials cannot visit the emigrant community working in the southern Mexican state of Chiapas as often as they would like. In this regard, Edgar Ruano, the former Guatemalan consul in Chiapas, has remarked that:

> One of the main difficulties we have as consuls is the lack of resources in the Ministry of Foreign Affairs. They have not provided consuls with cars, and we need them to pay visits to the emigrant workers in [the southwest Chiapas region of] Soconusco. I have been using my own car to visit them in recent years. (E. Ruano, personal communication, June 1, 2012)

The implementation of consular supervision in Mexico is a hard task without the necessary means, and the documented human rights violations in temporary foreign workers' programs demonstrate the need for and importance of consular visits (Gesualdi-Fecteau et al., 2017).

The reception of deported citizens is another policy area where a lack of policy implementation and enforcement is evident. While the aim of these programs is to provide protection to emigrants detained abroad and later deported to their countries of origin, in the cases of Guatemala and Honduras, they often end up merely providing services. Both states delegate their functions to international organizations, such as the IOM or USAID, and to religious NGOs for the implementation and enforcement of the reception of deported nationals (Rosales Sandoval, 2021). Although there is a program for deported nationals, they come back to a country of origin without any effective state program for reception and integration. To the deported migrant, deportation usually represents a catastrophe. To the receiving state, the deportee represents a burden. Stripped of his or her economic capacity, the "migrant hero" of the remittance-dependent state instantly becomes "deportee trash" (Sørensen 2011). Deported migrants are kept out of sight, with their planes arriving at the Military Air Force portion of the facility. Inside the building, the deported migrants are assigned a plastic chair and given sandwiches and coffee, along with information (e.g. from the Casa del Migrante or the IOM). The deported migrants are welcomed by government posters saying, "You are finally in your own country and with your own people—Welcome to Guatemala," and given a pep talk by a government representative: "Welcome home! No worries, there is surely chicken broth waiting for you at home." Despite this welcome, the deportees are subject to state authority. They are not, for instance, allowed to go to the toilet or make phone calls before they have gone through the ordinary migration control procedures followed by a second check by the national police for felonies committed in Guatemala, a process that can take hours. Apart from the meal, the service offered consists of a voluntary health check, a free phone call to a relative in Guatemala, and a bus ride to the central bus terminal. Those arriving on afternoon planes and whose communities are located long bus rides away from Guatemala City are dropped off at the Casa del Migrante, the migrant shelter operated by the Catholic Church. Ironically, the only existing reception program is the Guatemalan Repatriates Project, funded by USAID (in other words, aid from the country that deported them) and operated by the IOM. Apart from a few basic, immediate services, there is no long-term reintegration plan for deportees (Wainer, 2012).

Deported Honduran citizens face a fate very similar to that of the deported Guatemalans. State engagement ceases the moment the deportees leave the reception area. Outside the gate, money exchangers, "coyotes"—professional people smugglers—and loan sharks line up alongside family members to "welcome" deported emigrants. The Center for the Reception of Returned Migrants (CAMR), Casa Alianza, the Network of Migrant Committees and Families (RED COMIFAH), and other civil society members of the National Forum on Honduran Migration, FONAMIH, provide vital social infrastructure and humanitarian assistance to migrants and deported citizens, as well as information. Much of the work is done on a voluntary basis. Over the years these NGOs, particularly the religious organizations, have had success at improving some areas of public policy, like programs for unaccompanied minors, compensating for a lack of public policies in other areas, such as migrant shelter and receiving deported citizens. "Welcome to Honduras, a country of five stars, and you are one of the seven million stars that inhabit this beautiful country" is the encouraging message that Sister Valdette Willemann, who represents the CAMR at the airport in Tegucigalpa, gives to arriving deported nationals when she steps up to greet them off the flights arriving daily.

7.4.5 Efficiency

The inefficiency of NTCA states is evident in the states' policies for missing emigrants. Until recently, for example, Guatemala did not keep records on kidnappings, missing persons, or the murder of Guatemalan nationals on Mexican territory. August 24, 2021 marks 11 years since the discovery of 72 emigrants, the majority from NTCA countries, who were killed by a criminal group in San Fernando, Tamaulipas, a state in northern Mexico. The tragedy is an emblematic case, not only of the violence and dangers that migrants face when traveling through Mexico, but also of the Mexican and NTCA governments' failure to address and prevent those abuses.

Few cases are reported to the Ministry of Foreign Affairs in Guatemala and Honduras, as the process is complicated. Before filing a complaint, family members must present themselves to the Ministry of Justice and obtain a certificate proving a complaint has been made. They are then sent to the Office for Victim Attention, which sends the cases to a prosecutor, such as the Prosecutor of Crimes against Life or the Prosecutor of Organized Crime. Due to a lack of funding, no special prosecutor for migrant affairs has been appointed to date, and the family members of missing emigrants depend on the Ministry of Foreign Affairs, through its understaffed consular offices, to present each case to the Mexican or American governments (Sørensen, 2019). Apart from the complicated processes, many citizens are afraid to report a missing family member because they are undocumented. A joint analysis conducted by the Institute of Studies and Dissemination on Migration and INCEDES points to restrictive border control policies as the main factor behind Guatemalan migrants who go missing while in transit in Mexico (INEDIM & INCEDES, 2011). Civil society organizations advocating for missing migrants use a powerful symbol connected to missing persons that was produced by survivor groups during the wars in the context of forced disappearances: showing a picture of the lost family member with the political demand, "Alive you took them, alive we want them back" (Sørensen, 2019).

Central American migrants are often fleeing from extreme violence or the fear of death produced by threats, extortion, or the assassination of a close relative by the criminal gangs or drug cartels who operate with impunity in the region. There are estimates of more than 20,000 kidnapped emigrants on Mexican territory every year, of between 72,000 and 120,000 migrants having gone missing between 2006 and 2016, of 24,000 bodies buried in unmarked graves in municipal cemeteries, of 40,000 unidentified bodies brought to public morgues, and of 174 mass graves that have so far been acknowledged and keep appearing throughout the country (Sørensen, 2019).

Evidence produced by international organizations confirms that current migration from the NTCA constitutes a humanitarian security crisis, in which people are running for their lives (Médicos sin Fronteras, 2017). In response to the missing migrant crisis, the Forensic Anthropology Foundation of Guatemala (FAFG) diversified its traditional activities in transitional justice to include disappearances related to migration, citizen security, and natural disasters. In the cases in which people have gone missing during migration, the FAFG focuses on identifying them by taking DNA samples from family members that can be later matched with unidentified migrants in mass graves or morgues in Mexico. While the Guatemalan state has so far been inefficient in providing justice to the victims of the missing migrant phenomenon, a proposal to include missing migrants was put on the congressional agenda in 2019, although it has not yet been passed (Briere, 2019). In any case, once again the NGOs are taking the lead in this situation, perhaps because the states do not find any economic or political benefit in missing, deported, or deceased emigrants.

7.4.6 Public Regardedness

Regarding the degree to which policies pursue the public interest, Honduras is the only country in Central America that—after demands from civil society organizations—has approved state funding to repatriate Hondurans abroad in situations of extreme vulnerability. Likewise, El Salvador's CONMIGRANTES institution approved public funding for the emigrant community. El Salvador is the state with the highest public regardedness score, because it has taken active steps to take civil society into account, as noted by the Foreign Affairs Vice-Minister for Salvadorans Abroad: "We have tried with everything we do to connect with civil society in all policies we want to implement, because they are the ones who are going to give the United States the necessary legitimacy in all these processes" (J. J. García, personal communication, February 27, 2012). With respect to Guatemala, in turn, according to Erick Maldonado, former Executive Secretary of CONAMIGUA, "The situation in Guatemala is different because public funding for the emigrant community depends on the percentage of annual remittances in the national income. This generates financial instability due to constant fluctuations of remittance flows to Guatemala" (E. M. Maldonado Ríos, personal communication, January 24, 2012).

These examples illustrate the different levels of public regardedness in the three states in terms of the use of public funding to create institutions and initiatives for the emigrant community. Public expenditure in these areas is an indicator of state interest in migration issues. When the public budget is planned for emigrant policy, the states assume a leading role because of fiscal accountability obligations. On the contrary, when states do not have the money, or choose not to invest to it in their emigrant community, they delegate their role to international organizations that end up performing what should be public functions. The lack of interest in public regardedness by some states regarding deported, missing, or deceased emigrants may be due to the fact that when migrants return to their country of origin, they represent neither votes nor remittances.

7.5 Different Degrees of State-led Transnationalism Regarding Emigrant Policy

The degree of state-led transnationalism, the dependent variable in this study, is seen in the emigrant policy mechanisms employed by the states to engage with their emigrant community and through state involvement. Emigrant policy mechanisms are the policies that states use to either build or integrate emigrant communities, as described in detail in Part II of this publication. On the other hand, state involvement uses the following indicators:

1) the key actors involved in each policy;
2) the degree of state participation in setting the agenda for emigrant policy; and
3) how state influence is exercised.

This section discusses the degree to which state-led transnationalism differs regarding emigrant outreach in El Salvador, Guatemala, and Honduras. I argue that these differences are strongly related to a specific policy theme (policy mechanism), to the relationship between state and non-state actors (key actors involved in each policy), to the degree of state participation in setting the agenda for emigrant policy, and how states exert influence, e.g., funding, lobbying, and consensus. In the NTCA, a combination of actors is involved in each policy. These actors either facilitate or impede particular policies in the pursuit of their interests, which are sometimes oblivious to the collective welfare.

7.5.1 State Emigrant Policy Mechanisms

The NTCA states have followed different paths in their emigrant policies. Programs to build relationships with the emigrant community (emigrant community policy building mechanisms) are divided into a) recognizing the emigrant community and b) cultivating loyalties in the emigrant community. Figure 10 shows the emigrant community building policy mechanism promoted by each sending state.

Emigrant Community Building Mechanisms

The three states have put more effort towards recognizing the emigrant community than towards cultivating a relationship. This is the first step, acknowledging that there is an emigrant community worth recognizing. Related policies include creating institutions and improving statistics on how many migrants have left and how many come back, and El Salvador is the leading state in this regard.

Figure 7   Emigrant Community Building Mechanisms in the NTCA

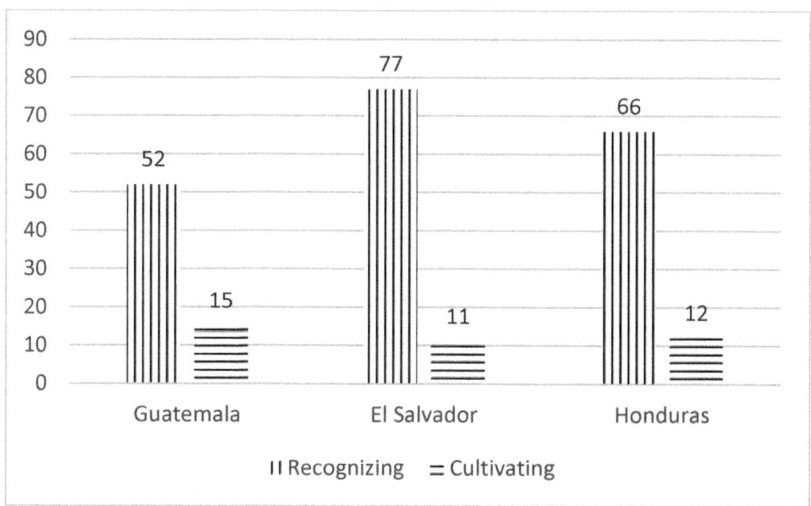

Note. Prepared by the author based on the fieldwork database.

The states have paid less attention to cultivating their relationship with the emigrant community by, for instance, taking responsibility for the migrants or creating symbolic days and an imagined territorial constituency, although all three states do have some policies of that nature, because they are not costly and are largely symbolic.

Emigrant Community Integration Mechanisms

Figure 8 shows the policies to integrate the emigrant community (emigrant community integration policy mechanisms) promoted by each sending state, divided into the categories of extending emigrant rights and extracting emigrant resources.

Figure 8   Emigrant Community Integration Mechanisms in the NTCA

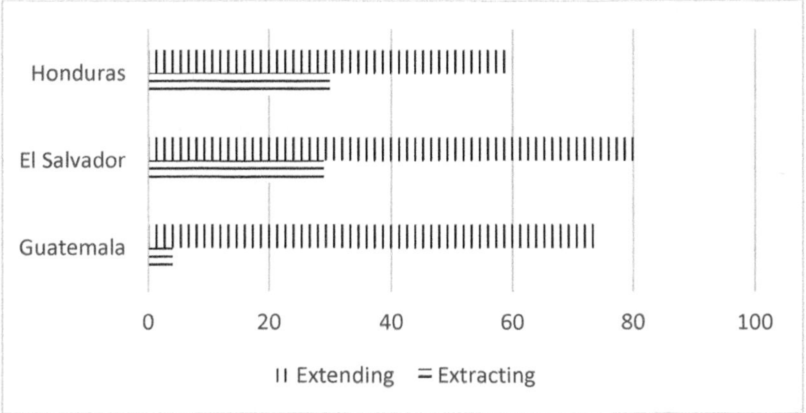

[Bar chart showing Honduras, El Salvador, and Guatemala with two bars each representing "Extending" and "Extracting" on a scale from 0 to 100. Honduras: Extending ~35, Extracting ~35. El Salvador: Extending ~70, Extracting ~30. Guatemala: Extending ~60, Extracting ~10.]

Note. Prepared by the author based on the fieldwork database.

This figure shows that El Salvador is the state that puts the most emphasis on extending rights to the emigrant community, followed by Guatemala. In the area of extracting resources in the form of remittances and all things related to money that can be taken from the emigrant, Honduras and El Salvador take the lead. It is most likely that Guatemala does not have as many programs to profit from the emigrant community not because it is not interested, but because the state does not have the capacity to enact such programs.

7.5.2 State Involvement

The Key Actors Involved in each Policy

In Central America, civil society has sought to take instrumental control over migration programs related to human rights as part of cultivating state outreach to the emigrant community. The role of civil society in advocating for emigrant policy often varies in each NTCA country. In Guatemala, for example, civil society was already highly organized by 1996, after the peace agreements were signed, and in many ways the internal structures of these organizations are highly democratic (May, 2005). However, in the last 25 years, with young democracies developing in Central

America, civil society has needed to organize in new and more efficient ways to be able to influence both emigrant policy and the state, which has proven to be a difficult task. This can be explained by the diverging regime trajectories in Central America during the 19th and 20th centuries. Mahoney, for instance, argues that the 19th-century liberal reform period was a critical juncture that locked the Central American countries onto divergent paths of long-term development, culminating in sharply contrasting regime outcomes (Mahoney, 2001). Today, each of the NTCA states has different democratic scores, as determined by the NGO Freedom House, as seen in Table 22.

Table 22   Global Freedom in the NTCA

Country	Total Score and Status	Political Rights	Civil Liberties
El Salvador	63 Partly Free	30	33
Guatemala	52 Partly Free	21	31
Honduras	44 Partly Free	19	25

Note. (Freedom House, 2021).

El Salvador has the strongest global freedom, political rights, and civil liberties scores out of the three countries in the region, which may explain why the Salvadoran state takes the lead on emigrant policy in the NTCA. When asked about the state's responsibility towards the emigrant community, the Foreign Affairs Vice-Minister for Salvadorans Abroad stated:

> Who is going to aid migrants in transit? Should we leave them to the Church's charity? No, it is the state's obligation to protect them, and this is what we have been doing. However, we are on a thin line between the functions performed by a consulate and the functions of an NGO. (J. J. García, personal communication, February 27, 2012)

Figure 9 presents the different actors participating in setting the agenda for emigrant policies in the NTCA, providing some idea of who is behind the initiatives to engage with the emigrant community.

Figure 9   **Number of Emigrant Policies Proposed by each Actor in the NTCA**

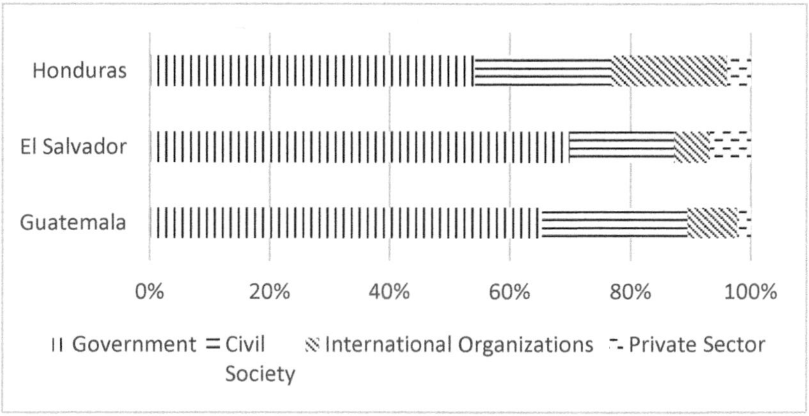

[Bar chart showing, for Honduras, El Salvador, and Guatemala, the percentage breakdown of emigrant policies proposed by Government, Civil Society, International Organizations, and Private Sector, from 0% to 100%.]

Legend: || Government = Civil Society ⦚ International Organizations ⁻ Private Sector

Note. Prepared by the author based on the fieldwork database.

As seen in the figure, compared to other actors such as international organizations, civil society, and the private sector, the NTCA states take the lead in promoting emigrant policies. Civil society and IOs are the second most important actors in the region, and in Honduras, the IOs play the most important role after the state. State leadership is weakened when civil society and IOs take over their functions, and Honduras provides one such example of a state delegating public functions to international organizations. This gives IOs discretionary power to conduct programs and even to propose laws and create institutions that end up operating without efficient control in the long run. State involvement also varies because IOs and NGOs apply pressure to sending states, especially regarding emigrant policies related to security and economic development. The sending states, in turn, react to this pressure by signing bilateral and multilateral cooperation programs and agreements, which are at times simply a formality, a way to comply with international cooperation demands without any concrete results for the emigrants.

The situation of deported nationals exemplifies how international pressure triggers the participation of sending states. The three countries here have been quite active in terms of signing agreements and creating programs with Mexico and the United States, especially when border vulnerability is involved and migration becomes a security issue. Examples include the IOM's migrant reception and care programs in Guatemala and the CAMR project in Honduras which, as noted above, offer deportees services like a free phone call, food, and a bus ticket to return to their communities. By implementing short-term and aid-oriented measures, international organizations help cover areas where the state lacks funds of its own, of course, but at the same time they remove the responsibility these states have to take care of their own citizens. Although El Salvador's program for deported citizens was initially managed by Catholic Relief Services and other organizations, the Directorate-General of Migration, a state institution, took over the program and now manages it alone.

The figures below show the emigrant policy building mechanism being promoted in the agenda of each actor.

Figure 10   Recognizing the Emigrant Community by Actor in the NTCA

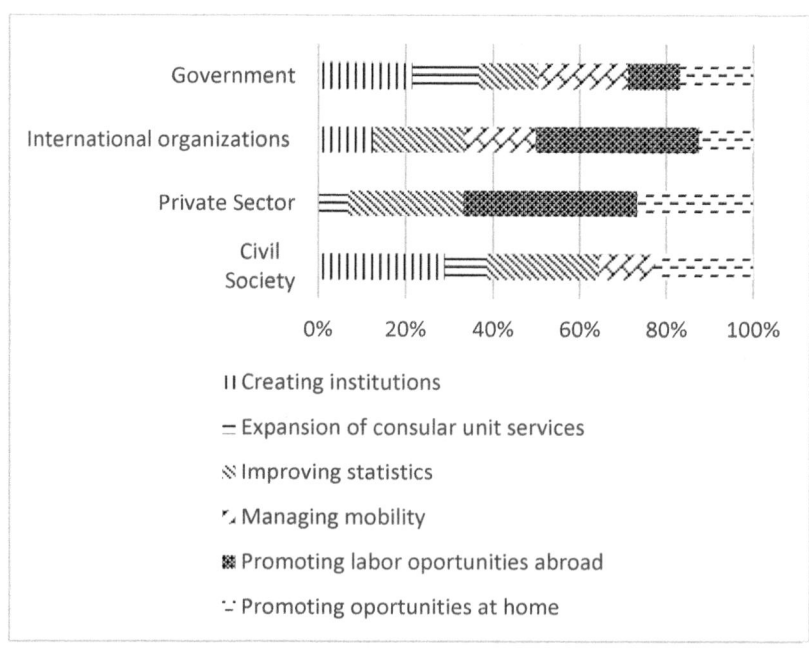

Note. Prepared by the author based on the fieldwork database.

States propose more emigrant policies related to managing mobility, which includes security policies. IOs and the private sector, on the other hand, place special focus on promoting labor opportunities abroad and promoting opportunities at home, which makes sense if they can offer jobs to deported nationals or profit from contracts they enter into with foreign companies to send cheap labor abroad.

Figure 11   Cultivating Loyalties by Actor in the NTCA

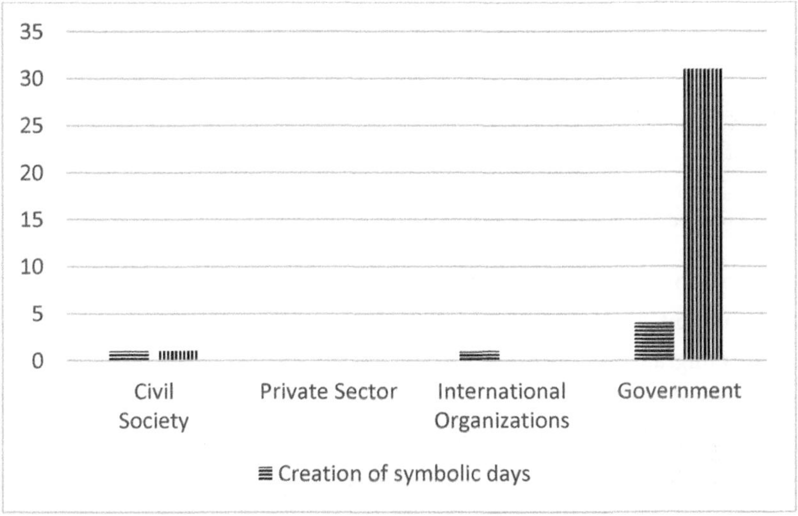

Creation of symbolic days

Note. Prepared by the author based on the fieldwork database.

The above figure shows that the states emphasize symbolic policies, such as offering to take responsibility for deceased, missing, or deported emigrants. This can be explained by the fact that such policies generally remain at a discursive level, rather than translating into real, and costly, benefits for the emigrant community.

The following figure shows both elements of the integration mechanism: extending rights to the emigrant community and extracting resources from them, by actor.

Figure 12   Integration Mechanism by Actor in the NTCA

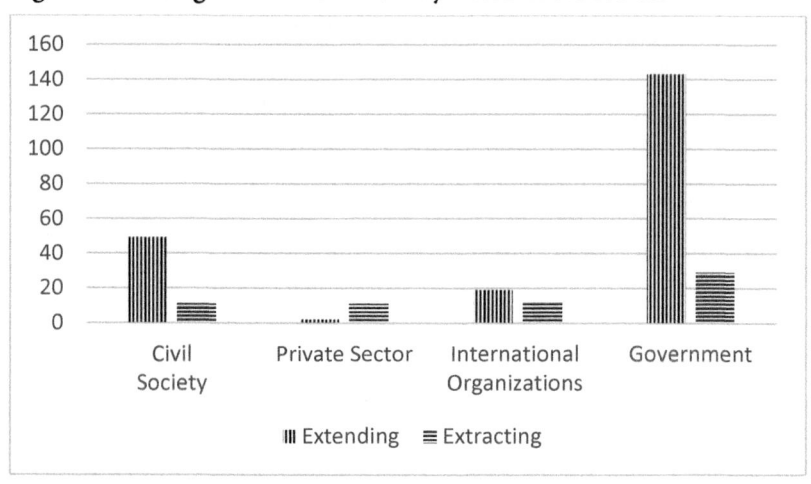

Note. Prepared by the author based on the fieldwork database.

As seen, governments and civil society promote the extension of rights to the emigrant community, while all the actors are involved in the extraction of the emigrants' resources.

Honduras organizes and finances projects to invest remittances, in most cases following the directions of IOs and civil society, such as the IOM and the Catholic Church, respectively. The Honduran state delegates a large number of its functions to IOs and civil society. The Guatemalan state often contradicts itself, focusing, on the one hand, on human rights policies, as promoted by civil society, but also managing mobility and the securitization of borders, as promoted by regional agreements and IOs, which often clashes with the human rights focus.

Degree of State Participation in Setting the Agenda for Emigrant Policy

This section explains how the state's type of participation contributes to its degree of state-led transnationalism, analyzed as follows:

a) a high role played by the government in leading the political agenda;

b) a medium role played by the government (civil society/international actors, NGOs); and
c) a low role played by government (the state is not seen as a source of policy leadership)

Figure 13   Degree of NTCA State Participation in Setting the Agenda for Emigrant Policy

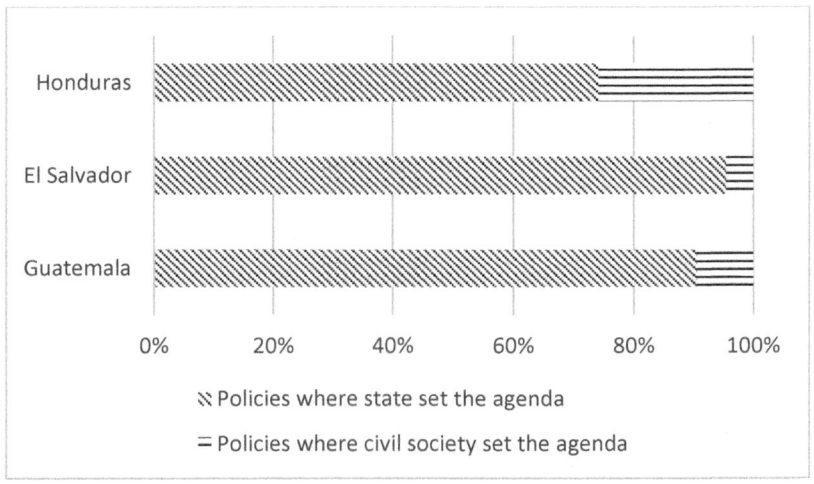

Note. Prepared by the author based on the fieldwork database.

This figure shows that the Guatemalan and Salvadoran states have a higher role than Honduras in setting the agenda in the NTCA region. The states tend to take the lead with some policy areas and delegate their functions with others. For instance, the large number of deported nationals is an economic concern for the sending states, but as seen above, some states have a low participation capacity, so they tend to ally with other actors or even delegate their functions.

The use of remittances, providing labor opportunities abroad, and arranging opportunities at home are three areas where IOs and businesses interact with sending states, and the states appear to have a medium degree of participation in setting the agenda for emigrant policy. Initiatives regarding the use of remittances tend to come from international organizations such as the UNDP and IOM. Temporary foreign worker programs, on the other hand, tend to be promoted by private companies in receiving states. Other programs, such as Temporary Protected Status in the United States, are designed to ensure the flow of temporary or permanent workers to the receiving states and, likewise, to guarantee the flow of remittances to the sending state.

In Honduras, the UNDP supports the creation of individual businesses in communities with high levels of migration. Rather than use the remittances, the goal of the program is to provide opportunities at home when there are no employment prospects. This type of program is characterized by a low degree of state participation. The programs, for example, limit state participation in hiring the person who will monitor the program. As a result, the state is not involved in creating public mechanisms to evaluate the programs and remains uninvolved in job creation. With many emigrant policies, the Honduran state delegates its functions to the UNDP, which manages the financial resources from the international loans received by the government. This country is an example of the strong delegation of public functions to an international organization. Similar situations have occurred in the past, as with the creation of the Human Rights Secretariat after the 2009 coup d'état in the country. Just as with many institutions and policies in Honduras, this secretariat lacks accountability systems, but was created in response to international cooperation pressure and offers to fund the office. However, as observed by a human rights defender, "the protection mechanism for defenders lies in that secretariat; their actions for the human rights crisis in Honduras is completely irrelevant" (C. Espinoza, personal communication, June 30, 2021).

How State Influence is Exercised

While the previous section analyzed the different degrees of state-led transnationalism regarding the key actors involved and the degree of state participation in setting the emigrant policy agenda, this section examines how influence can be exerted to establish a policy within the agenda, via:

a) state creates consensus;
b) state allocates funding for the policy;
c) state invites international organizations;
d) state promotes interinstitutional coordination; and
e) state invites the private sector.

Figure 14 presents these sources of influence in the NTCA states:

Figure 14   State Influence on Emigrant Policy in the NTCA

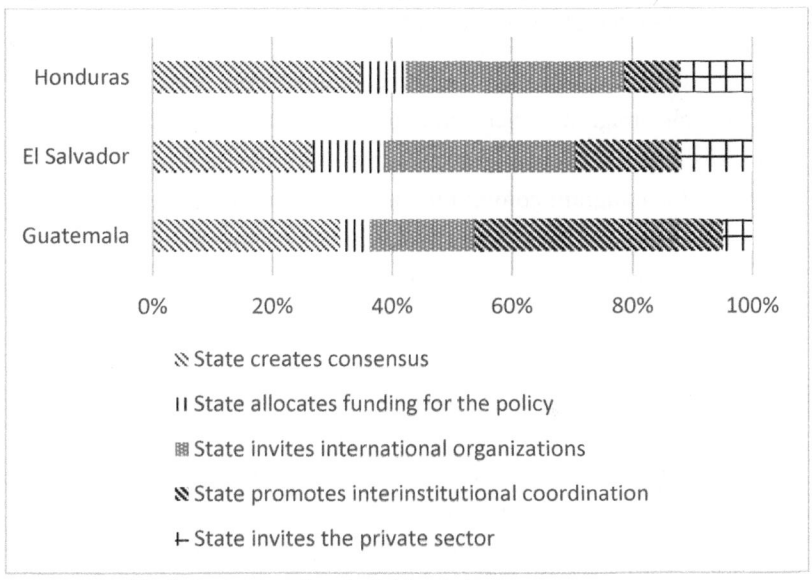

Note. Prepared by the author based on the fieldwork database.

One of the main findings here is that El Salvador and Honduras have managed to put their migration policies on the political agenda when IOs are present. As shown in the figure, the three NTCA states seem to have a better chance of putting a policy on the agenda when there is consensus among all the actors involved. In line with this idea, the Vice-Minister for Salvadorans Abroad stated in an interview that "We have done our best to include civil society in all the policies we want to implement, because they are the ones who are going to provide the United States with the required legitimacy in all these processes" (J. J. García, personal communication, February 27, 2012). This statement summarizes how El Salvador and the other two states find it easiest to set the agenda when they reach a consensus with all the parties involved. The Guatemalan government relies on civil society and other actors to take part in setting their agenda, and to have interinstitutional coordination when working with emigrant policy in particular. El Salvador and Honduras find it easier to set the agenda for emigrant policies when they have the support of business partners and, thus, funding.

7.6 Concluding Remarks

This chapter has established the three variables that explain why states adopt certain emigrant policies and the different degrees of state-led transnationalism. It did so by analyzing the importance of the size and potential impact of the emigrant community in the country of origin, divided into a) the importance of the size of the emigrant community; b) the history of the emigrant community; c) the emigrant community degree of organization; d) current remittances from the emigrant community; and e) out-of-country voting rights for emigrants.

Even though El Salvador and Guatemala score higher with regard to the size and history of their emigrant community because of the armed conflicts in the region, El Salvador and Honduras are the countries with a higher dependence on remittances and have the highest percentage of their population living abroad. For those two sending states, out-of-country voting has been functioning the longest and has had an actual impact on electoral results. However, because the Honduran emigrant community has a shorter history of going to the United States, it is less organized and, thus, obtains a lower score regarding the importance of the size and history of the emigrant community, indicating the explanatory power of social capital. The country that scores high for every indicator of this independent variable is El Salvador.

This chapter also compared party system competitiveness in the NTCA, divided into a) fragmentation and b) polarization. In El Salvador, the effective number of electoral parties continues to be two, despite the appearance of new political parties and the fact that the country no longer has the bipolar system featuring competition between ARENA and the FMLN that characterized the country's politics for more than two decades. Consequently, the battle for the loyalty of the emigrant community continues. Honduras ranked second out of the three countries in this variable, with between two and three effective parties during a period of almost 10 years. Consequently, the few parties in the electoral arena keep the emigrant community at the center of the competition for votes, although since President Hernández's fraudulent reelection in 2018, the emigrant vote is no longer an object of competition. Finally, Guatemala is home to the least competition for the migrant vote for two main reasons: first, the electoral law only enacted out-of-country voting for one election in 2019, and second, the effective number of electoral parties rose from 4 to 8 between 2011 and 2019. The high level of party fragmentation relegates the demands of the emigrant community to the back burner and emigrants end up without a voice. Additionally, the parties are not particularly interested in lobbying the emigrant community, because they know their votes do not guarantee a victory.

On the subject of polarization, the results of this chapter show that in El Salvador, the FMLN has taken the emigrant community into consideration more than the far-right ARENA or right-wing GANA. On the other hand, political competition over the emigrant communities is absent in the Guatemalan parties. During the last three legislative terms, only a few political parties have presented migration initiatives as part of their political platforms. Interparty ideological distance is simply not an issue in Guatemala. Finally, Honduras has had two parties competing since the end of the 19th century and is a stable two-party system. Even though its system is currently classified as being multiparty, there is not much competition over the emigrant community, particularly because of the lack of ideological difference in a country where all of the parties are on the right side of the spectrum.

This chapter also analyzed a third independent variable, the institutional capacity of the sending states. With results based on the analytical framework established by Stein et al., the key features of public policies were determined to be: a) adaptability; b) stability; c) coordination: d) implementation and enforcement; e) efficiency; and f) public regardedness (2005).

Adaptability is the characteristic where El Salvador is the only country from the NTCA to have a high score. The country adapts its policies to changing economic conditions or in response to institutional failures. In Honduras, an illegitimate government implements emigrant policies that it finds personally convenient, adapting opportunistic, one-sided policies that reflect the politicians' preferences. Finally, the Guatemalan state's adaptability has resulted in volatility, with emigrant policies shifting back and forth as different groups alternate in power. Regarding stability, in turn, El Salvador and Honduras score the highest. This can be explained by the fact that they were two-party systems for decades, making them capable of sustaining most policies over time and building upon the achievements of previous administrations through consensus. By contrast, Guatemala, with its volatile policy environment, receives a medium score and is characterized by large swings and a lack of consultation with different groups in society.

When it comes to coordination and coherence, the three states all score medium. In these countries, policymaking—even beyond emigrant policy—involves a large number of actors who do not communicate adequately with each other, producing what Cox and MaCubbins have called a balkanization of public policies, in other words the fragmentation or division of a region into smaller regions that are often uncooperative with each other regarding policy (Cox & McCubbins, 2007). With implementation and enforcement, Guatemala scores low. This is associated with a lack of capable, independent bureaucracies, as well as an absence of incentives and resources to invest in policy capacities for policymakers. Looking at efficiency, El Salvador is the only state that obtains a high score, meaning that this state can allocate its scarce resources to those activities where they have the greatest returns. This is noteworthy because El Salvador is also the state that delegates the fewest number of its functions to non-state actors, while still managing to make its public spending most effective. El Salvador again scores high in public regardedness, meaning it can produce and promote policies for the general welfare. This dimension is closely tied to inequality, particularly since individuals favored by policies tend, in turn, to favor individuals well-connected to policy decisions, as in the case of Honduras. Low public regardedness is related to the extent to which the government represents diffuse, unorganized interests, as in Guatemala.

Last, this chapter put forward possible explanations both for the repertoire of policies that states employ, and for how far states are willing to go to ensure that migrants maintain an enduring long-distance membership in their country. To that end, the study focused on the degree of state-led transnationalism as the dependent variable, operationalized as a) emigrant policy mechanisms, divided into policy building and policy integration; and b) the variation in state involvement, operationalized in three indicators. Looking at emigrant policy mechanisms, the three states have made more of an effort to recognize the emigrant community. States have paid less attention to cultivating a relationship with the emigrant community, for instance announcing responsibility for migrants, or creating symbolic days and an imagined territorial constituency. With regard to the emigrant community integration policy mechanism, El Salvador is the state with the fullest focus on extending rights to the emigrant community, followed by Guatemala. Here, El Salvador obtains high scores in state capacities.

Finally, this chapter analyzes the variations in state involvement, first by providing a comprehensive list of the key actors involved in policy-making. As seen in the chapter, the NTCA states take the lead in promoting emigrant policies. Civil society and international organizations are the second most important actors in the region, while in Honduras IOs play the most important role after the state. This chapter also examines the degree of state participation in setting the agenda for emigrant policy, arguing that a state's leadership is weakened when civil society and IOs take over its functions. By contrast, El Salvador and Guatemala have a higher role in setting their agendas.

State-led transnationalism is explained by assessing how states exercise their influence to set the agenda. When the public budget is planned for emigrant policy, NTCA states assume a leading role due to fiscal accountability obligations. In the case of Guatemala, there is high interinstitutional coordination, which allows for public and private alliances on certain policy topics. El Salvador and Honduras manage to put their migration policies on the political agenda when IOs are involved, and the three NTCA states have better opportunities to achieve their policy goals when there is consensus between all the actors.

Chapter 8
Conclusion

8.1 Key Question Answered

This book addresses the question of how and why sending states adopt policies to engage with their emigrant communities abroad. The study has two main aims. To answer the first question of "how," the thesis provides a systematic and detailed description of what sending states do—emigrant policy—and compares their overall levels. Part II lays out the argument through two policy mechanisms divided into four policy categories, all designed by the sending states to reinforce the emigrants' sense of enduring membership. The discussion of the programs related to the emigrant policy building mechanism describes how sending states recognize the emigrant community through the creation of institutions and how states cultivate loyalties in the emigrant community through symbolic policies. Part II then analyses the forms of emigrant policy integration mechanisms, which include extending emigrant rights and extracting resources by incorporating emigrants into the national economy.

Part III addresses the second goal of the thesis, to answer "why" the levels of the engagement of sending states differ; in other words, to provide explanations for the determinants of emigrant policies and state efforts to reach out to their emigrant community, defined as state-led transnationalism. In doing so, it clarifies the importance of three variables that explain the differences in state-led transnationalism: 1) the importance of the size and potential impact of the emigrant community in the country of origin; 2) interparty system competitiveness; and 3) the sending states' institutional capacity. The study shows how states employ different emigrant policy mechanisms to engage with their emigrant community and that state involvement varies regarding the different sets of actors and how they influence the policy agenda.

These findings are explained by the argument that home country institutions are increasingly engaged in reaching out to their emigrants to further their domestic agendas. A most different systems design is used to compare the three cases of El Salvador, Guatemala, and Honduras, in which emigrant outreach is dominated by the states, in other words, state-led transnationalism.

Although some scholars have highlighted the importance of policies aimed at emigrants, not enough attention has been paid to why different states adopt differing policies. Thus, my aim with this investigation was to contribute to the study of the sending states and their emigrant policies, as well as the defining factors that explain the differences in state-led transnationalism.

8.2 Key Findings

Sending states matter. Contrary to the affirmation that managing migration continues to be a foreign policy issue for receiving states, I argue that sending states are capable and, through my empirical results, I show that they are an important piece of the transnational emigrant policy puzzle. The best case in this regard is El Salvador, which has a policy that aims to respect migrants' human rights, more than the other two countries in the region. This could be explained by past human rights violations. In El Salvador, human rights has long been an important topic, first because the army withdrew from political life after the Peace Accords in 1992 and second, because the FMLN as a political party made human rights a priority of its political agenda.

International relations, new institutionalism, and policymaking together hold a greater explanatory power in migration studies. Migration has been traditionally researched from an international relations approach, leaving institutions, actors, and the policy process under-researched, thus underestimating the actions and interests of sending states both in the political realm and in academia.

Emigrant policy is very often a response to international pressure on the issue of border security. There is a strong tendency in the NTCA states to establish collaboration practices through bilateral and multilateral agreements with receiving states, specifically Mexico and the United

States, most often to their own detriment. One such example is the Safe Third Country Agreement that Guatemala was pressured to adopt by the United States upon threat of a reduction in financial support in other areas.

The significant presence of international organizations managing migration jeopardizes state initiatives. One specific example of this phenomenon is the presence of the International Organization for Migration in Guatemala and Honduras. In Honduras, moreover, the Catholic Church basically manages reception and care programs for migrants. The Honduran and Guatemalan governments have outsourced several humanitarian services to NGOs, primarily because of a lack of state capacity, but also because large portions of their social and humanitarian funds have been provided by the international community which, due to state corruption, have made their economic assistance conditional on outsourcing.

Several NGOs acknowledge their business function. Even if their main concern is the creation of migration policies to protect the emigrant community, the actual activities of many NGOs are focused on deportation reception and anti-trafficking campaigns, because these issues receive international funding and states do not make any profit off of detained, deceased, missing, or deported nationals. At the same time, secular and faith-based NGOs compete over the same meager national and international resources available for information campaigns, migrant shelters, and deportee reception. NGOs are especially competing for funding related to migration now, since the caravan phenomenon began, because of the recent decrease in international funding for Central America.

Some migrants do not matter to states, because they do not represent votes or remittances. For many states, the question of deported citizens seems to be a problem of economic imbalance. Deportation is not in the best interest of sending states, because it does not maintain remittance flows. As a result, states invest the least in policies for missing, deceased, or deported emigrants, where families of migrants often need the most support.

Political parties will compete for emigrant community loyalty if their votes matter. Both El Salvador and Honduras, where the effective number of electoral parties continues to be two or three, are sites of competition over the emigrant community. However, if all parties fall along the same ideological spectrum, as in the case of Honduras, this does not occur. Only in El Salvador, where there are still left- and right-wing parties, has the emigrant community continued to participate.

8.3 Theoretical Implications

This study has examined how sending states are increasingly institutionalizing policies to include emigrants beyond their national territory and demonstrated the ways in which state-led transnationalism is challenging traditional concepts of sovereignty, the nation-state, and citizenship. The role of emigrant policy and receiving states has been the subject of important academic debates in migration studies. As a consequence, there is a significant amount of literature on migration policy from the perspective of receiving states, with sending states only considered at the implementation phase. One significant problem with this type of approach is that it underestimates the role of sending states and the policies specifically designed for emigrants.

New approaches argue that emigrant policymaking should be understood as a cooperative process in which both sending and receiving states have a voice. This literature highlights the ability and interest of sending states to guarantee their emigrant citizens more inclusive treatment, by establishing closer ties, extending social, political, and economic rights for emigrants, protecting their human rights, providing better reintegration opportunities when they return, and lobbying with receiving states.

The theoretical aim of this study is to contribute to the academic understanding of the determinants that make some sending states more reluctant than others to reach out to their citizens abroad. The starting point is the concept of state-led transnationalism, which includes policies and programs that attempt to expand the scope of a state's political, economic, and social regulation to include emigrants and their families outside the national territory. To explain the empirical problem of why some states are more active than others with respect to emigrant policy, the study relies on existing theoretical approaches. At a broader level, the fact that sending states are increasingly addressing citizens who live outside their national territory presents a paradox. States are implicitly undermining the basic principle of sovereignty, which has been defined by their political authority and has characterized the international system since the Peace of Westphalia in 1648. This has affected the nature of international relations and global governance policies. State boundaries are defined in social rather than geographical terms, and sending states engage in "re-territorializing" their citizens abroad by launching polices that re-include them not only in the nation, but also in the national economy and political life of their country of origin. In line with this argument, it is my contention that the state matters and that, rather than disappearing or being subordinated to international regimes, sending states can potentially play a major role, along with other institutions such as civil, religious, political, and migrant associations.

8.4 Implications for Policy and Practice

Researching Central America is a challenge, methodologically speaking, due to the lack of information in public institutions, or an unwillingness to share the information because it is not systematized. Second, although they have been the object of important debates by scholars of transnationalism, conceptualizing policies that go beyond the nation-state still poses a challenge for the field of International Relations. Finally, the actors in Central America that participate in the emigrant policy process do not perform only one role. For instance, some members of civil society now work for the state, and understanding the actions of this type of actor is far more complex than imagined. Notwithstanding these challenges, this study contributes both on a theoretical base—to the literature on sending states and state-led transnationalism—and on an empirical base—to the current data about states in Central America and the region itself. It is my hope that these contributions will reinforce the argument that strengthening the state is absolutely necessary if better results in emigrant policy are to be achieved, and that this is not (only) a task of civil society, political parties, or even the migrants, because states matter.

8.5 Avenues for Future Research

This thesis suggests many potential areas for future study. As mentioned, there is a policy category related to "extending rights" that includes the concept of providing opportunities at home for deported citizens. Beyond the numbers of deportees, almost nothing is known about the policies that exist or what happens to deported citizens once they return to their communities. The fact that governments are not doing enough to provide their deported citizens with jobs, health, education, or reintegration opportunities once they are back in their home country suggests that they are applying a "policy of no policy," encouraging migrants to emigrate again so that they will continue to send remittances. Likewise, there is still little research on the role of the IOs, NGOs, and private companies that profit from undocumented emigrants and the impact of public and private alliances for emigrant policy.

Furthermore, few studies have investigated the policies designed for detained, deported, missing, and deceased migrants, possibly because of the difficulty entailed in obtaining data. There are also fewer emigrant policies for migrants who fall into one of these categories, perhaps because they represent neither a political nor an economic gain for governments.

Finally, this study has analyzed how emigrant outreach is dominated by the states of emigrant communities in the United States. However, more research is needed into state outreach to the emigrant community from Latin America in Europe, a growing and quite unexplored trend.

Bibliography

Abella, M. I. (2004). The Role of Recruiters in Labor Migration. In D. S. Massey & E. J. Taylor (Eds.), *International Migration. Prospects and Policies in a Global Market* (pp. 201–211). Oxford University Press.

Abuelafia, E., Del Carmen, G., & Ruiz-Arranz, M. (2019). *Tras los pasos del migrante: Perspectivas y experiencias de la migración de El Salvador, Guatemala y Honduras en Estados Unidos.* Interamerican Development Bank. https://publications.iadb.org/publications/spanish/document/Tras_los_pasos_del_migrante_Perspectivas_y_experiencias_de_la_migraci%C3%B3n_de_El_Salvador_Guatemala_y_Honduras_en_Estados_Unidos.pdf

Aguayo, S. (1985). *El éxodo centroamericano: Consecuencias de un conflicto* (1st ed.). Secretaría de Educación Pública.

Aguirre, L. (2012, February 12). *Director of the General Directorate of Human Rights Protection and Human Management, Ministry of Foreign Affairs, El Salvador* [Personal communication].

Ajenjo, N. (2004). El papel y la función de los parlamentos centroamericanos: Cuatro casos comparados. *América Latina Hoy, 038*, 125–139.

Ajenjo, N. (2008). *Legislative Procedures and Lawmaking in Central America.* VDM Verlag Dr. Müller.

Alcántara Sáez, M. (2008a). *Proyecto de élites parlamentarias.* Universidad de Salamanca.

Alcántara Sáez, M. (2008b). *Sistemas políticos de América Latina: Vol. México, América Central y el Caribe.* Tecnos.

Aleinikoff, T. A., & Klusmeyer, D. B. (Eds.). (2001). *Citizenship Today: Global Perspectives and Practices.* Carnegie Endowment for International Peace.

Alemán, M. (2019, December 19). *Sale grupo de salvadoreños a EEUU con visa de trabajo.* https://www.sandiegouniontribune.com/en-espanol/noticias/story/2019-12-19/sale-grupo-de-salvadorenos-a-eeuu-con-visa-de-trabajo

Algazi, L. B. (2009). *¿Qué pasa con la representación en América Latina?* Porrua Miguel Angel.

Altolaguirre Larraondo, M. (2006, November). *El Ministerio de Relaciones Exteriores y la Atención al Migrante.* Guatemalan Foreign Affairs Vice Ministry Meetings with Emigrant Community in the US, United States. Retrieved June 9, 2022, from <http://www.crmsv.org/sites/default/files/Presentaciones/guatemala_-_encuentro_con_el_migrante_nov._2006.ppt >.

Álvarez, L. (2010). *El IGSS ofrecerá seguros de salud y pensión a migrantes.* El Periódico. http://www.elperiodico.com.gt/es/20100603/economia/155340

Amnesty International. (2010). *Invisible Victims: Migrants on the Move in Mexico*. Amnesty International Publications. http://www.amnesty.org/en/library/as set/AMR41/014/2010/en/8459f0ac-03ce-4302-8bd2-3305bdae9cde/amr41 0142010eng.pdf

Andrade-Eekhoff, K. (2003). *Mitos y realidades: El impacto económico de la migración en los hogares rurales*. FLACSO El Salvador.

Andrade-Eekhoff, K., & Silva-Avalos, C. M. (2003). *Globalización de la Periferia: Los desafíos de la migración transnacional para el desarrollo local en América Central*. FLACSO Programa El Salvador.

Angenendt, S. (2007). International Migration—Just a Matter of State Security? In J. Sommer & A. Warnecke (Eds.), *The Security-Migration Nexus. Challenges and Opportunities of African Migration to EU Countries*. Bonn International Center for Conversion BICC. http://www.bicc.de/uploads/tx_bicctools/brief36.pdf

Angenendt, S., & Parkes, R. (2008). Arbeitsmigration in der EU. *Stiftung Wissenschaft Und Politik/Deutsches Institut Für Internationale Politik Und Sicherheit, SWP Aktuell*(38).

Appadurai, A. (1996). *Modernity At Large: Cultural Dimensions of Globalization* (1st ed.). University of Minnesota Press.

Arciniegas, Y. (2021, June 3). *Guatemala acogerá el primer centro para migrantes promovido por Estados Unidos*. France 24. https://www.france24.com/es/ee-uu-y-canad%C3%A1/20210603-guatemala-primer-centro-migrantes-esta dos-unidos

Aristegui, C. (2020, January 21). *Esto es lo que ha cambiado para los migrantes en México*. CNN. https://cnnespanol.cnn.com/video/migracion-caravana-cen troamericanos-gobierno-amlo-seguridad-leticia-calderon-elba-coria-ariste gui/

Arnold, K. R. (2011). *American Immigration After 1996: The Shifting Ground of Political Inclusion*. Penn State University Press.

Art, D. (2011). *Inside the Radical Right: The Development of Anti-Immigrant Parties in Western Europe*. Cambridge University Press.

Artiga-González, Á. (2000). *La política y los sistemas de partidos en Centroamérica* [Doctoral dissertation]. Universidad de Salamanca.

Asis, M. M. B. (2008). How International Migration can Support Development: A Challenge for the Philippines. In S. Castles & R. Delgado Wise (Eds.), *Migration and development: Perspectives from the South* (pp. 175–202). IOM International Organization for Migration.

Avci, G., & Kirişci, K. (2008). Turkey's Immigration and Emigration Dilemmas at the Gate of the European Union. In S. Castles & R. Delgado Wise (Eds.),

Migration and development: Perspectives from the South (pp. 203–253). IOM International Organization for Migration.

Avelar, R. (2019, July 19). *Manuel Alcántara: "Los partidos ARENA y FMLN sobrevivirán, están enraizados en la sociedad."* ElSalvador.com. https://www.elsalvador.com/eldiariodehoy/manuel-alcantara-los-partidos-arena-y-fmln-sobreviviran-estan-enraizados-en-la-sociedad/622552/2019/

Barahona, M. A. (2012, March 14). *Legislator. President of International Relations Committee* [Personal communication].

Baringhorst, S., Hollifield, J., & Hunger, U. (Eds.). (2006). *Herausforderung Migration – Perspektiven der vergleichenden Politikwissenschaft* (1st ed.). LIT-Verlag.

Basch, L., Glick Schiller, N., & Szancton-Blanc, C. (1995). *Nations unbound*. Gordon and Breach.

Battistella, G. (2004). Return Migration in the Philippines: Issues and Policies. In D. S. Massey & E. J. Taylor (Eds.), *International Migration. Prospects and Policies in a Global Market* (pp. 212–229). Oxford University Press.

Bauböck, R. (2003). Towards a Political Theory of Migrant Transnationalism. *International Migration Review, 37*(3), 700–723.

Bauböck, R. (2006). Interaktive Staatsbürgerschaft. In S. Baringhorst, J. Hollifield, & U. Hunger (Eds.), *Herausforderung Migration – Perspektiven der vergleichenden Politikwissenschaft* (1st ed., pp. 129–166). LIT-Verlag.

Baumeister, E., Acuña, G., & Fernández, E. (2008). *Estudio sobre las migraciones regionales de los nicaraguenses: Remesas y Desarrollo en América Latina*. Editorial de Ciencias Sociales. http://www.remesasydesarrollo.org/estadisticas/estudio-sobre-las-migraciones-regionales-de-los-nicaraguenses/

Betts, A. (2009). *Forced Migration and Global Politics*. John Wiley & Sons.

Betts, A. (2011). Introduction. In A. Betts (Ed.), *Global Migration Governance*. Oxford University Press.

Biden, J. (2021). *Joe Biden for President: Official Campaign Website: El Plan de Biden para fortalecer la seguridad y la prosperidad en colaboración con los pueblos de Centroamérica*. https://joebiden.com/es/el-plan-de-biden-para-fortalecer-la-seguridad-y-la-prosperidad-en-colaboracion-con-los-pueblos-de-centroamerica/

Biermann, F., Pattberg, P., Asselt, H., & Zelli, F. (2010). The Fragmentation of Global Governance Architectures: A Framework for Analysis. *Global Environmental Politics, 9*, 14–40.

Bogusz, B., Cholewinski, R., & etc (Eds.). (2004). *Irregular Migration and Human Rights: Theoretical, European and International Perspectives*. Brill.

Bonnici, G. L. (2009). *Respecting the Will to Work: A Foundation for Rights-Based Temporary Migration Programs*. INEDIM.

Bosques, G. (2018). *Observatorio: Acontecer de la política exterior de México* (No. 39). Senado de la República LXIV Legislatura. https://centrogilbertobosques.senado.gob.mx/docs/OPE_039.pdf

Boswell, C. (2007). Theorizing Migration Policy: Is There a Third Way? *International Migration Review, 41*(1), 75–100.

Brady, H. E., & Collier, D. (2004). *Rethinking social inquiry: Diverse tools, shared standards*. Rowman & Littlefield.

Brettell, C. (2000). Theorizing Migration in Anthropology. The Social Construction of Networks, Identities, Communities, and Globalscapes. In C. Brettell & J. Hollifield (Eds.), *Migration Theory: Talking Across Disciplines* (1st ed., pp. 97–136). Routledge.

Brettell, C., & Hollifield, J. (2000). Introduction: Migration Theory. In C. Brettell & J. Hollifield (Eds.), *Migration Theory: Talking Across Disciplines* (1st ed., pp. 1–26). Routledge.

Briere, J. P. (2016, March 17). *Outstanding Migrant of the Year* [Facebook].

Briere, J. P. (2017, October 22). De parte del Congreso se reconoció a varios Guatemaltecos residentes en Los Angeles, gracias a la labor de Doña Rosita y Dip. Ovidio Monzon. [Twitter]. *@PAULBRIERE*. Retricved June 9, 2022, from <https://twitter.com/PAULBRIERE/status/922185713470251008>.

Briere, J. P. (2018, May 28). Jean Paul Briere on Twitter: "Placa en el Consulado de Los Angeles: 'En memoria de los que se fueron y no pueden volver, por las familias que los desean volver a ver, por los sueños que quieren alcanzar y por los que emprendieron el viaje sin poderlo finalizar. Paul B.' No más casos como el de Claudia Gómez. Https://t.co/XEgBJPDAyF"/Twitter [Twitter]. *@PAULBRIERE*. https://twitter.com/PAULBRIERE/status/1001106101100843009

Briere, J. P. (2019, October 18). Jean Paul Briere on Twitter: "Hoy presentamos con varios compañeros la Iniciativa: 'Ley Marco de Búsqueda de Personas Desaparecidas'. Entre varios temas contiene el estandarizar procesos, incluidos procesos de búsqueda para migrantes que sus familias los dan por desaparecidos o puedan encontrarse fallecidos. Https://t.co/DrJbdMyjZT"/Twitter [Twitter]. *@PAULBRIERE*. https://twitter.com/PAULBRIERE/status/1184979511982604294

Brubaker, R. (1998). *Citizenship and Nationhood in France and Germany*. Harvard University Press.

Bustamante, J. (2008). *Misión a Guatemala: Promoción y protección de todos los derechos humanos, civiles, políticos, económicos, sociales y culturales, incluido el derecho al desarrollo.* https://www.gloobal.net/iepala/gloobal/fichas/ficha.php?entidad=Textos&id=7586&opcion=documento#s17

Caballeros, Á., & Lorenzana, J. (2006). *Herederos de pobreza: Diagnóstico sobre condiciones socioeconómicas de los Trabajadores Agrícolas Migrantes Temporales internos: Los casos de Rabinal, Baja Verapaz y Zacualpa, El Quiché*. MENAMIG.

Calderón, L. (2010). Migración latinoamericana y derechos políticos transnacionales: El proceso de extensión del voto en el exterior. In E. Oteiza (Ed.), *Patrones Migratorios Internacionales en América Latina* (pp. 413–426). Eudeba.

Camayd-Freixas, E. (2009). *Postville: La Criminalización De Los Migrantes* (1st ed.). F&G Editores.

Campos, G., & Huete, C. (2020). *El Salvador: No habrá voto en el exterior y escrutinio de votos en elecciones 2021 será 100% digital, anuncia TSE*. El Economista. https://www.eleconomista.net/actualidad/El-Salvador-no-habra-voto-en-el-exterior-y-escrutinio-de-votos-en-elecciones-2021-sera-100-digital-anuncia-TSE-20200930-0031.html

Camus, M. (Ed.). (2007). *Comunidades en movimiento. La migración internacional en el norte de Huehuetenango* (1st ed.). CEDFOG/INCEDES.

Castillo, M. Á. (1994). A Preliminary Analysis of Emigration Determinants in Mexico, Central America, Northern South America and the Caribbean. *International Organization for Migration (IOM), XXXII*(2), 269–306.

Castillo, M. Á., & Palma, S. I. (1996). *La emigración internacional en Centroamérica: Una revisión de tendencias e impactos*. FLACSO Guatemala.

Castillo, M. Á., & Palma, S. I. (2003, March 27). Las políticas migratorias de México y Guatemala: Un desafío para la congruencia de principios. *XXIV International Congress of the Latin American Studies Association*.

Castillo, M. Á., Toussaint, M., & Vázquez Olivera, M. (2011). *Historia de las relaciones internacionales de México, 1821–2010* (M. de Vega, Ed.; Vol. 2). Secretaría de Relaciones Exteriores/Acervo Histórico Diplomático.

Castles, S. (2002). Migration and Community Formation under Conditions of Globalization. *International Migration Review, 36*(4), 1143–1168.

Castles, S. (2004a). *The age of migration*. Guildford Press.

Castles, S. (2004b). The Factors that Make and Unmake Migration Policies. *International Migration Review, 38*(3), 852–884.

Castles, S. (2004c). Why Migration Policies Fail. *Ethnic and Racial Studies, 27*(2), 205–227.

Castles, S., & Alastair, D. (2000). *Citizenship and Migration*.

Castles, S., & Delgado Wise, R. (2008). *Migration and development: Perspectives from the South*. IOM International Organization for Migration.

Castles, S., & Miller, M. J. (2009). *The age of migration* (4th ed.). Guilford Press.
CEDOH. (2005). *Honduras: Migración, política y seguridad*. Centro de Documentación de Honduras CEDOH.
CEPAL. (2019). *Hacia un nuevo estilo de desarrollo: Plan de Desarrollo Integral El Salvador-Guatemala-Honduras-México. Diagnóstico, áreas de oportunidad y recomendaciones de la CEPAL* (LC/MEX/TS.2019/6). Naciones Unidas. https://www.gob.mx/cms/uploads/attachment/file/462720/34.Hacia_un_n uevo_estilo_de_desarrollo___Plan_de_Desarrollo_Integral_El.pdf
CEPAL. (2020, December 8). *CEPAL resaltó el enfoque innovador del Plan de Desarrollo Integral del norte de Centroamérica y México para abordar las causas estructurales de la migración, agudizada por el COVID-19*. CEPAL. https://www.cepal.org/es/comunicados/cepal-resalto-enfoque-innovador-plan-de sarrollo-integral-norte-centroamerica-mexico
Cerdas, R. (1995). Los partidos políticos en Centroamérica y Panamá. In C. Perelli & D. Zovato (Eds.), *Partidos y clase política en América Latina en los 90* (pp. 3–28). Instituto Interamericano de Derechos Humanos.
Chappell, L., & Glennie, A. (2009). Maximising the Development Outcomes of Migration: A Policy Perspective. *Global Development Network and Institute for Public Policy Research*.
Choate, M. I. (2007). Sending States' Transnational Interventions in Politics, Culture, and Economics: The Historical Example of Italy. *International Migration Review*, 41(3), 728–768.
Ciornei, I., & Østergaard-Nielsen, E. (2020). Transnational Turnout. Determinants of Emigrant Voting in Home Country Elections. *Political Geography*, 78, 102145.
CIVICUS. (2021). *CIVICUS Monitor Tracking conditions for citizen action*. https://monitor.civicus.org/
Clemens, E. S. (1997). *The People's Lobby: Organizational Innovation and the Rise of Interest Group Politics in the United States, 1890–1925*. University of Chicago Press.
Coppedge, M. (1998). The Dynamic Diversity of Latin American Party Systems. *Party Politics*, 4(4), 547–568.
Cornelius, W., & Lewis, J. (Eds.). (2007). *Impacts of Border Enforcement on Mexican Migration: The View from Sending Communities*. Lynne Rienner Pub.
Cornelius, W., Martin, P., & Hollifield, J. (Eds.). (2004). *Controlling Immigration: A Global Perspective* (1st ed.). Stanford University Press.
Cox, G. W., & McCubbins, M. D. (2007). Agenda Power in the U.S. House of Representatives, 1877 to 1986. In D. W. Brady & M. D. McCubbins (Eds.),

Party, Process, and Political Change in Congress: New Perspectives on the Hisotry of Congress. Stanford University Press.
CRM. (2020). *Regional Conference on Migration*. http://crmsv.org/en
Cuc, S. (2012, January 26). *Former Director of the International Migration Studies Department at CONAMIGUA* [Personal communication].
Curruchich, S. (2016, December 9). *Entregan reconocimiento a migrante guatemalteco*. https://www.deguate.com/artman/publish/migrantes_actualidad/entregan-reconocimiento-a-migrante-guatemalteco.shtml
Dalby, C., & Carranza, C. (2019, January 22). *Balance de InSight Crime sobre los homicidios en 2018*. https://es.insightcrime.org/noticias/analisis/balance-de-insight-crime-sobre-los-homicidios-en-2018/
Dardón, J. (2009). Dos rostros en un mismo vuelo: Las personas guatemaltecas deportadas de Estados Unidos. In M. E. Anguiano & R. Corona (Eds.), *Flujos migratorios en la frontera Guatemala-México* (1st ed., pp. 333–369). SEGOB/Instituto Nacional de Migración/Centro de Estudios Migratorios: DGE Ediciones; Colegio de la Frontera Norte.
de Haas, H. (2008a). Irregular Migration from West Africa to the Maghreb and the European Union: An Overview of Recent Trends. *IOM Migration Research Series, 32*.
de Haas, H. (2008b). Migration and development. *International Migration Institute, 9*.
de Haas, H. (2008c). North African Migration Systems: Evolution, Transformations, and Development Linkages. In S. Castles & R. Delgado Wise (Eds.), *Migration and development: Perspectives from the South* (pp. 143–174). IOM.
de Haas, H., Czaika, M., Flahaux, M., Mahendra, E., Natter, K., Vezzoli, S., & Villares-Varela, M. (2019). International Migration: Trends, Determinants, and Policy Effects. *Population and Development Review, 45*(4), 885–922.
Délano, A. (2009). From Limited to Active Engagement. *International Migration Review, 43*(4), 764–814.
Délano, A., & Mylonas, H. (2017). The microfoundations of diaspora politics: Unpacking the state and disaggregating the diaspora. *Journal of Ethnic and Migration Studies, 45*(4), 473–491.
DIGESTYC. (2017). *Encuesta de Hogares de Propósitos Múltiples*. Ministerio de Economía.
Diner, C. (2000). History and the Study of Immigration Narratives of the Particular. In C. Brettell & J. Hollifield (Eds.), *Migration Theory: Talking Across Disciplines* (1st ed., pp. 27–42). Routledge.

Dirección General de Migración y Extranjería de El Salvador. (2020). *Retorno a casa.* http://www.migracion.gob.sv

Domenech, E. (2009). *Migración y política: El Estado interrogado. Procesos actuales en Argentina y Sudamérica.* Universidad Nacional de Córdoba.

Duverger, M. (1974). *Los Partidos políticos.* Fondo de Cultura Económica.

EFE. (2019a, April 10). *Honduras comienza un programa de migración laboral temporal con Estados Unidos.* http://www.laconexionusa.com/noticias/2019041 0292725_lc29272510.asp

EFE. (2019b, May 20). *El presidente de Honduras viajará a España para buscar inversiones y empleos.* https://www.eldiario.es/politica/presidente-Honduras-viajara-Espana-inversiones_0_901159902.html

El Heraldo. (2020, August 21). *Segunda fase del enrolamiento será en el exterior* [Newspaper]. https://www.elheraldo.hn/pais/1402780-466/segunda-fase-d el-enrolamiento-será-en-el-exterior

Elizondo Breedy, G. (2011). *Derechos laborales y acceso al a justicia laboral de las personas migrantes.* PACT.

Engels, A. (Ed.). (2016). *Global Transformations towards a Low Carbon Society.* Universität Hamburg.

Engels, A. (2018). Understanding how China is Championing Climate Change Mitigation. *Palgrave Communications, 4*(1), 1–6.

Escrivá, M. A., Bermúdez, A., & Morales, N. (2009). *Migración y participación política: Estados, organizaciones y migrantes latinoamericanos en perspectiva local-transnacional.* Consejo Superior de Investigaciones Científicas.

Espinoza, C. (2021, June 30). *Project Officer at Centro de Derechos de Mujeres, Honduras* [Personal communication].

Expofer Guatemala USA. (2018). *Feria de Guatemala en USA.* http://guatefe rusa.com/

Faist, T. (2007). Migrants as transnational development agents: An inquiry into the newest round of the migration–development nexus. *Population, Space and Place, 14*, 21–42.

Faist, T., Gerdes, J., & Rieple, B. (2004). Dual Citizenship as a Path-Dependent Process. *International Migration Review, 38*(3), 913–944.

Falla, R. (2008). *Migración Transnacional Retornada* (AVANCSO).

Falla, R., & Yojcom, E. (2012). *El sueño del Norte en Yalambojoch: Migrantes retornados de EE.UU.* AVANCSO.

Feria Chapina. (2021). *Feria Chapina | Facebook.* https://www.facebook.com/feri achapinaoficial/?__xts__[0]&__xts__[1]&__xts__[2]=68.arceyhbbeii1…

Fischer, F., Miller, G. J., & Sidney, M. S. (Eds.). (2007). *Handbook of Public Policy Analysis.* Taylor & Francis.

Fitzgerald, D. (2000). *Negotiating Extra-Territorial Citizenship. Mexican Migration and the Transnational Politics of Community*. University of California Press.

Fitzgerald, D. (2008). *A Nation of Emigrants: How Mexico Manages Its Migration*. University of California Press.

Fox, J. (2006). Repensar lo rural ante la globalización: La sociedad civil migrante. *Migración y Desarrollo*, 5, 35–58.

Freedom House. (2021). *Global Freedom Scores*. Freedom House. https://freedomhouse.org/countries/nations-transit/scores

Freeman, G. (1994). Can Liberal States Control Unwanted Migration? *The ANNALS of the American Academy of Political and Social Science*, 534(1), 17–30.

Freeman, G. (2004). Immigrant Incorporation in Western Democracies. *International Migration Review*, 38(3), 945–969.

Freeman, G., & Birrell, B. (2001). Divergent paths of immigration politics in the United States and Australia. *Population and Development Review*, 27(3), 525–551.

Freeman, G., & Kessler, A. (2008). Political Economy and Migration Policy. *Journal of Ethnic and Migration Studies*, 34(4), 655–678.

Fuentes, F. (2012, May 24). *Vice Chair of the Migrant Rights Commission, City and County of San Francisco. Elected member of CONAMIGUA Emigrants Abroad*. [Personal communication].

FUNDAUNGO, UCA, Universidad Don Bosco, & FLACSO El Salvador. (2019). *Memorándum de propuesta de reforma electoral. Voto desde el exterior para elecciones legislativas y municipales en El Salvador*.

Gallagher, M. (2015). Election indices dataset. *Comparative Political Studies*, 1–48.

Gamlen, A. (2008). The emigration state and the modern geopolitical imagination. *Political Geography*, 27(8), 840–856.

Gamlen, A. (2019). *Human Geopolitics: States, Emigrants, and the Rise of Diaspora Institutions*. OUP Oxford.

Gamlen, A., Cummings, M. E., & Vaaler, P. M. (2019). Explaining the rise of diaspora institutions. *Journal of Ethnic and Migration Studies*, 45(4), 492–516.

Gamlen, A., & Marsh, K. (2011). Introduction: Modes of governing global migration. In A. Gamlen & K. Marsh (Eds.), *Migration and Global Governance* (pp. xiii–xxxiii). Edward Elgar Publishing.

Gammeltoft-Hansen, T. (2011). *Access to asylum*. Cambridge University Press.

Gammeltoft-Hansen, T., & Sørensen, N. N. (2013). Introduction. In T. Gammeltoft-Hansen & N. N. Sørensen (Eds.), *The Migration Industry and the Commercialization of International Migration* (pp. 1–23). Routledge.

Gándara, N. (2017, February 13). *Deportados a Guatemala ante el reto de volver a trabajar*. Prensa Libre. https://www.prensalibre.com/economia/poca-opcion-laboral-para-deportados/

García, J. J. (2012, February 27). *Entrevista. Viceministerio de Relaciones Exteriores para los Salvadoreños en el Exterior* [Personal communication].

García, M. C. (2006). *Seeking Refuge: Central American Migration to Mexico, the United States, and Canada*. University of California Press.

García Montero, M. (2009). *Presidentes y Parlamentos: ¿quién controla la actividad legislativa en América Latina?* (Vol. 269). Centro de Investigaciones Sociológicas.

Geiger, M., & Pécoud, A. (2010). *The politics of international migration management*. Palgrave Macmillan.

George, A. L., & Bennett, A. (2005). *Case Studies and Theory Development in the Social Sciences*. The MIT Press.

Gerring, J. (2004). What Is a Case Study and What Is It Good for? *American Political Science Review, 98*(2), 341–354.

Gesualdi-Fecteau, D., Thibault, A., Schivone, N., Dufour, C., Gouin, S., Monjean, N., & Moses, É. (2017). *Who, How and How Much? Recruitment of Guatemalan Migrant Workers to Quebec*. On the Move Partnership.

Ghosh, B. (2000). *Managing Migration: Time for a new International Regime?* Oxford University Press.

Gianopoulos, K. (2015). *Unaccompanied Alien Children. Improved Evaluation Efforts could Enhance Agency Programs to Reduce Migration from Central America*. United States Government Accountability Office. https://www.gao.gov/assets/680/673414.pdf

Gillivray Mac, J. (2009, 23–24). *Programa de Migración Laboral Temporal: El Salvador, Honduras, OIM*. Taller sobre los Programas de los Trabajadores Migratorios Temporales, San Salvador, El Salvador. Retrieved June 9, 2022, from <http://www.crmsv.org/es/eventos/taller-sobre-los-programas-de-los-trabajadores-migratorios-temporales>.

Glick Schiller, N., & Fouron, G. (2001). All in the Family: Gender, Transnational Migration, and the Nation-State. *Identities: Global Studies in Culture and Power, 7*(4), 539–582.

Gobiernos de El Salvador, Guatemala y Honduras. (2015). *Triángulo Norte: Construyendo confianza, creando oportunidades. Acciones estratégicas del Plan de la Alianza para la Prosperidad del Triángulo Norte El Salvador, Guatemala y Honduras*. United Nations. https://www.un.int/honduras/sites/www.un.int/files/Honduras/1-acciones_estrategicas_del_plan_de_la_alianza_para_la_prosperidad_del_triangulo_norte_folleto_07abril20151.pdf

Goldring, L. (2001). Disaggregating Transnational Social Spaces: Gender, Place and Citizenship in Mexico-US Transnational Spaces. In L. Pries (Ed.), *New Transnational Social Spaces: International Migration and Transnational Companies in the Early Twenty-First Century* (pp. 1–59). Routledge.

Goldring, L. (2002). The Mexican State and Transmigrant Organizations: Negotiating the Boundaries of Membership and Participation. *Latin American Research Review, 37*(3), 55–99.

González, S., & Montenegro, R. M. (Eds.). (2003). *Sueños truncados. La migración de hondureños hacia Estados Unidos.* Guaymuras.

Grupo Articulador. (2010). *Informe Alternativo de Guatemala sobre la aplicación de la Convención Internacional sobre la Protección de los Derechos de todos los Trabajadores Migratorios y de sus Familiares.* Grupo Articulador.

Grupo Articulador. (2021, June 3). *Comunicado de OSC ante visita de Vice-presidenta Kamala Harris.* Grupo Articulador En Materia Migratoria Para Guatemala. https://grupoarticuladormigraciones.org/2021/06/03/comunicado-de-osc-ante-visita-de-vice-presidenta-kamala-harris/

Guarnizo, L. E. (1998). The Rise of Transnational Social Formations: Mexican and Dominican State Responses to Transnational Migration. *Political Power and Social Theory, 12*, 45–94.

Guild, E., & van Selm, J. (2005). *International Migration and Security: Opportunities and Challenges: Immigrants as an Asset or Threat?* Routledge Chapman & Hall.

Guo, M. (2020). *Immigration Enforcement Actions: 2019* (Annual Flow Report). Homeland Security. https://www.dhs.gov/sites/default/files/publications/immigration-statistics/yearbook/2019/enforcement_actions_2019.pdf

Gutiérrez, B., & Manzanedo, C. (2019, July 12). Los invisibles de las políticas migratorias: Los deportados. *El País.* https://elpais.com/elpais/2019/07/10/3500_millones/1562794341_175507.html

Guzmán, M. (2012, January 24). *Legislator, Former President of the Migrant Committee in the Guatemalan Congress* [Personal communication].

Hernández-León, R. (2013). Conceptualizing the migration industry. In T. Gammeltoft-Hansen & N. N. Sørensen (Eds.), *The Migration Industry and the Commercialization of International Migration* (pp. 24–44). Routledge.

Herrera, G., Espinosa, M. C. C., & Torres, A. (2005). *La Migración Ecuatoriana: Transnacionalismo, Redes e Identidades.* FLACSO Ecuador.

Hoffmann, B. (2008). Bringing Hirschman Back In: Conceptualizing Transnational Migration as a Reconfiguration of "Exit", "Voice", and "Loyalty." *GIGA German Institute of Global and Area Studies, 91*(GIGA Working Papers).

Hollifield, J. (1986). Immigration Policy in France and Germany: Outputs versus Outcomes. *The ANNALS of the American Academy of Political and Social Science, 485*(1), 113–128.

Hollifield, J. (1998). Migration, Trade, and the Nation-State: The Myth of Globalization. *UCLA Journal of International Law and Foreign Affairs, 3*, 595–636.

Hollifield, J. (2000). The Politics of International Migration. How Can We "Bring the State Back in"? In C. Brettell & J. Hollifield (Eds.), *Migration Theory: Talking Across Disciplines* (1st ed., pp. 137–186). Routledge.

Hollifield, J. (2004). The Emerging Migration State. *International Migration Review, 38*(3), 885–912.

Hugo, G. (2010). *The Future of Migration Policies in the Asia-Pacific Region* [Background Paper WMR 2010]. International Organization for Migration.

Hujo, K., & Piper, N. (Eds.). (2010). *South-South Migration: Implications for Social Policy and Development*. Palgrave Macmillan.

Huntington, S. (1998). *The Clash of Civilizations and the Remaking of World Order* (1st ed.). Simon & Schuster.

IIDH/CAPEL. (1989). *Diccionario Electoral: Vol. II*. IIDH/CAPEL.

INE Guatemala. (2019). *Principales Resultados Censo 2018*. Gobierno de la República de Guatemala.

INE Honduras. (2019). *Población Total 2019*. https://www.ine.gob.hn/V3/

INEDIM, & INCEDES. (2011). *Security for Migrants: Building a Policy and Advocacy Agenda* (INEDIM; INCEDES). INEDIM.

INM. (2016). *Embajada y Consulados de Honduras*. https://www.inm.gob.mx/gobmx/word/index.php/honduras/

International Monetary Fund. (2019). *World Economic Outlook: Global Manufacturing Downturn, Rising Trade Barriers*. World Economic Outlook-IMF.

IOM. (2010a). *IOM Managed Temporary Labour Migration Programme to Canada Assists More than 12,000 Guatemalans*. https://www.iom.int/news/iom-managed-temporary-labour-migration-programme-canada-assists-more-12000-guatemalans

IOM. (2010b). *World Migration Report 2010—The Future of Migration: Building Capacities for Change* (International Organization for Migration).

IOM. (2013). *Central American Officials attend workshop on labour migration management*. https://www.iom.int/news/central-american-officials-attend-workshop-labour-migration-management

IOM. (2018). *Migration and the 2030 Agenda: A Guide for Practitioners*. International Organization for Migration. http://migrationdataportal.org/tool/migration-and-2030-agenda-guide-practitioners

IOM. (2019). *Global Migration Data Portal.* http://migrationdataportal.org/es/data
Itzigsohn, J., & Villacrés, D. (2008). Migrant Political Transnationalism and the Practice of Democracy: Dominican External Voting Rights and Salvadoran Home Town Associations. *Ethnic and Racial Studies, 31*(4), 664–686.
Jann, W., & Wegrich, K. (2003). Phasenmodelle und Politikprozesse: Der Policy Cycle. In K. Schubert & N. Bandelow (Eds.), *Lehrbuch der Politikfeldanalyse* (pp. 71–106). Oldenbourg Verlag.
Jonas, S. (2011). *Increasing Visibility of Guatemalan Immigrants. The Great Raid of Postville, Iowa.* ReVista Harvard Review of Latin America.
Joppke, C. (1998). *Immigration and the Nation-State: The United States, Germany, and Great Britain.* Oxford University Press.
Joppke, C. (1999). How immigration is changing citizenship: A comparative view. *Ethnic and Racial Studies, 22*(4), 629–652.
Juss, S. (2004). Free Movement and the World Order. *International Journal of Refugee Law, 16*(3), 289–335.
Kaye, J. (2010). *Moving Millions. How Coyote Capitalism Fuels Global Immigration.* John Wiley & Sons, Inc.
Khagram, S., & Levitt, P. (Eds.). (2008). *The transnational studies reader.* Routledge.
Koslowski, R. (2005). International migration and the globalization of domestic politics: A conceptual framework. In R. Koslowski (Ed.), *International Migration and the Globalization of Domestic Politics* (pp. 19–46). Routledge.
Kron, S. (2001, January 25). *Regional Responses to Transnational Migration in North and Central America.* Annual Globalisation and Latin American Development (GLAD) Lecture, London.
Kron, S. (2011). Gestión Migratoria en Norte y Centroamérica: Manifestaciones y Contestaciones. *Anuario de Estudios Centroamericanos, Universidad de Costa Rica, 37,* 53–85.
La Prensa. (2011, November 28). *Lobo inaugura programa de Seguro Social en EUA.* Diario La Prensa. https://www.laprensa.hn/honduras/sanpedrosula/337448-98/lobo-inaugura-programa-de-seguro-social-en-eua
La Prensa. (2019, April 30). *Alcalde Calidonio fue retenido dos horas en Houston, EEUU.* Diario La Prensa. https://www.laprensa.hn/honduras/1280392-410/armando-calidonio-alcalde-san-pedro-sula-honduras-retenido-aeropuerto-estados-unidos-migracion
Laakso, M., & Taagepera, R. (1979). "Effective" Number of Parties: A Measure with Application to West Europe. *Comparative Political Studies, 12*(1), 3–27.

Lafleur, J.-M., & Chelius, L. C. (2011). Assessing Emigrant Participation in Home Country Elections: The Case of Mexico's 2006 Presidential Election. *International Migration, 49*(3), 99–124.

Lafleur, J.-M., & Martiniello, M. (Eds.). (2009). *The transnational political participation of immigrants*. Routledge.

Lakhani, N. (2015, April 6). Violence escalates in El Salvador as end to gang truce proves deadly. *The Guardian*. https://www.theguardian.com/world/2015/apr/06/el-salvador-violence-end-to-gang-truce-proves-deadly

Landolt, P. (2001). Salvadoran Economic Transnationalism: Embedded Strategies for Household Maintenance, Immigrant Incorporation, and Entrepeneurial Expansion. *Global Networks, 1*(3), 217–241.

Levitt, P. (2001). *The Transnational Villagers*. University of California Press.

Levitt, P., & de la Dehesa, R. (2003). Transnational migration and the redefinition of the state: Variations and explanations. *Ethnic and Racial Studies, 26*(4), 587–611.

Levitt, P., & Sørensen, N. N. (2004). The transnational turn in migration studies. *Global Migration Perspectives, 6*, 2–13.

Lind, D. (2018, October 24). *The migrant caravan, explained*. Vox. https://www.vox.com/2018/10/24/18010340/caravan-trump-border-honduras-mexico

López, A. I. (2018). Economic Remittances, Temporary Migration and Voter Turnout in Mexico. *Migration Studies, 6*(1), 20–52.

López, A. M. (2005). *Migrantes y Estados: La respuesta política ante la cuestión migratoria*. Anthropos Editorial.

Lungo, M., & Kandel, S. (1999). *Transformando El Salvador: Migración internacional, sociedad y cultura*. Fundación Nacional para el Desarrollo.

Macías, J. L. (2019, July 22). *Alejandro Giammattei en Los Ángeles: "Tengo una misión, no ambición."* La Opinión. https://laopinion.com/2019/07/22/alejandro-giammattei-en-los-angeles-tengo-una-mision-no-ambicion/

Maguid, A. (2010). Gente en movimiento: La migración internacional en Centroamérica. In E. Oteiza (Ed.), *Patrones Migratorios Internacionales en América Latina* (pp. 67–98). Eudeba.

Mahler, S. J. (2000a). Constructing International Relations: The Role of Transnational Migrants and other Non-State Actors. *Identities: Global Studies in Culture and Power, 7*(2), 197–232.

Mahler, S. J. (2000b). *Migration and Transnational Issues. Recent Trends and Prospects for 2020*. Institut für Iberoamerika-Kunde.

Mahoney, J. (2001). Radical, Reformist and Aborted Liberalism: Origins of National Regimes in Central America. *Journal of Latin American Studies, 33*, 221–256.

Maldonado Ríos, E. M. (2012, January 24). *Ex-Viceministro de Relaciones Exteriores y Ex-Secretario Ejecutivo del Consejo Nacional de Atención al Migrante de Guatemala* [Personal communication].

Maldonado Ríos, E. M., Zea, E. M., & Caballeros, Á. (2010). *Marco general y descripción de acciones del Estado de Guatemala en materia migratoria*.

Marfaing, L., & Hein, W. (2008). Das EU-Einwanderungsabkommen—Kein Ende der illegalen Migration aus Afrika. *GIGA Focus, Global*(8). http://www.giga-hamburg.de/dl/download.php?d=/content/publikationen/pdf/gf_global_0 808.pdf

Margheritis, A. (2007). State-led Transnationalism and Migration: Reaching out to the Argentine Community in Spain. *Global Networks, 7*(1), 87–106.

Margheritis, A. (2011). "Todos Somos Migrantes" (We Are All Migrants): The Paradoxes of Innovative State-led Transnationalism in Ecuador. *International Political Sociology, 5*(2), 198–217.

Mármora, L. (1994). Desarrollo sostenido y políticas migratorias: Su tratamiento en los espacios latinoamericanos de integración. *OIM, 12* (April–December), 5–49.

Marquardt, M. F., Steigenga, T. J., Williams, P. J., & Vasquez, M. A. (2011). *Living "Illegal": The Human Face of Unauthorized Immigration* (1st ed.). The New Press.

Martínez, C. (2019, November 21). *"Los migrantes son muy importantes, pero la prioridad es México."* Elfaro.Net. https://elfaro.net/es/201911/el_salvador/23790/"Los-migrantes-son-muy-importantes-pero-la-prioridad-es-México".htm

Martínez, J. F. (2008). *Diagnóstico. Situación de los Trabajadores Centroamericanos en Guatemala*. MENAMIG.

Martínez, J., & Reboiras, L. (Eds.). (2012). *Development, Institutional and Policy aspects of International Migration between Africa, Europe and Latin America and the Caribbean* (United Nations). ECLAC.

Martínez Rodas, A. (2017). *La Acción Colectiva Migrante Guatemalteca en Estados Unidos*. OBIMID.

Massey, D., Arango, J., Graeme, H., Kovaouci, A., Pellegrino, A., & Taylor, E. (1994). An Evaluation of International Migration Theory; The North American Case. *Population and Development Review, 20*(4), 699–751.

Massey, D., & Taylor, E. (Eds.). (2004a). *International Migration. Prospects and Policies in a Global Market*. Oxford University Press.

Massey, D., & Taylor, E. (2004b). Introduction. In *International Migration. Prospects and Policies in a Global Market* (pp. 1–19). Oxford University Press.

Matamoros, D. (2012, March 14). *Entrevista. Magistrado del Tribunal Supremo Electoral Honduras* [Personal communication].
May, R. A. (2005). Human Rights NGOs and the Role of Civil Society in Democratization. In R. A. May & A. K. Milton (Eds.), *Un Civil Societies: Human Rights and Democratic Transitions in Eastern Europe and Latin America* (pp. 1–10). Lexington Books.
Médicos sin Fronteras. (2017). *Forzados a huir del Triángulo Norte de Centroamérica: Una crisis humanitaria olvidada.* https://arhp.msf.es/sites/default/files/Informe-MSF_Forzados-a-huir-del-triangulo-norte-de-Centroamerica.pdf
MENAMIG. (2006). *Diagnóstico sobre menores de edad y mujeres trabajadores agrícolas temporales en las fincas de Chiapas, México.* MENAMIG/Oficina de Derechos Humanos, Casa del Migrante Tecún Umán San Marcos.
Meyer, P. J., & Seelke, C. R. (2015). *Central America Regional Security Initiative: Background and Policy Issues for Congress.* Congressional Research Service. https://fas.org/sgp/crs/row/R41731.pdf
Meyers, E. (2000). Theories of International Immigration Policy—A Comparative Analysis. *International Migration Review, 34*(4), 1245–1282.
Meza, V. (Ed.). (2011). *Honduras: Retos y desafíos de la reconstrucción democrática.* Centro de Documentación de Honduras CEDOH.
Ministerio de Trabajo y Previsión Social de Guatemala. (2019, July). *Ministerio de Trabajo y Previsión Social y autoridades de Estados Unidos suscriben acuerdo para programa de trabajadores agrícolas temporales.* https://www.mintrabajo.gob.gt/index.php/noticias/142-suscriben-acuerdo-para-programa-de-trabajadores-agricolas-temporales
Miranda, V. (2018, December 19). *Comienza proceso para ofrecer oportunidades de empleo a salvadoreños en Canadá.* Noticias de El Salvador—elsalvador.com. https://www.elsalvador.com/noticias/internacional/salvadorenos-podran-aplicar-a-empleos-en-canada/550758/2018/
Money, J. (1999). *Fences and Neighbors: The Political Geography of Immigration Control.* Cornell University Press.
Morales, A. (2007). *La diáspora de la posguerra. Regionalismo de los migrantes y dinámicas territoriales en América Central.* FLACSO Costa Rica.
Morales, A., Kandel, S., Ortiz, X., Díaz, O., & Acuña, G. (2011). *Trabajadores migrantes y megaproyectos en América Central.* PNUD/UCA.
Morales, S. (2019, June 17). *¿Cuánto costaron los 734 votos de los guatemaltecos en EE. UU.?—Prensa Libre.* Prensa Libre. https://www.prensalibre.com/guatemala/politica/cuanto-costaron-los-737-votos-de-los-guatemaltecos-en-ee-uu/

MRE El Salvador. (2010, November 25). *Día del Salvadoreño y Salvadoreña en el Exterior.* https://www.youtube.com/watch?v=yoXzUHW-sX8

MRE El Salvador. (2015a). *Memoria de Labores 2014–2015.* https://issuu.com/cancilleriasv/docs/memoria_de_labores_rree_2016_17_sma

MRE El Salvador. (2015b, July 31). *Consulado General de El Salvador en Los Ángeles, California—LosAngeles.* http://consuladolosangeles.rree.gob.sv/index.php/component/k2/itemlist/category/21-cos-losangeles?start=70

MRE El Salvador. (2016). *Experiencia del espacio de coordinación local TRICAMEX, para la Protección Consular.* Mexican Consular Diplomacy in Trump's Era. https://www.cepal.org/sites/default/files/events/files/32_tricamex.pdf

MRE El Salvador. (2017). *Memoria de Labores 2016–2017.* https://issuu.com/cancilleriasv/docs/memoria_de_labores_rree_2016_17_sma

MRE El Salvador. (2018). *Ministerio de Relaciones Exteriores de El Salvador. Áreas de Trabajo.* https://rree.gob.sv/areas-de-trabajo/

MRE El Salvador. (2019a). *Directorio de Embajadas y Consulados de El Salvador.* http://embajadasyconsulados.rree.gob.sv/index.php?option=com_content&view=featured&Itemid=323

MRE El Salvador. (2019b, August 29). *Compatriotas en Des Moines, Houston, y Phoenix, en Estados Unidos, recibirán atención consular en jornadas móviles.* Embajada de El Salvador en Washington D.C. http://www.elsalvador.org/index.php/actualidad/avisos/item/7754-compatriotas-en-iowa-y-tucson-en-estados-unidos-recibiran-atencion-consular-en-jornadas-moviles

MRE Guatemala. (2007). *Política de Protección, Asistencia y Atención al Guatemalteco en el Exterior.*

MRE Guatemala. (2011). *Acciones y Logros en Materia Consular y Migratoria.* Departamento de Reproducciones MRE.

MRE Guatemala. (2015a, June). *Proyecto de Liderazgo Ciclo Escolar 2015–2016.* https://www.consuladoguatemalanuevayork.org/noticias-del-consulado.html

MRE Guatemala. (2015b, July). *Reunión de alcaldes de Trenton, New Jersey y Salcajá, Quetzaltenango.* https://www.consuladoguatemalanuevayork.org/noticias-del-consulado.html

MRE Guatemala. (2019). *Consulado General de Guatemala en Nueva York—Servicios de Asistencia y Orientación Básica en Salud.* https://www.consuladoguatemalanuevayork.org/noticias-del-consulado.html

MRE Guatemala. (2020). *Directorio de Embajadas y Consulados de Guatemala.* https://www.minex.gob.gt/Directorio.aspx?ID_TIPO=6

Naylor, R. T. (2004). *Wages of Crime: Black Markets, Illegal Finance, and the Underworld Economy.* Cornell University.

NDI. (2009). *2009 Honduran General Elections.* https://www.ndi.org/sites/def ault/files/NDI_Honduras_Final_Report_International_Election_Assessme nt_Mission_%20English.pdf

Nolte, D. (2016). Regional Governance from a Comparative Perspective. In V. M. González-Sánchez (Ed.), *Economy, Politics and Governance Challenges for the 21st Century* (pp. 1–15). Nova.

Noticiero Lourdes. (2019, October 15). *Tocan puertas en Canadá y Europa para extender oportunidades laborales a salvadoreños.* https://noticiaslourdes.co m/tocan-puertas-en-canada-y-europa-para-extender-oportunidades-labor ales-a-salvadorenos/

Novick, S. (2008). Migración y políticas en Argentina: Tres leyes para un país extenso (1876–2004). In S. Novick (Ed.), *Las migraciones en América Latina* (pp. 131–151). Catálogos.

Ögelman, N. (2003). Documenting and Explaining the Persistence of Homeland Politics Among Germany's Turks. *International Migration Review, 37*(1), 163–193.

OIM. (2020a, September 8). *ONU brinda asistencia humanitaria a las personas migrantes retornadas en el contexto de la COVID-19 en el TNCA.* https://trian gulonorteca.iom.int/es/news/onu-brinda-asistencia-humanitaria-las-perso nas-migrantes-retornadas-en-el-contexto-de-la-covid

OIM. (2020b, September 11). *OIM lanza campaña informativa sobre la migración y COVID-19 en idiomas mayas en el Triángulo Norte de Centroamérica.* https://triangulonorteca.iom.int/es/news/oim-lanza-campa%C3%B1a-info rmativa-sobre-la-migraci%C3%B3n-y-covid-19-en-idiomas-mayas

Olán, E. (2015, February 20). *Statistics Director, General Directorate of Migration* [Personal communication].

Onuf, N. (1991). Sovereignty: Outline of a Conceptual History. *Alternatives: Global, Local, Political, 16*(4), 425–446.

Orozco, M. (2000). *Latino Hometown Associations as Agents of Development in Latin America.* Inter-American Dialogue.

Orozco, M. (2006). *Diasporas, philanthropy and hometown associations: The Central American experience.* Inter-American Dialogue. http://www.thedialo gue.org/page.cfm?pageID=32&pubID=1012

Orozco, M. (2012). *Future Trends in Remittances to Latin America and the Caribbean.* Inter-American Dialogue.

Orozco, M. (2020). *Remittances to Latin Amerca and the Caribbean in 2019. Emerging Challenges.* Inter-American Dialogue. https://www.thedialogue.org/wp-content/uploads/2020/03/Remittances-to-the-LAC-2019_Emerging-Chall enges-1.pdf

Orozco, M., & Klaas, K. (2021). *A Commitment to Family: Remittances and the COVID-19 Pandemic* (p. 16). Inter-American Dialogue.

Osorio, L. (2019, October 14). *XIX Binational Health Week*. XIX Binational Health Week. https://binationalhealthweek.org/

Østergaard-Nielsen, E. (2001). Diasporas in World Politics. In D. Josselin & W. Wallace (Eds.), *Non-state Actors in World Politics* (pp. 2018–2234). Palgrave.

Østergaard-Nielsen, E. (2003a). *International Migration and Sending Countries: Perceptions, Policies and Transnational Relations*. Palgrave Macmillan.

Østergaard-Nielsen, E. (2003b). The Politics of Migrants' Transnational Political Practices. *International Migration Review, 37*(3), 760–786.

Østergaard-Nielsen, E. (2016). Sending Country Policies. In B. Garcés-Mascareñas & R. Penninx (Eds.), *Integration Processes and Policies in Europe* (pp. 147–165). Springer International Publishing.

Oteiza, E. (comp) (Ed.). (2010). *Patrones Migratorios Internacionales en América Latina*. Eudeba.

Paarlberg, M. (2017). Competing for the diaspora's influence at home: Party structure and transnational campaign activity in El Salvador. *Journal of Ethnic and Migration Studies*, 539–560.

Palma, S. I. (Ed.). (2004). *Despues de nuestro deñor, Estados Unidos: Perspectivas de análisis del comportamiento e implicaciones de la migración internacional en Guatemala*. FLACSO Guatemala.

Palma, S. I. (2012, February 8). *Executive Director, Instituto Centroamericano de Estudios Sociales y Desarrollo* [Personal communication].

PARLACEN. (2020, June 3). *Declaración APEX/04-02/2019-2020 para Apoyar a la Población Migrante Centroamericana, no Documentada, que Reside en los Estados Unidos de América y que está Extremadamente Vulnerable a la Pandemia por el COVID-19*. https://firebasestorage.googleapis.com/v0/b/parlac en-back.appspot.com/o/parliament-docs%2FDEC-APEX-04-02-2019-202 0.pdf?alt=media&token=6284a893-9709-4050-9149-3d5f205275ff

Pedroza, L. (2020). A Comprehensive Framework for Studying Migration Policies (and a Call to Oberve Them beyond Immigration to the West). *GIGA Working Papers, 321*. https://www.giga-hamburg.de/de/system/files/publications /wp321_pedroza.pdf

Pedroza, L., Palop, P., & Hoffmann, B. (2016). *Emigrant Policies in Latin America and the Caribbean*. FLACSO Chile.

Pellegrino, A. (2010). Tendencias de la migración internacional en América Latina y el Caribe en la segunda mitad del siglo XX. In E. (comp) Oteiza (Ed.), *Patrones Migratorios Internacionales en América Latina* (pp. 27–46). Eudeba.

Periódico Equilibrium. (2012, February 25). *Canadá ofrece 135 empleos temporales para salvadoreños.* https://www.periodicoequilibrium.com/canada-ofrece-135-empleos-temporales-para-salvadorenos/

Piper, N. (2006). Gendering the Politics of Migration. *International Migration Review, 40*(1), 133–164.

Piper, N. (2010). Migration and Social Development: Organizational and Political Dimensions. In K. Hujo & N. Piper (Eds.), *South-South Migration. Implications for Social Policy and Development* (pp. 120–157). Palgrave Macmillan.

Popkin, E. (2003). Transnational Migration and Development in Postwar Peripheral States: An Examination of Guatemalan and Salvadoran State Linkages with Their Migrant Populations in Los Angeles. *Current Sociology, 51*(3/4), 347–374.

Portes, A., Guarnizo, L. E., & Landolt, P. (1999). The study of transnationalism: Pitfalls and promise of an emergent research. *Ethnic and Racial Studies, 22*(2), 217–237.

Pozzebon, S. (2021, May 5). *What to know about the political drama raising fears over El Salvador's democracy.* CNN. https://www.cnn.com/2021/05/05/americas/el-salvadors-political-crisis-intl-latam/index.html

Pradilla, A. (2019). *Caravana: Cómo el éxodo centroamericano salió de la clandestinidad.* Penguin Random House.

Reglamento de Ejecución de la Ley Especial para la Protección y Desarrollo de la Persona Migrante Salvadoreña y su Familia, Pub. L. No. 80, 408 Diario Oficial Nr. 158 (2015).

Pries, L. (2007). *Die Transnationalisierung der sozialen Welt: Sozialräume jenseits von Nationalgesellschaften.* Suhrkamp Verlag.

Pries, L. (2008). *Rethinking Transnationalism: The Meso-Link of Organisations.* Routledge Chapman & Hall.

Proceso Digital. (2015, March 12). *Honduras y PNUD firman acuerdo para reactivar Programa de Remesas Solidarias.* https://www.proceso.hn/component/k2/item/98407-honduras-y-pnud-firman-acuerdo-para-reactivar-programa-de-remesas-solidarias.html

PTAT-C. (2010). *Reglamento de Normas y Conductas en Alberta Canadá.* FLACSO Guatemala.

Puerta, R. (2012, February 27). *Researcher and professor, Universidad Católica de Honduras* [Personal communication].

Puerta, R. (2020, December 14). *Plan Biden para Centroamérica.* Proceso Digital. https://proceso.hn/plan-biden-para-centroamerica/

RELAF, Save the Children, & UNICEF. (2015). *Niños, Niñas y Adolescentes Migrantes Retornados. Un Análisis de los Contextos y las Respuestas de los Servicios y las Políticas de Protección en El Salvador, Guatemala, Honduras y México.* RELAF, Save the Children & UNICEF. https://resourcecentre.savethechildren.net/node/9072/pdf/informe_migrantes_retornados_final.pdf

Reynosa, F. (2012, January 30). *Defensoría del Migrante, Procuraduría de Derechos Humanos, Guatemala* [Personal communication].

Ríos, C. (2011). *Lineamientos para la construcción de una política migratoria inclusiva en El Salvador.* Friedrich Ebert Stiftung.

Ríos, C. (2018, February 23). *Executive Director of Instituto Salvadoreño del Migrante (INSAMI) and of Asociación Salvadoreña de Educación Financiera (ASEFIN)* [Personal communication].

Rivas, D. (2012, February 20). *Director General Directorate of Migration Policy, Ministry of Foreign Affairs, El Salvador* [Personal communication].

Rivera, A. D. (2012, August 2). *Former Technical Secretary Regional Parliamentary Council on Migration (COPAREM)* [Personal communication].

Rocha, J. L. (2006). *Region Torn Apart: The Dynamics of Migration in Central America.* Central American Jesuit Service for Migrants.

Rocha, J. L. (2010). *Expulsados de la globalización: Políticas migratorias y deportados centroamericanos.* IHNCA-UCA.

Rocha, J. L. (2011). Remittances in Central America: Whose Money is it Anyway? *Journal of World-Systems Research, XVII*(2), 463–481.

Rodas Melgar, H. (2010). Propuesta de una estrategia integral regional centroamericana para el abordaje del tema migratorio. *Impactos de La Crisis Económica En Migración y Desarrollo: Respuestas de Políticas y Programas En Iberoamérica.* II Foro Iberoamericano sobre Migración y Desarrollo, San Salvador, El Salvador.

Rosales Sandoval, I. (2013). Public officials and the migration industry in Guatemala: Greasing the wheels of a corrupt machine. In T. Gammeltoft-Hansen & N. N. Sørensen (Eds.), *The Migration Industry and the Commercialization of International Migration* (pp. 215–237). Routledge.

Rosales Sandoval, I. (2021). "Migrant trash" or humanitarian responsibility? Central American government state responses to deported nationals. In T. J. Dunne & N. Ribas-Mateos (Eds.), *Handbook on Human Security, Borders and Migration* (pp. 148–164). Edward Elgar Publishing.

Rosales Sandoval, I., & Marvic García, G. (2021). Análisis de las políticas regionales de contención de movilidades entre el Sur de México y el Norte de Centroamérica: Desde el Plan Sur hasta el Plan de Desarrollo Integral. In S. Giorguli, D. Lindstrom, J. Nájera, & L. Gandini (Eds.), *Migraciones en Centroamérica y México*. COLMEX.

Rosenblum, M. (2002). *Moving Beyond the Policy of No Policy: Emigration from Mexico and Central America*. The Center for Comparative Immigration Studies.

Rosenblum, M., & Ball, I. (2016). *Trends in Unaccompanied Child and Family Migration from Central America*. Migration Policy Institute. https://www.migrationpolicy.org/research/trends-unaccompanied-child-and-family-migration-central-america

RROCM. (2021, March 6). *Red Regional de Organizaciones Civiles para las Migraciones*. https://saludymigracion.org/es/red-regional-de-organizaciones-civiles-para-las-migraciones

Ruano, E. (2012, June 1). *Ex Cónsul de Guatemala en Chiapas, México* [Personal communication].

Ruhs, M. (2008). The Potential of Temporary Migration Programmes in Future International Migration Policy. *International Labour Review, 145*, 7–36.

Salazar Grande, C. (2012, April 12). *President of the Central American Court of Justice* [Personal communication].

Salt, J., & Stein, J. (1997). Migration as a Business. *International Migration, 35*, 467–494.

Sandoval, V. (2021, June 17). *Director of Grupo de Monitoreo Independiente de El Salvador* [Personal communication].

Sardiña, M. (2021, June 8). *Kamala Harris sobre la migración en Centroamérica: "Si vienen a nuestra frontera, serán devueltos."* France 24. https://www.france24.com/es/am%C3%A9rica-latina/20210607-kamala-harris-migracion-centroamerica-devueltos

Sartori, G. (1992). *Partidos y Sistemas de Partidos*. Alianza Universidad Textos.

Sassen, S. (2000). Regulating Immigration in a Global Age: A New Policy Landscape. *The ANNALS of the American Academy of Political and Social Science, 570*(1), 65–77.

Schmitter Heisler, B. (1985). Sending Countries and the Politics of Emigration and Destination. *International Migration Review, 19*(3), 469–484.

Serrano, R. (2019, June 4). *Con nuevo presidente al frente de la comisión de relaciones exteriores, se continuará abogando por los migrantes salvadoreño*. Asamblea Legislativa de El Salvador. https://www.asamblea.gob.sv/node/8967

SICA. (2021a, February 11). *SICA y ACNUR impulsan diálogo político para la atención y protección de las personas refugiadas y desplazadas en la región.* https://www.sica.int/noticias/sica-y-acnur-impulsan-dialogo-politico-para-la-atencion-y-proteccion-de-las-personas-refugiadas-y-desplazadas-en-la-region_1_126329.html

SICA. (2021b, June 14). *Comisión de Autoridades Migratorias de los países miembros del SICA OCAM.* https://www.sica.int/ocam/breve

SICA. (2021c, June 14). *El Convenio Centroamericano de Libre Movilidad (CA-4).* https://www.sica.int/ocam/ca4

SICA. (2021d, June 14). *El Parlamento Centroamericano.* https://www.sica.int/organos/parlacen

Smith, M. P. (2003). Transnationalism, the State, and the Extraterritorial Citizen. *Politics & Society, 31*(4), 467–502.

Solís, O. (2012, March 13). *Legislator, previously in charge of migration matters in the Honduran Congress* [Personal communication].

Sørensen, N. N. (2004). *The Development Dimension of Migrant Transfers* (DIIS Working Paper No. 16). Danish Institute for International Studies.

Sørensen, N. N. (2007). *Living Across Worlds.* IOM.

Sørensen, N. N. (2010). The Rise and Fall of the "Migrant Superhero" and the New "Deportee Trash": Contemporary Strain on Mobile Livelihoods in the Central American Region. *Border-Lines, 5,* 90–120.

Sørensen, N. N. (2013a). Central American Migration, Remittances and Transnational Development. In D. Sanchez-Ancochea & S. M. i Puig (Eds.), *Handbook of Central American Governance* (pp. 45–58). Routledge.

Sørensen, N. N. (2013b). Jumping the Remains of the Migration Train Honduran migration and criminal co-optation of the migration industry. In T. Gammeltoft-Hansen & N. N. Sørensen (Eds.), *The Migration Industry and the Commercialization of International Migration* (pp. 256–279). Routledge.

Sørensen, N. N. (2019). Wars and Migration Crises in Central America: On Missing Persons during Armed Conflict and International Migration. In C. Menjívar, M. Ruiz, & I. Ness (Eds.), *The Oxford Handbook of Migration Crises* (pp. 389–406). Oxford University Press.

Sosa, K. (2012, February 15). *Legislator, Former President of the International Relations Committee in the Salvadorian Congress* [Personal communication].

Soysal, Y. (1994). *Limits of Citizenship: Migrants and Post-national Membership in Europe.* University of Chicago Press.

SRE Honduras. (2011). *Directorio Consulados de Honduras en EEUU.* http://www.hondurasemb.org/consulados.html

SRE Honduras. (2017). *Observatorio consular y migratorio de Honduras, CON-MIGHO.* https://www.conmigho.hn/

SRE México. (2018, December 18). *Declaración entre México y Estados Unidos sobre los Principios de Desarrollo Económico y Cooperación en el sur de México y Centroamérica.* Comunicado No. 012 de la SRE del Gobierno de México. http://www.gob.mx/sre/prensa/declaracion-entre-mexico-y-estados-unidos-sobre-los-principios-de-desarrollo-economico-y-cooperacion-en-el-sur-de-mexico-y-centroamerica

Stanley, W. (1993). Blessing or Menace? The Security Implications of Central American Migration. In M. Weiner (Ed.), *International Migration and Security* (pp. 229–262). Westview Press.

Stein, E., Tommasi, M., Echebarría, K., Lora, E., & Payne, M. (Eds.). (2005). *The Politics of Policies: Economic and Social Progress in Latin America: 2006 Report.* Inter-American Development Bank/David Rockefeller Center for Latin American Studies, Harvard University.

Stepputat, F. (1999). Politics of Displacement in Guatemala. *Journal of Historical Sociology, 12*(1), 54–80.

Suhari, M. (2016). Transformation von Energielandschaften an der Nordseeküste: Ein explorativer Vergleich der Diffusion und Governance des Windenergieausbaus in Deutschland, Dänemark und den Niederlanden. In A. Engels (Ed.), *Global Transformations towards a Low Carbon Society* (pp. 1–25). Universität Hamburg.

Taylor, E. (2004). Remittances, Savings, and Development in Migrant-Sending Areas. In D. Massey & E. Taylor (Eds.), *International Migration. Prospects and Policies in a Global Market* (pp. 157–173). Oxford University Press.

Tiempo Digital. (2015, October 26). *Migrantes podrán estudiar como si estuvieran en Honduras.* Tiempo Digital Honduras. https://tiempo.hn/migrantes-podran-estudiar-como-si-estuvieran-en-honduras/

Torres-Rivas, E., & Jiménez, D. (1985). Informe sobre el estado de las migraciones en Centroamérica. *Anuario de Estudios Centroamericanos, Univ. Costa Rica, 11*(2), 25–66.

Trump, D. J. (2018, October 22). Guatemala, Honduras and El Salvador were not able to do the job of stopping people from leaving their country and coming illegally to the U.S. We will now begin cutting off, or substantially reducing, the massive foreign aid routinely given to them. [Twitter]. *@realDonaldTrump.* https://twitter.com/realDonaldTrump/status/1188909031403900928

TSE El Salvador. (2009). *Memoria Especial Elecciones 2009.* https://archivo.tse.gob.sv/documentos/memoria-de-elecciones/memoria-elecciones-2009.pdf

TSE El Salvador. (2014). *Primera elección presidencial 2014.* https://archivo.tse. gob.sv/2014/escrutiniofinal_1ray2davuelta/pres1/pais.html
TSE El Salvador. (2019). *Memoria Especial Elección 2019.* https://www.tse.gob.sv/ TSE/Documentos/Memorias-de-Elecciones/2019
TSE El Salvador. (2020). *Tribunal Supremo Electoral de El Salvador.* http://www. tse.gob.sv/
TSE Guatemala. (2011). *Memoria de Elecciones Generales y al Parlamento Centroamericano 2011. Tomo I.* https://tse.org.gt/memoria-electoral-2011.pdf
TSE Guatemala. (2015). *Memoria de Elecciones Generales y al Parlamento Centroamericano 2015.* https://www.tse.org.gt/images/memoriaselec/me2015.pdf
TSE Guatemala. (2019). *Elecciones Generales y al Parlamento Centroamericano 2019.* https://resultados2019.tse.org.gt/201901/#
TSE Honduras. (2013). *Elecciones Generales 2013.* https://web.archive.org/web/20131217132154/http://siede.tse.hn/app_dev.php/divulgacionmonitoreo/reporte-presidente
TSE Honduras. (2017). *Elecciones Generales 2017.* https://web.archive.org/web/20171129212943/https://resultadosgenerales2017.tse.hn/
TSE Honduras. (2020). http://www.tse.hn/web/elecciones_2017_EG/index.html
United Nations. (2020a). *International Migration 2020 Highlights.* https://www.un.org/en/desa/international-migration-2020-highlights
United Nations. (2020b). *United Nations Treaty Collection.* https://treaties.un.org/Pages/ViewDetails.aspx?src=TREATY&mtdsg_no=IV-13&chapter=4&clang=_en
UNODC. (2019). *Global Study on Homicide 2019.* https://www.unodc.org/documents/data-and-analysis/gsh/Booklet2.pdf
Valladares, K. (2012, March 12). *Executive Director of FONAMIH* [Personal communication].
Vertovec, S. (2004). Migrant Transnationalism and Modes of Transformation. *International Migration Review, 38*(3), 970–1001.
Vertovec, S. (2007). *Circular Migration: The Way Forward in Global Policy?* International Migration Institute, James Martin 21st Century School, University of Oxford.
Vertovec, S. (2009). *Transnationalism.* Routledge.
Villafuerte, D. (2018). Seguridad y control geopolítico: Crónica de la Iniciativa para la Prosperidad del Triángulo Norte de Centroamérica. *Revista CS, 24,* 91–118.
Waever, O., Buzan, B., Kelstrup, M., & Lemaitre, P. (1993). *Identity, migration and the new security agenda in Europe.* Pinter.

Wainer, A. (2012). *Exchanging People for Money: Remittances and Repatriation in Central America* (No. 18; Briefing Paper, p. 18). Bread for the World Institute. https://www.bread.org/sites/default/files/downloads/briefing-paper-18.pdf

Waldinger, R. (2013). Engaging from Abroad: The Sociology of Emigrant Politics. *Migration Studies, 2*(3), 319–339.

Warnecke, A. (2007). In Search of a Balanced Approach. In J. Sommer & A. Warnecke (Eds.), *The Security-Migration Nexus. Challenges and Opportunities of African Migration to EU Countries* (pp. 57–60). Bonn International Center for Conversion BICC.

Watts, J. (2015, August 22). One murder every hour: How El Salvador became the homicide capital of the world. *The Guardian.* http://www.theguardian.com/world/2015/aug/22/el-salvador-worlds-most-homicidal-place

Weber, C. (1992). Writing Sovereign Identities: Wilson Administration Intervention in the Mexican Revolution. *Alternatives: Global, Local, Political, 17*(3), 313–337.

Wehr, I. (Ed.). (2006). *Un continente en movimiento. Migraciones en América Latina.* Iberoamericana/Vervuert.

Weiner, M. (Ed.). (1993a). *International migration and security.* Westview Press.

Weiner, M. (1993b). Security, Stability and International Migration. *International Security, 17*(3), 91–126.

Weiner, M. (1995). *The Global Migration Crisis: Challenge to States and to Human Rights.* Harper Collins College Publications.

Willeman, V. (2012, June 3). *Scalabrinian missionary director of Centre for Returned Migrants (CAMR)* [Personal communication].

Williams, P. J. (2009). *A Place to Be: Brazilian, Guatemalan, and Mexican Immigrants in Florida's New Destinations.* Rutgers University Press.

Worby, P. (2002). *Los refugiados retornados guatemaltecos y el acceso a la tierra: Resultados, lecciones y perspectivas.* AVANCSO.

World Bank. (2019). *Migration and Remittances Data.* World Bank. https://www.worldbank.org/en/topic/migrationremittancesdiasporaissues/brief/migration-remittances-data

Zhou, M. (2004). Immigrants in the U.S. Economy. In D. Massey & E. Taylor (Eds.), *International Migration. Prospects and Policies in a Global Market* (pp. 131–153). Oxford University Press.

Zolberg, A. (1999). Matters of State: Theorizing Immigration Policy. In C. Hirschman, P. Kasinitz, & J. DeWind (Eds.), *The Handbook of International Migration: The American Experience* (pp. 71–92). Russell Sage.

Zolberg, A. (2006). *A Nation by Design: Immigration Policy in the Fashioning of America*. Harvard University Press/Russell Sage Foundation.

Zolberg, A., Suhrke, A., & Aguayo, S. (1989). *Escape from Violence: Conflict and the Refugee Crisis in the Developing World*. Oxford University Press.

Legal Sources

Código de Migración, Pub. L. No. 44–2016 Guatemala (2016).

Código de Trabajo de Guatemala, Pub. L. No. 1441, CLXII-14–145 228 (1961).

Constitución Política de la República de Honduras, Pub. L. No. 131, 60 (1982).

Creación de la Tarjeta de Identificación Consular, Pub. L. No. 18–2005 (2005).

Declárase el 26 de Noviembre de cada Año como Día Nacional de los Salvadoreños en el Exterior, Pub. L. No. 825 (2005).

Fondo de Actividades Especiales para la Atención de los Salvadoreños en el Exterior y para las personas Retornadas, Pub. L. No. 617, 414 45 (2017). https://www.asamblea.gob.sv/sites/default/files/documents/decretos/177C 245B-FD3D-4272-AF40-E233CF2F9A2E.pdf

Iniciativa que Dispone Declarar el 18 de Diciembre de cada Año "Día Nacional del Migrante", en la República de Guatemala, no. 4572 (2013).

Ley de Protección de los Hondureños Migrantes y sus Familiares, Pub. L. No. 106–2013 (2013).

Ley del Consejo Nacional de Atención al Migrante de Guatemala, Pub. L. No. 46–2007 (2007).

Ley Especial para el Ejercicio del Sufragio de los Hondureños en el Exterior, Pub. L. No. 72–2001, 29,507 Diario Oficial La Gaceta (2001).

Ley Especial para el Ejercicio del Voto desde el Exterior en las Elecciones Presidenciales, Pub. L. No. 273, 398 Diario Oficial, Asamblea Legislativa de la República de El Salvador (2013). https://www.asamblea.gob.sv/sites/default/fil es/documents/decretos/67AA4625-BF93-4DD6-ACD0-235149AC16A1.pdf

Ley Especial para la Protección y Desarrollo de la Persona Migrante Salvadoreña y su Familia, Pub. L. No. 655 (2011).

Reforma a la Ley Especial para la Protección y Desarrollo de la Persona Migrante Salvadoreña y su Familia, Pub. L. No. 311, 89 Diario Oficial (2019).

Reforma al Artículo 29 de la Ley de Protección de los Hondureños Migrantes y sus Familiares, Pub. L. No. 15–2015, 33,686 Diario La Gaceta (2015).

Reformas al Decreto Número 1-85 de la Asamblea Nacional Constituyente, Ley Electoral y de Partidos Políticos, Pub. L. No. 26–2016, 1, Congreso de la República de Guatemala (2016).

Régimen Especial de Migración Legal de Trabajadores Hondureños para Trabajar en el Sector Agrícola de Estados Unidos y otros Países, Pub. L. No. 69-2010 (2010).

Reglamento de Ejecución de la Ley Especial para la Protección y Desarrollo de la Persona Migrante Salvadoreña y su Familia, Pub. L. No. 80, 408 Diario Oficial Nr. 158 (2015).

Reglamento Interno del Consejo Asesor de CONAMIGUA, Pub. L. No. 01–2009 (2009). https://issuu.com/conamigua/docs/reglamento_del_consejo_asesor_del_c